Born in Wimbledon in 19.. Rose Collis has worked i... performer, singer, song... forming extensively thro... began her career in journalism in... articles and reviews have appeared in over thirty publica- tions on both sides of the Atlantic, including the *Independent, Time Out, Diva* and *Gay Times.* She is the author of several critically acclaimed books, including *Portraits to the Wall* and *A Trouser-Wearing Character: The Life and Times of Nancy Spain.*

Colonel BARKER'S
MONSTROUS REGIMENT

A TALE OF FEMALE HUSBANDRY

ROSE COLLIS

Virago

A *Virago* Book

Published by Virago Press, 2002
First published in Great Britain by Virago Press, 2001

Copyright © Rose Collis, 2001

The moral right of the author has been asserted.

A CIP catalogue record for this book is
available from the British Library.

ISBN 1 86049 893 0

Typeset in New Baskerville by M Rules
Printed and bound in Great Britain
by Clays Ltd, St Ives plc

Virago
An imprint of
Time Warner Books UK
Brettenham House
Lancaster Place
London WC2E 7EN

www.virago.co.uk

For Sally, with love

*In memory of my 'lost' uncle, Cyril George Austin
(1929–2000)*

*And, with all respect, to the memory of Brandon Teena
(1972–1993)*

'His legacy lives on . . . to be ourselves, follow our hearts and
not conform. I pray for the day when we not only accept our
differences, but celebrate our diversity'

CONTENTS

INTRODUCTION

I do wonder about myself sometimes.

Each time I complete a book, I vow that the next project I tackle will be simpler, better-funded and will leave me less wasted, mentally, physically and financially.

This book has left me even further from keeping that promise.

When I completed *A Trouser-Wearing Character: The Life and Times of Nancy Spain*, I had no clear idea of what I would embark upon next. All I knew was that after years of painstaking, expensive, exhausting research into a fascinating and rewarding subject, I wanted a break.

I chanced upon Victor Barker when I was researching Nancy Spain: the odd story in an old newspaper, a reference or two in various compendia, especially Andrew Barrow's endlessly useful *Gossip 1920–1970*.

I mentioned this curious character to my friend Tom Sargant of the Brighton Ourstory Project, who told me how their archive had come to have material about Colonel Barker, and of the public presentation they had given, based on these cuttings, about the case. I also discovered that Julie Wheelwright had given a brief account of the Barker case in her ground-breaking book *Amazons and Military Maids*.

Perhaps that was all there was to it, I thought.

I realised there was more to it when, shortly after completing *A Trouser-Wearing Character*, I had a dream which featured Victor Barker and Nancy Spain performing in the same play, in some small provincial theatre. Such a scenario was, of course, a chronological impossibility. But I took it as a sure sign that I should take the story further; just how much further it could be taken, I was not so certain.

In the last decade or so, the subject of female husbands has proved inspirational for a number of authors: it has featured in plays like *Ladies and Gentlemen* by Emma Donoghue and *Eugenia* by Lorae Parry; in the novels *The Hide and Seek Files* by Caeia March, *Trumpet* by Jackie Kay, *James Miranda Barry* by Patricia Duncker and *Tipping the Velvet* by Sarah Waters; and in the biography *Suits Me: The Story of Billy Tipton*, by Diane Wood Middlebrook.

What makes the story of Victor Barker considerably different from those of Billy Tipton, James Miranda Barry and others is that they were 'unfrocked' at death – whereas Barker spent most of his adult life being 'discovered', again and again.

When the Billy Tipton book was published, Julie Wheelwright, reviewing it in *The Independent*, wrote that she was astonished by the story, 'since I had assumed that gender reassignment had ended a centuries-old phenomenon'. I was equally astonished by this statement: it seemed an uncharacteristically blinkered view of what had motivated a surprising number of nineteenth- and twentieth-century women to take on male identities. Everything tells us that it has rarely been a simple case of someone desiring a physiological transformation – a snip and a cut here, a hormone shot there, and 'just call me Uncle Bob'.

Nothing is as cut and dried as we, in our cynical twenty-first century, like to imagine it is – or would prefer it to be.

There are stories – and then there are stories within those stories. Virginia Woolf wrote that 'a biography is considered complete if it merely accounts for six or seven selves, whereas a person may well have as many as a thousand'. Victor Barker may not have had a thousand selves, but there were certainly many, many more than I, or anyone else, had originally believed. I have written about as many of them as I could find. As to any others that may have existed – well, they will have been consigned to the same unmarked grave that their creator went to, deliberately and skilfully concealed.

There are many other 'selves' featured in this book – not Barker's, not all of them complete, but stories which, when I discovered them (or they discovered me), had almost all lain unmarked and unearthed. And so, though this book is not intended to be any sort of definitive collection, these stories had so many resonances with Barker's story, and with each other, that there was clearly a place for them all within it.

Writing about someone like Victor Barker presents real challenges – as a researcher, as a writer and as an individual. After all, this was someone who left no body of work behind him, no archive of private documents and pictures. There were very few living witnesses and, in published sources, a tangle of conflicting public records and personal testimonies – including those of Barker himself.

Nonetheless, this story screamed out for my attention. As much as I tried to ignore Victor Barker, he loomed large on my consciousness and, when – like other women before me – I finally succumbed to his charms, I was only too happy to embrace him, regardless of all his flaws, his complexities and his contradictions. I have never regretted doing so – far from it.

While the unorthodox structure of *Colonel Barker's Monstrous Regiment* might suggest otherwise, nothing in it is fictional: it is, in its entirety, drawn from the factual evidence I uncovered during several years' research.

The documents relating to Colonel Barker in the Mass-Observation Archive at the University of Sussex were accessible and at least one researcher had studied them. However, for reasons best known to them, they chose not to use certain substantial, and illuminating, sections; much of this information, therefore, is published for the first time in this book.

Lengthy searches at the Public Record Office turned up Home Office and Metropolitan Police files containing a wealth of documents relating to Barker – previously unaccessed. Much of the information in those documents appears in print for the first time, as do photographs of Barker's birthplace, his family's graves, the church where he was first married and the churchyard where he lies. I was also able to locate a previously unknown photograph of his father, Thomas, published here for the first time since 1895.

I paid visits to St Clement's in Jersey, Milford in Surrey and Lowestoft in Suffolk, and spent months in the Public Record Office, the British Newspaper Library and the British Library. All traces of Barker's children have been well covered; his son's real full name was kept well-concealed and, hence, so was virtually everything else about the young man who, we do know, lies in some corner of a foreign field that is forever England.

Another, lesser, dilemma was what to call this complex person I was unravelling. What *do* you call such a person? And does it really matter? Barker has been called many things: *deviant, lesbian, transsexual, man-woman, transvestite, gene, pervert, he, she, it.* For the purposes of this book, I decided that, until the official appearance of Victor Barker, Valerie Arkell-Smith would be referred to as 'she'; after this, 'she' becomes 'he', mirroring the actual transformation that took place. Other than that, I quote only the names bestowed by others. Victor Barker was many things to many people – but never a category.

For me, as both a writer and someone who is viewed by certain people as queer, Victor Barker was a refreshingly ambivalent and challenging subject. This was no obvious heroine or hero: as both a man and a woman, Barker was, at best, appallingly naïve and obtuse; at worst, arrogant, snobbish and reactionary. But during the course of all the historical research on queer subjects I have undertaken in the last ten years or so, I have discovered that the most fascinating subjects to investigate have been those with whom I have had the least in common. It was also something of a revelation to me that I could feel compassion and sympathy for another human being who, in all probability, would have found me, and all I believe in, utterly repellent.

For an author – and, hopefully, for any reader – the endless paradoxes of Colonel Barker's story are part of its appeal. It's about lies and truth. Victims and crimes. Punishment and forgiveness. Ignorance and knowledge. Searching and finding. Trust and betrayal. It is neither a comfortable nor a comforting story. But, I contend, it is all the more fascinating for that.

Some would – and do – classify Barker and others like him as impostors. But what exactly *is* an 'impostor'? The author Sarah Burton stated that '[the impostor] takes control of his or her life, utterly changing its direction, whether just for a single day or for a whole lifetime'. But, as

Patricia Duncker has said, 'If you live as a man, that *is* your reality . . . Why do we have to know if someone is a man or a woman? The only possible reason for wanting to know is that you'd treat them differently.'

Being a man was certainly a reality for Victor Barker, and for most of those who came into contact with him. As a man, he *was* treated differently – by both men and women – and it was screamingly obvious that he preferred the way he was treated as a man to the way he was treated as a woman.

In this, he was not alone: Cora Anderson, a Native American woman who lived as Ralph Kerwinieo in Milwaukee for thirteen years, told a Chicago newspaper, 'This world is made by man – for man alone . . . do you blame me for wanting to be a man – free to live life as a man in a man-made world? Do you blame me for hating to again resume a woman's clothes and just belong?'

Patricia Duncker also said, 'What you expect to see, you will see.' And, whether we intend to or not, that is precisely what we do.

This is nothing new, of course – as Stormé DeLarverié, a male impersonator of the 1950s and 60s, put it: 'I model myself after me. All I had to do was just be me. And let people use their imaginations.'

And how people use those imaginations, given the opportunity.

In the 1920s and 30s, Grey Owl, the Native Canadian environmentalist, was a folk hero to millions worldwide. After his death in 1938, it was revealed that he was actually Archie Belaney, a native of East Sussex born and raised in Hastings. 'It must have been a great stress for him to live this lie – but he couldn't go back on it,' one commentator observed. Then there was the time the notoriously shortsighted E. M. Forster attended the wedding of his friend Lord Harewood. At the reception, he bowed to the ornate, multi-tiered white wedding cake – he thought he was looking at the often ornate and white Queen Mary.

And, just in case you think these incidents are all firmly in the dim and distant past, take the time I was on holiday in Paphos, Cyprus, in October 1999. My partner and I went to buy some beer and wine. When we got to the check-out, the chap serving at the till, giving us no more than a cursory glance, declared: 'The man drinks beer, the woman drinks wine.' I'm not sure who was the most confused: me, Sally or the chap behind the till.

We all see what we want to see – and this was never more true than for those who believed what they saw in the person they knew as Victor Barker.

Despite Barker's many and varied published statements, he spoke very little about what it *felt* like to be a man – especially in later life, when menopause came to remind him of his basic femininity.

I have been fortunate enough to learn from a contemporary voice on this subject: that of Peggy Shaw, veteran performer and founder of Split Britches, who went through these experiences on and off stage. She told me stories of how, during the 1970s, she was 'kicked out of women's toilets everywhere' – even though her blonde hair was waist-length at the time. 'The worst one was in Portobello Road,' she recalled. 'The police came in and kicked the door down.'

Shaw also talked a lot about the fear and vulnerability felt by a woman who chooses to present herself to the world in a male identity. This had a good deal of resonance: at first sight, many of the carefully posed pictures of Victor Barker, in all his and her incarnations, appear to portray a confident, almost strutting, slightly arrogant figure. But the more I looked at the photographs, the more I saw fear and panic in those eyes: fear of being 'found out', by his child, by neighbours, by colleagues, by the press, by the police, by the judiciary. These were real, justifiable fears, for Victor Barker and all the others of the 'monstrous regiment' – and in most instances, those fears were realised.

In *The Microcosm*, Maureen Duffy's classic novel of life in a queer world-within-a-world, it is said that 'There are dozens of ways of being queer and you have to find what your kind is and then make something of it'. Victor Barker defies any neat little label we might want to pin on him next to his medals. But he most certainly *was* queer, in many ways, and he tried to make the best of it – which is the most any of us can do.

Jean Genet once wrote that 'Crimes of which a people is ashamed constitute its real history'; many centuries earlier, Virgil declared: 'From a single crime know the nation.' When we reflect on the 'crimes' detailed in this book, and who were adjudged to be the 'victims', it is painfully obvious that what has been done to Colonel Barker's 'monstrous regiment' by different nations in different eras tells us a great deal about those societies and their histories. Monstrous, indeed. But more monstrous were this to be left buried and forgotten.

And, for all the monstrosity, there is still much to learn and enjoy in all of these tales of female husbandry: courage, romance, tenderness, idealism, audacity and moments of high camp and pure farce – elements as much a part of our lives as theirs.

PROLOGUE

◈

Beware: Man at Work

We are used to pieces of flotsam and jetsam like old drift-wood turning up on the beach – but nothing like this.

Guardian, 3 March 2000

The world is damned queer – it really is.
But people won't recognize the immensity of its queerness.

Lytton Strachey to Duncan Grant, June 1908

She had been a tarry sailor bold
And stemmed the briny water
This she he barman we are told
Spruce Mary Tommy Walker

Some time ago, we understand,
She lived near Burton Crescent,
Where she fell in love with lots of girls,
And made them lots of presents.

They jealous was of Mary Tom,
And one damsel like a fairy,

Did swear one day in the family way
She was by Tommy Mary

When dressed so fine, she was so kind,
With her trousers on her legs, sir,
She sent a handsome crinoline,
And a dozen new laid eggs, sir –

To pretty Jane of Ivy Lane,
Who she had long been wooing,
But very bad and naughty tricks,
Tommy Mary had been doing.

He she Tom, and she he Poll,
The world had been deceiving,
And every place he she was in,
The rogue she had been thieving.

She did not wear a crinoline
Gown or petticoat, I vow, sir,
But a pork pie hat and pilot coat
And a handsome pair of trousers.[1]

Kessingland, Suffolk, Thursday 22 June 2000

This is a queer place to end up.

Even in summer, a sinister atmosphere permeates the dunes that lie below the cliffs at Kessingland, where families staying at the nearby holiday camps and cottages come to play. But with a bitter wind whipping over the vast expanses of sand, all traces of the warmth left by happy, relaxed bodies vanish and the bleakness is grim indeed. Perhaps it's the North Sea, always a menacing presence, with its water which never warms, even in the height of summer, and its swift tides which threaten to scoop up anything in their way.

All manner of things are washed up here.

Which probably explains why, at first, no one noticed him amongst Kessingland's flotsam and jetsam, stranded like a landed whale. There was no particular reason why anyone would: it's not unknown for unusual creatures to be observed in the vicinity, and not just on the beach. A few miles away is the most easterly point in Britain – an ideal spot for concealment.

There is no doubt, it is a place that can fire the imagination. Sir Henry Rider Haggard, author of King Solomon's Mines *and* She, *owned a holiday home, Kessingland Grange, and knew the village and coastline well. The Grange is long gone, but Rider Haggard Lane and its holiday cottages commemorate his presence here.*

His daughter Lilias spent some of her holidays here and, in 1912, wrote to her father, telling him she had seen a large animal of unfamiliar shape and indeterminate identity. Seeking some explanation, her father wrote to the local paper, asking, 'Has anybody else seen a peculiar creature in the sea off the East Coast?' and discovered that others had indeed heard about the supposed existence of this mythical creature.

It took its place in Kessingland's folklore, as did others who have subsequently become part of the history and mystery of this village.

They have left a scant trail of disparate clues as evidence of their existence. At one time, men's clothing was washed up on the shoreline; at another, a framed photograph of a nameless young airman and a packet of letters, dog-eared from the innumerable times they had been read and reread. The biggest clue was photographs and cuttings featuring a tall, dark, handsome man, resplendent in military uniform and proudly bearing medals and decorations on his broad chest.

Each clue tells a story. Each photograph tells a story. Different stories, in different times, of different crimes.

Central London, Thursday 28 February 1929

In London's Piccadilly Circus, the reception clerk of the Regent Palace Hotel, dressed in his customary smart morning clothes, is on duty, dealing with the many new faces that pass through a busy West End hotel. The clerk's main duties are to receive guests and then to direct them either to the head waiter, to be seated in the restaurant, or to the reception office, if they wish to take a room.

Five months ago, when he first took up the position, the clerk was required to wear a black tail coat and stiff white shirt, but this made him indistinguishable from a waiter, so after a few weeks he was allowed to wear less formal attire. Some of his colleagues have asked him about the exceptionally tight belt he often wears. 'He told us a long story of how he was blown up in the war, and now he could not move unless he had this surgical belt,' according to a hotel superintendent.

The reception clerk gets on well with the other hotel workers, with whom he shares a communal dressing room, and they enjoy the colourful stories he tells them about his life, especially those concerning his war experiences. Most days, he receives a visit from a woman he calls his wife; she often telephones him at the hotel, too. They seem a happy couple. Once, she had an accident and sprained her wrist, and her husband asked for some time off to attend to her.

He takes his meals at the hotel, but after he has finished his day's work and changed clothes, he often goes for a drink at the bar of the Adelphi Hotel in John Street or, as often as not, at the Marquis of Granby pub at Cambridge Circus. He is a familiar figure to the manager and staff there. Everyone seems to like him.

Everything appears to be normal.

Except, this morning, one of the hotel's visitors is High Court bailiff James Glover, who, upon his arrival, asks to see the staff manager. Glover is in possession of a warrant for the arrest of a gentleman, the proprietor of a failed West End restaurant. It seems this unfortunate chap, though thoroughly respectable, amassed a number of debts during the running of his dining rooms in Litchfield Street, and several months ago, one of his creditors, Ubique Film Sales Ltd, took legal action to obtain the money due to them – £103.14s. rent and insurance on the restaurant premises.

The gentleman who owes the money was served with a summons from the Official Receiver's department on 5 December 1928, but failed to appear in court. Thus the warrant for his arrest has been issued and, somehow, he has been traced to this hotel.

The debtor is a married man, by all accounts, but it's believed he's actually separated from his wife and raising his young son by himself. The lady friend he calls his wife has been living with him for a while; the boy is at a boarding school somewhere on the south coast. The debtor is known to have once resided at an expensive apartment in 8 Hertford Street, in the heart of Mayfair, a very desirable address – the current Recorder of London, the highly respected Sir Ernest Wild QC, used to live at number 7.

During the time the debtor lived at Hertford Street, he even had his own valet, but such luxuries have been absent since his recent move to a flat in Markham Square, Chelsea. After all, a hotel reception clerk's wages cannot provide all the trappings of life a gentleman might be used to.

And it is a gentleman – the Regent Palace Hotel's reception clerk – that the bailiff is seeking. The man is sent for.

Ever obedient and courteous, the clerk makes his way to the manager's office, where Bailiff Glover tells him, 'I have a warrant for your arrest and am going to take you to Brixton gaol.' The clerk pales, and is heard to mutter, 'This is terrible. It is the end for me.'

The hotel staff all think it's terrible too. Word quickly spreads that their debonair colleague is being arrested, and will have to undergo the indignities of temporary incarceration in Brixton prison – not a suitable fate for an officer and a gentleman. And a war hero to boot: after all, he was awarded a DSO and other military honours. It's bad enough that he has been compelled to take what is quite a lowly job for one so distinguished, without being hauled off to prison in front of all the hotel staff and guests.

After all, the Regent Palace's management was glad to have such a tall, distinguished-looking and courteous gentleman as their mere reception clerk. In his black coat, waistcoat and dark striped trousers, this ex-army officer created a most favourable first impression to visitors.

He has shown no signs of regarding this job as being beneath his dignity – in fact, it could be said that he has embraced his work with more than the usual amount of enthusiasm, bordering on gratitude.

But Bailiff Glover is not surprised that there should be such a turn of events in a respectable gentleman's life; after all, bankruptcies are not uncommon nowadays – though it will be some months before the Wall Street Crash, British industry is already suffering a depression, and the New Year began dismally for the 1½ million people throughout the country without a job.

The clerk, after being told of his arrest and quickly re- alising the full extent of what it will mean, manages to recover his composure slightly and voices his concern for his 'wife'. He is allowed to spend half an hour with her in a Piccadilly teashop, making arrangements for his legal representation. Once the couple have agreed a suitable course of action, the ex-soldier kisses his wife, tells her not to worry, and then gets into a taxi with Bailiff Glover, who gives the driver their destination: 'Brixton prison.'

'It is the end,' Glover's prisoner had said. And, in at least one sense, he was right: it *was* all over, even if the world didn't yet know exactly what had come to such an inglorious end for Colonel Victor Barker.

For a fortunate few, however, this is a time of happy begin- nings: a new, highly prolific and lengthy career beckons for a lady writer. The finishing touches are being put to a detective novel, due to be published in the summer of 1929. *Speedy Death* will not only introduce a new crime writer to the world, but also a new, eccentric amateur sleuth. It will be the first of many murder mysteries by author Gladys Mitchell involving her fictional creation, Adela – known as Beatrice – Lestrange Bradley. Miss Mitchell will go on to write over sixty novels; for some of them, she will take on male pseudonyms and write as Stephen Hockaby and Malcolm Torne.

This joint debut is particularly memorable for another reason. The first *Speedy Death* murder victim is Everard Mountjoy, a well-known explorer, recently engaged to be married to Eleanor Bing. At a birthday dinner for his fiancée's father, Alastair Bing, the unfortunate Everard is found dead in his bath – which is when it becomes unmistakably apparent that he is, in fact, a woman. On learning that his now-deceased future son-in-law would have been his daughter-out-of-law, Bing can only say, 'It is a most incomprehensible thing to me, most incomprehensible that a woman could have masqueraded so long without being detected.'[2]

But, after all, this is a time when women are starting to enter arenas from which previously they have been excluded: after the long struggle to win the vote, more women are considering a career in parliamentary politics, especially working-class women inspired by the example of the Labour MP and trade unionist Margaret Bondfield, the former shop-worker and first woman delegate to a TUC conference who, in June, will become the first ever female Cabinet minister. This will be by way of a payback by new Labour Prime Minister Ramsay MacDonald to the millions of first-time women voters who, benefiting from the reduction in the female voting age to twenty-one, chose to support his party.

Upper-class women are being set different examples, as wealthy titled ladies such as Lady Dailey and the Duchess of Bedford enter the field of aeronautics.

Many women of similar social strata to these daring young women in their flying machines – especially those from the upper classes, the daughters of the military, and those with deeply held religious beliefs – are being drawn to a new breed of politics that is already hugely popular in Italy: fascism. These women are attracted to it by the prevalent twin forces of extreme patriotism, and fear of communism. With the cries of the Russian Revolution still ringing in their ears, any form of communism threatens to sweep away everything they believe in and represent; everything they saw their fathers, husbands and brothers fight and die for little more than a decade before. Fascism supports capitalism and the maintenance of a strong military. Moreover, there are many women whose lives have not been entirely enriched by attaining the right to vote. And since, as the writer Hilda Browning observed, '. ... equality had not in any way alleviated the lot of the middle-class and proletarian women, they longed backwards for the inequality of past times'.[3]

However, one female fascist sympathiser has been having rather a rough time of it in recent months.

In 1928, the obscenity trial concerning Radclyffe Hall's novel, *The Well of Loneliness*, has led to both author and book being simultaneously *causes célèbres* and *bêtes noires*. The legal furore caused by the story of Hall's lesbian – or, as she has it, 'invert' – heroine Stephen Gordon has brought the real Everard Mountjoys of the world into the headlines and on to British breakfast tables. It has caused the likes of the *New Statesman* to declare that lesbianism is now 'a comparatively widespread social phenomenon, having its original roots no doubt in the professional man-hating of the Pankhurst Suffragette movement'.[4] According to the judge at the Hall trial, it is preferable for young women to swallow prussic acid than for them to read about 'inverts'. The book's publication in Britain has been outlawed, copies of it seized and destroyed. Hall has been able to get it published in Paris, but because of the ban, she hasn't been able to see any proofs of her book. Some 60,000 copies of this French-produced edition will be sold, many being bought by British women visiting Paris and smuggling copies back for their friends in the wide sleeves of their coats. A diarist in the *Daily Telegraph* is appalled at the way Hall and her supporters have been able to subvert the law and turn her book into a bestseller: this development is 'very depressing and shows how difficult it is to control public morals by regulation'.[5]

This notorious episode of repression and injustice did not itself engender a climate of intolerance in Britain, but exposed and endorsed its existence. The government, the justice system and the press displayed their official disapproval of 'inverts' and their 'unnatural practices'; or, indeed, of anyone who appeared to fly in the face of the law, convention and God. These institutions showed that when the 'unnaturals' reared their heads, the full force of the legal, political and religious establishments would be wielded against them. And it was.

> *When you feel really good about yourself, and then you're put some place where you're not safe – suddenly, you're a freak. It happens just like that. It's a very thin line.*

Peggy Shaw, November 2000

1

<svg>꧁ꦾ꧂</svg>

Simple Gentlemen

*My father always told me that if you have a crease in your
pants, a fresh haircut and a shine on your shoes, you can
do anything.*

Peggy Shaw, November 2000

Jersey, September 1895

Victorian Jersey – then, as now: affluent, aloof, conservative, insular, consumed by its own history, clean, but with
something a little grubby under its nails. (In 1999, it would
be the Nazi collaborators left unnamed and unshamed,
with their identities protected for nearly fifty years by their
own government, and unable to be touched by any
European law.) In the late Victorian period, an ongoing
debate concerning 'Decency in Bathing' prompted this
representative pronouncement from a Mr Henry Pelton: 'I
have been told to go to Brighton and other places. Jersey
has nothing to do with other places. Let them wallow in
immorality as they live; but let us, as far as we can, be more
clean.'[1] That was Jersey, then as now: neither British, nor
French, nor European.

Truly, an island unto itself.

And an ideal place, then as now, for private gentlemen of independent means to play golf or ride, raise dogs and a small quota of children, and lead a life of kindly, harmless but ultimately purposeless activity.

Thirty-nine-year-old Thomas William Barker was one such Victorian gentleman. The son of James Barker, an Oldham businessman, Thomas had worked as an architect in Brighton, but the inheritance that came to him on his father's death enabled him to abandon his career and join the ranks of the unlanded gentry, dedicating his time to gentlemanly pursuits and ensuring his wife and children enjoyed a genteel existence.

September 1895 was a busy time for Thomas Barker. The annual Jersey Dog Club Show was taking place and, as its longstanding Honorary Secretary, he was responsible for ensuring that all the prize money was paid out to the winners and for distributing the ornamental prize cards. Then there were the dogs themselves to worry about, not least those he and his wife were showing. There was Thomas's smooth-haired fox terrier, Longueville Rollicker, while his wife had her two bloodhounds, Commonwealth and Lady Jane, competing.

And there was another pressing, non-canine matter that he had to attend to: he needed to pay a visit to the District Registrar's Office and register the birth of his first child.

Thomas had married relatively late in life for a Victorian bachelor. He was thirty when he and his eighteen-year-old bride, Lillias Adelaide Hill, were wed by the Revd H. Newton at St Mark's Church, Kemp Town, Brighton, on 26 January 1887. As was then customary, Thomas had bought the ring and arranged the service, and the wedding itself was a quiet affair. The church was unusual, in that it was aimed at its poorer parishioners and gentry alike.

'A simple gentleman' – Valerie's father Thomas
(left) enjoying his duties as Honorary Secretary of
the Jersey Dog Club, 1895

The first family of Kemp Town, the Herveys, had been
keen to erase the memory of their infamous ancestor Lord
John Hervey, whose close relationships with prominent
society gentlemen, fondness for wearing white make-up
and propensity for fainting spelt 'effeminacy' to his many
detractors. One of these, Lady Mary Wortley Montagu,

declared that 'The world consists of men, women and Herveys.'[2] Lord John's descendants spent many years and pious works attempting to attach more honourable associations to their name. And what could be more honourable than a parish church which opened its doors to poor and affluent alike?

Thomas Barker's bride, the tall, glamorous Lillias, was, according to her own daughter, 'a very lovely woman in the Lily Langtry style'.[3] She was the fourth daughter of ten children of recently deceased country parson Nicholas Frank Hill and his wife Lillias Gilfillan Cotesworth. The extensive Hill family tree included such illustrious figures as Olave Baden-Powell, wife of Robert Baden-Powell, founder of the Boy Scouts and Girl Guides.

Born on 26 May 1868, in High Crosby, near Carlisle, Lillias Hill had latterly been a pupil at St Mary's Hall, a boarding institution for educating the daughters of the poorer clergymen. A marriage settlement had been made on her; the purpose of such settlements was to enable a woman to keep a 'separate estate' of money or property, or both, free from her husband's.

The Barkers spent the early years of their marriage in Brighton before moving to Jersey in 1889. They settled in the Samarés district of St Clement, Jersey's smallest parish, situated on the south-east tip of the island, a few miles from St Helier, the capital. St Clement was noted for its 'Moonscape Beach' and, during the sixteenth and seventeenth centuries, the prevalence of witchcraft and the subsequent trials of its practitioners. According to local folklore, the witches had been particularly fond of dancing around Rocqueberg, the forty-foot granite rock at Samarés beach. Despite the Latin word from which the town took its name – *clemens*, meaning merciful –

little mercy was shown to those tried and convicted of witchcraft in the parish, and many were sent to the gallows.

Witchhunts, of a kind, periodically still went on in Victorian Jersey. It had never been easy for anyone remotely outside the norm to remain unnoticed on the island, and it was common for those who didn't fit in to be sought out and punished – or made to disappear.

In 1898, Jean Marie Lucas and William Pallot were charged with committing gross indecency in a field situated at the foot of Fort Regent in St Helier. They were discovered not by a policeman, but by one Charles Frederick Malzard. This was no coincidence: there was a history of antagonism between Lucas and Malzard, and William Pallot had few friends in the town. No fewer than eleven witnesses came forward to give evidence against him. When he came before the court, the place 'was crowded but, of course, no women were admitted'.[4]

At the trial, Prison Surgeon Dr Hind said that he

> believed Pallot to be of unsound mind and had
> formed this impression from the eccentric manner in
> which he had seen him parading in the streets –
> dressed partially like a woman, with curled hair,
> powdered face, bracelets, etc. He had the voice and
> gait of a woman, as well as the mind of a woman. He
> was not responsible for his acts and the best place for
> him was the Asylum . . . the mere fact of a man
> committing such an act tended to shew [*sic*] insanity.[5]

In their defence, Pallot said they had gone to the field so that he could tell Lucas's fortune for a shilling by 'cutting the cards'. A pack of cards was found in Pallot's possession, but, according to the Attorney General, '. . . they chose an obscure spot, and it was so dark that one of the witnesses had to strike a match to see them'.[6]

It took just ten minutes for the jury to find both defendants guilty, only to recant in the case of Pallot, who they then declared to be innocent on the grounds of insanity. He was sent to the asylum, while Lucas was sentenced to six months' imprisonment.

Most crime committed in Jersey during the 1890s involved brothel-keeping, illegal fortune-telling or bathing without full costume. But beneath the respectable veneer, all was clearly not well: this small island, with its population of barely 55,000, had a disproportionately high rate of suicide and attempted suicide – on average, two a month. This could explain why, at that time, there were over five times as many people incarcerated in the Jersey public asylum than in the prison. Perhaps, to these people, there seemed no other way of escape.

This, then, was the island that the Barkers had chosen as their ideal domicile. An island where, apparently, it was infinitely easier to be regarded as a witch or a lunatic than a criminal, just by the slightest hint of being 'different'. All kinds of insanity could be found there. Sometimes it sprang from the island itself, sometimes it was brought to its shores – and sometimes it could be married.

As Julia Marquand was said to have done.

When Julia Marquand got married in the Ballarat Presbyterian Church, west of Melbourne, on 19 September 1868, she was about as far away from her Jersey birthplace as she could be. She had arrived in Australia some twelve years previously, and worked as a dressmaker. Her bridegroom was widower Edward John de Lacy Evans, 'an active, wiry little fellow, about 5′6″ in height, with broad shoulders and muscular arms and hands that bore evidences of hard work'.

For many years, Julia had been good friends with Helen Moore, whose sister Sarah had been the second Mrs de Lacy Evans. Edward had wed Sarah in 1862; some time afterwards, they went to work as general servants on a farm in Sandhurst, Victoria. Edward's multifarious skills soon made him much sought after – he could turn his hand to anything, from blacksmith work to cutting up and preserving slaughtered pigs. A year later, the Evanses decided to move on, and settled in the town of Eaglehawk, where their fortunes took a downward turn. Edward became a miner, but the couple soon fell into debt; when Sarah died in August 1867, it was said her husband was so poor, his wife's body was kept in their house until he could rustle up the money to have her buried.

Unfortunately for Edward, this was the second time he had been made a widower. No one seemed to know a great deal about his first wife, Mary Montague, other than that she had died on 17 May 1859 and was buried in North Melbourne's new cemetery. But there had been a story going around that she and Edward had gone to work for a farmer in a small town near Melbourne, purporting to be servant girls. One week, the farmer had to go away for a few nights and his wife asked one of the girls to sleep with her 'for company'. For some reason, the very next day she sent word for her husband to return, whereupon he inflicted a horsewhipping on Edward de Lacy Evans.

Such was the story.

Edward, however, appeared devoted to his third wife. He built her a house and named it Jersey Cottage to remind her of the island she came from, where they lived happily for four years; a baby daughter completed their joy.

The happiness ended when Edward began working as a miner in Sandhurst. He lived apart from his wife, at the Hibernia Hotel where, to amuse the other residents, he would dress up as a woman and sing. But the japes ended after Edward was injured in an accident at the mine, and became increasingly aggressive and moody. Finally, his behaviour caused such concern that it was brought to the attention of the local police, and on 22 July 1880, Edward de Lacy Evans was brought before magistrates at Sandhurst Police Court on a charge of lunacy. He was examined by doctors, who certified that he was suffering from amentia, or softening of the brain, and recommended he be taken to a lunacy ward.

Within hours of his arrival, Edward escaped from the ward and went home, but was persuaded by his wife and friends to return to the hospital. During his six weeks there, he shared a room with a Guardsman called Gundry. 'He was continually smoking, and could chew tobacco in the most approved style,' observed Gundry, who also noticed that his room-mate never undressed or washed in front of anyone.

Julia visited her husband more than a dozen times, usually bringing their daughter with her, but the flow of visits was interrupted when Edward was transferred to a hospital in Melbourne for further examination. This revealed that Edward de Lacy Evans really wasn't quite himself.

He was, in fact, Ellen Tremaye.

In 1857 Tremaye had set sail from Plymouth on board the Ocean Monarch, bound for Hobson's Bay, Victoria. On the journey, her trunk bore the label 'Edward de Lacy Evans', and another that read 'Not Wanted During the Voyage'. Under her dress, Ellen wore a man's shirt and trousers, and she told other female passengers she was a man. The Ocean Monarch arrived in Australia on 22 June, and within months, Edward de Lacy Evans had become a married man for the first time.

All eyes now turned towards the third Mrs Evans, who faced some tricky questions from the police and the doctors. She was *adamant: yes, of course, all along she had believed Edward was a man, that he was the father of their child. But, yes, she had to admit that her opinion on that matter had changed. Now her official opinion was that 'One night, when she expected her husband to return from work, some other man came in his place, and she did not find out the mistake till he was gone. Such is her story'.*[7]

And the story was having quite an effect on the towns throughout Victoria where Edward de Lacy Evans had lived, worked and wed, as a kind of madness spread through the district:

> People could not believe that for so long they had entertained an angel . . . and a general suspicion of each other was engendered. Anyone who had a married friend that was not blessed with encumbrances, regarded him with a doubting scrutiny, and the genders of the pronouns used became so mixed, that they were almost being abolished altogether.

A local tract dubbed Evans an 'amphi-sex individual',[8] while Evans himself summed up the prevailing mood perfectly when he said, 'Everything coming together was enough to drive a man mad.'[9]

While people were prevaricating over their pronouns and eyeing each other for encumbrances, Evans was taken back to the hospital at Sandhurst, where he complained that the 'examination' he had been given in Melbourne had 'injured' him. He reaffirmed his commitment to his wife: 'I would work again for you, for you are my wife, and belong to me in spite of the world, and I defy them to take you from me,' he told her.[10] This was challenged by the doctors' diagnosis, which concluded that 'the circumstances of "his" life make it very probably [sic] that "his" chief ailment is cerebral mania, which has caused the insane desire of marrying women,

*and which of a necessity, causes amentia. The cause of none of the
wives exposing the deception practised on them has been, without
doubt, nymphomania.'*[11] *It was clear that, whatever else his fail-
ings may have been, Edward de Lacy Evans had been a most
successful husband.*

Such was his story.

*As for Ellen Tremaye, the anonymous author of the tract which
told of 'The History and Confession of the Man-Woman' proposed a happy ending for her:*

> *Pity for her misfortunes is the most charitable and most
> just sentiment, and if to that is added a little generous help
> to remove the unhappy creature to a country where her
> career of imposture is not known, our citizens will have
> earned the reward which attached to the performance of a
> good action, the sense of having done their duty as
> Christians and men.*[12]

*This, then, was the solution: put this curious 'amphi-sexual' back
on a boat and send her out of Australia – an inversion of the
country's own recent demographic history. It was enough to drive
a man mad. Mad as the sea and the wind.*

*For Louis Jobosch, it wasn't really the sea, just Southampton
Water.*

*It should actually have been somewhere along the English
Channel – especially the stretch between France and Jersey.*

But in the end, Southampton Water and the Solent Queen, *an
Isle of Wight steamer, would have to suffice. And so the elderly
man jumped over the bulwark and into the water. But not for the
first time, his intentions were thwarted. He was pulled from the
water and taken to the infirmary. When the staff undressed their
new patient, they were all at sea. But when they heard who had*

been rescued from Southampton Water, the people of Jersey weren't: 'In all probability, this is the same person who was sent away from the island.'[13]

Louis Herman Jobosch had arrived in St Helier, Jersey, aboard the SS Plymouth *on 2 April 1889. The ship's previous port of call had been St Brieuc, France, which is where Louis had wanted to disembark. But when the* Plymouth *docked there, the ship's captain summoned a doctor and asked him to examine a passenger who had been behaving in a suspicious manner. He had fallen down, insensible and apparently ill. It was ascertained that the passenger, who appeared to be German and in his late fifties, was suffering from slight concussion. The doctor also found a number of stones amongst the passenger's clothing. In fact, everything the doctor had found out about this man convinced the French authorities that he should not be allowed to land in France, and thus he no choice but to sail on to Jersey.*

After landing in St Helier, Jobosch took a cab to Mr Richards' boarding house in Bond Street, where he had lodged before on previous visits to the town. But another witchhunt was in progress: it had been started by the Plymouth's *captain and was being continued on land by local police officers, who had been tipped off by the captain that they should keep an eye on this passenger. So the officers watched Jobosch leave the ship, dressed in his fur waistcoat, hat and long overcoat, and followed him to his lodgings. There, they arrested him and he was taken to the General Hospital, pending further enquiries. The information passed to the Jersey police by the captain had been the same given to him by the doctor who had examined his passenger at St Brieuc: Louis Herman Jobosch was a woman.*

The Jersey police learned that Jobosch had been living as a man for forty-two years – after being orphaned at the age of thirteen, he had travelled the world working as a courier, and now spoke several languages. Jobosch had been in Jersey as recently as the *previous August and his behaviour had given cause for concern then: he scarcely left the boarding house and was often heard saying he wished he was dead. He also said he was having trouble sleeping and, as a result, had been taking large quantities of opiates. In St Helier's General Hospital, Jobosch was in poor health, eating very little, although he had been allowed to keep his men's clothes.*

After nearly four weeks in hospital, Jobosch was seen off the island by a local police officer, who accompanied him on board an outgoing steamer, bound for Antwerp via London.

A little generous help to remove the unhappy creature to a country where her career of imposture is not known.

Just over a month later, Louis Jobosch died of pneumonia in Southampton Infirmary, aged approximately fifty-seven. A number of letters had been found amongst his clothing, including one addressed to a Mr Doling, a Southampton restaurant owner: 'All I leave in my room is to pay my bill. I die of misery – trust God forgive me.'[14]

For most of the time they lived on Jersey, the Barkers' home was Maitland Villa, later to be renamed Baycroft, situated on La Grande Route De St Clement. It was a large though unostentatious house with a spacious walled garden, big enough to keep children and dogs happy. Thomas and Lillias always kept at least four dogs. The Barkers did not belong to the élite of Jersey society; they were never featured on the guest lists for the garden parties, dinner parties and musical soirées given by the island's most prominent hostess, Lady Otway, at her Gloucester Terrace home. Nonetheless, Thomas's stewardship of the Jersey Dog Club brought him many

'Baycroft', St Clements, Jersey: birthplace of Valerie Barker

friends, and his efforts for this parochial institution – only Jersey residents were allowed to exhibit at the annual show – greatly enhanced its reputation at home and abroad. Its members were observed to 'excel in personal zeal many societies that have a more widespread reputation'.[15]

Thomas's years as Honorary Secretary of the Jersey Dog Club made his name locally. 'It must never be forgotten that the success of our local Club and its annual exhibition is altogether due to its Treasurer Mr Torre-Picot in company with Mr T. W. Barker, being amongst the foremost of the energetic when its causes are to the fore.'[16]

Jersey was also the perfect place for Thomas to indulge in another of his enthusiams – golf. Though hunting was the most popular sport of Victorian gentlemen, an increasing number were being attracted to games that didn't involve contact between humans and animals. Thomas Barker played most of his golf at the Royal Jersey Golf Club, where he was a member; he served as club captain in 1898.

In 1895, the Jersey Dog Club was holding its 8th Annual Show at the Vegetable Market, Beresford Street, in St Helier, over 11 and 12 September. Thus Thomas Barker didn't register his daughter's birth until 13 September – though she had been born at Maitland Villa on 27 August. In the time-honoured Victorian tradition of their class, the Barkers bestowed on the baby a name already featured within the family: Lillias, a Hebrew name, meaning 'God is my satisfaction'. Her full name was to be Lillias Irma Valerie, but she would always be known as Valerie to family and friends.

In 1899, the Barkers decided to move back to England, though the family connection with Jersey didn't end there: one of Lillias's brothers, Captain F. W. R. Hill of the Royal Fusiliers, would return to the Samarés district at the outbreak of war in 1914, serving as the island's Chief Army Ordnance Officer. Valerie Barker never offered any explanation as to why her father decided to move the family away from Jersey while she was still so young. Whatever it was, leaving this strange island didn't seem to stop something of its intensity and quirkiness rubbing off on her, even though she always said she had no memories from this early part of her childhood.

The family settled in Surrey, at Nurscombe Grange, Bramley, 'a Tudor house with aged black beams', according to Valerie, and it was here that their second child, Tom Leslie, was born on 20 April 1899.

Married men of the late Victorian and early Edwardian

era 'looked for an offspring who would continue the family name and transmit the attributes of masculinity to posterity'. Young men's publications, such as the *Boys' Own Paper*, were unequivocal about what Britain expected from its male children during this era: 'People say "boys will be boys", but they are wrong – boys will be *men*. The weakling goes to the wall in the great battle of life.'[17] In comparison, little was expected of daughters – except to wait for a suitable husband to present himself.

Almost from the start, little Tom Barker buckled under the weight of his parents' – and society's – expectations. According to Valerie: 'The birth of my brother was a joy to my parents, for they had both felt a twinge of disappointment when their first-born was a girl. They were more disappointed when they found my brother did not like games or sports, in stern contrast to the tomboy me – who loved climbing trees and all sorts of pranks.'[18] Tom was overshadowed in all departments by his robust elder sister, not least physically: Valerie, though hardly a Lily Langtry, was growing to be as statuesque as her mother.

Thomas Barker, according to Valerie 'one of the gentlest, dearest men I ever remember', discovered the bond which he had expected to enjoy with his son now developing with his daughter. 'My father always treated me as a boy rather than a girl,' she said. 'It was from my father that I inherited a fondness for horses, dogs and the open life. Always have I liked boyish things. I always read boys' books and was fond of adventure stories.'[19]

Valerie's love of horses had started in Jersey, where they had been part and parcel of daily life, used in agriculture and industry, and as the main means of transporting goods and people. In Bramley, she had been trotted around on 'a fat shaggy pony . . . by the time I was four I was looked upon as an experienced "horse-woman", with my own jacket, breeches and riding boots'.[20]

The Barkers moved from Bramley to an old hunting lodge, Kennel Moor, on Rodborough Common, at Milford, where they enjoyed the luxuries of three servants, expansive gardens, a tennis court and a croquet lawn. Here, Thomas taught his tomboyish daughter the rudimentary skills of fencing, cricket and boxing – skills which she could never have imagined would prove to be so useful in a later life.

Her formal education continued along more conventional lines: she attended Huxley's School for young ladies at Priors Corner, Surrey, which was run by a son of biologist Professor Thomas Henry Huxley. There, Valerie was 'better at sport than scholarship' and more interested in riding her favourite hunter, Ladybird II, around Kennel Moor. Her next school, near Upavon, Wiltshire, was even less successful: 'I was intensely unhappy there. I tried to run away twice, but was caught because I had no money. My mother would not believe that I was unhappy simply because a cousin of mine had been to the same tutor's and was very happy.'[21]

Eventually, when Valerie was sixteen, the Barkers heeded her pleas to have her education completed elsewhere – at an institution where daughters could be 'finished off' before 'coming out' as young women of marriageable age and modest expectations.

The primary purpose of such finishing schools, especially in the late Victorian/early Edwardian era, was to hone a young lady's social education – what to wear, how to behave, table etiquette and so forth. James Bryce, Assistant Commissioner to the 1867 Schools' Inquiry Committee, correctly observed that 'The finishing school is not so much an educational agent as a tribute which the parent pays to his own social position.'[22] The Barkers' social position was respectable but modest, their means independent and comfortable but not opulent, and so they sent their daughter to an appropriate convent school at Graty, near Brussels, where she would be cloistered from the manly pursuits of life at home in Surrey. One of her schoolmates, Mrs Margaret White, remembered young Valerie Barker well: 'She had a craving for doing things that would attract notice and shocked the nuns by dressing up as a boy and smoking. She was always playing pranks.' Another classmate said that 'When we had tableaux at the convent, Valerie always wanted to take the men's parts. She liked dressing up and putting on moustaches.'[23]

Valerie herself told a different story: 'Of course, out there among the nuns I lived the entire life of a girl . . . this devout environment, there was nothing to implant any masculine tendencies in my young mind . . . but on my return home I again dressed as a boy. A boy's activities continued to appeal to me.'[24] In this, she was not alone. It was not regarded as 'feminine' for Victorian and Edwardian girls to want or achieve success – apart from the success of making a 'good' marriage, of course. But in the new century a new breed of women was evolving, women who sensed that ambition and success need not necessarily be a male prerogative. Appropriately enough, one such young woman was Charles Darwin's granddaughter, Gwen Raverat, who admitted: 'I wanted so much to be a boy that I did not dare to think about it at all, for it made me feel quite desperate to know that it was impossible to be one.'[25] Little wonder, then, that stories about career girls – teachers, nurses, students and journalists – and middle-class tomboy heroines written by pioneering female authors such as L. T. Meade were being avidly consumed by the women of Valerie Barker's generation.

And then there was 'Handsome Harry'.

Girls' Home was a halfpenny adventure story weekly that began publication in 1910 and ran for five years. It was largely full of tales concerning respectable middle-class girls doing what respectable middle-class girls seemed to excel at: getting into mischief at school and taxing their parents' patience. Their somewhat melodramatic titles – 'The Outcast of Crowthorpe College' and 'A Rod of Iron – The Story of a Pretty Girl and a Just But Stern Father' – were tales in themselves. But each issue usually contained at least one story featuring a girl who dared to be different.

And the story of 'Handsome Harry the Girl-Man' was nothing if not different.

It told the tale of Harriet Nash, a respectable but poor young woman dismissed from her job at the Stamford Tramway Depot after spurning the advances of her boss, Adolf Grattan. With no employer's reference and, after the presumed death of her only brother, no family to depend on, Harriet takes a pair of scissors to her hair and her name, dons her lost brother's clothes, parcels up her own clothes and tosses the package into the river: 'Fate was against her as a woman; she would now try her fortune as a man.'[26] And thus Harry Nash treads boldly in search of a new life.

It's not too long before Harry encounters some practical difficulties – when he visits the barber to have his hair cut, he's asked if he wants a shave; and then he discovers that men's shoes are not made in the petite size three that he takes. However, he has more luck with his kindly new land-lady, Mrs Gubbins, and her daughter Clara. Harry becomes a hero when he saves a child from being run over by a tram and is rewarded with a job as a tram-driver, at the depot owned by the evil Adolf Grattan. He also makes a new friend, Ben Jeffries, whose niece quickly becomes enamoured of the handsome chap – as does, it seems, every woman who comes into contact with the well-mannered, fresh-faced bachelor, who is regarded by one and all as 'an example for young men to copy'.

Harry is quite specific about the sort of man he has become: 'She posed as a man, firstly because it enabled her to get a living, and secondly because the masquerade appealed to her romantic nature. But for all that, boldness or coarseness of any kind were as repulsive to her as ever.'[27]

Handsome Harry joins a gym and takes up boxing; after just a fortnight, the sport of gentlemen makes him 'a dangerous opponent'. But not everyone is taken in by such manly displays: Ben Jeffries' small daughter thinks Daddy's new friend is a woman, although Mrs Jeffries dismisses this as an understandable mistake because Harry 'has such a clear complexion'; and awful Adolf Grattan, encountering his new tram-driver, hisses, 'I don't like his looks.'[28] But then Harry doesn't help his cause by spending his evenings embroidering cushion covers and a child's hat.

Matters become more complicated when Harry becomes friendly with one of his passengers, Miss Bertha Wells, and 'cut off from the company of women, she was attracted to the girl in pink, as one friend is attracted to another'.[29] Bertha's thoughts turn to possible marriage and her mother regards Handsome Harry as the perfect future son-in-law: 'A husband that loves you like the dearest of girl friends can't have much the matter with him.'[30]

But something *is* the matter, for 'Harry was the victim of her moods';[31] moreover, he has taken a fancy to Bertha's brother, Stanley.

And then comes the rather disappointing denouement, when long-lost brother Tom Nash returns from America, tracks down his sister and, being reconciled, reveals to all and sundry just who is supposed to be wearing the trousers in their family. The way is now clear for a double wedding to take place, between Harriet and Stanley, and Tom and Bertha. All that is left of Handsome Harry is the small oil portrait of him, wearing his uniform, left hanging in the men's room at the tram depot – an example for young men to copy.

Of course, Handsome Harry was also setting an example for young women to copy. But then the Edwardian era appeared to boast more than its fair share of women who had no need of this paragon – they had already been paving a way for other Harrys to follow.

When Percival Carol Redwood, said to be an archbishop's nephew, married Nessie Ottaway, his landlord's daughter, on 21 April 1909, in Port Molyneux, New Zealand, the lavish wedding was given generous coverage in the local newspapers. When the bride and groom spent the wedding night in separate rooms, there was more than a hint that the marriage might hit the headlines again.

The groomsman suspected that Redwood might not be the man everyone thought he was, and called in the police. One of the officers recognised his suspect immediately: he was wanted in connection with a number of cases of fraud, forgery and theft committed between 1886 and 1905. He had, in fact, already served a string of short sentences in gaol for similar offences.

Except that it wasn't Percival Redwood the police were looking for; it was Amy Bock. Redwood was just one of the identities she had used – there had been many other aliases, including the surnames Shannon, Channel, Vallane and Skevington.

For dressing as a man and marrying a woman, forty-five-year-old Bock was given two years' hard labour and declared an 'habitual criminal'. After her release from New Plymouth prison, she worked at boarding houses in Waitara and Mokau, but was convicted again in 1931, this time for 'false pretences'.

Sixty-eight-year-old Charlie Wilson worked as a sign painter; he was married twice, the second time for twenty-four years. When the police picked him up for drunkenness in Piccadilly in 1904, he admitted he had begun life as Katherine Coombe, though he hadn't gone by that name for over forty years.

In 1906, Nicolai de Raylan, the dashing secretary to the Russian Consul in Chicago, died in Arizona. Six months after his death, the publication of his diary and correspondence revealed that he was a wanted man in his native Russia, having fled to Finland and Belgium before making his way to America. Raylan was three times married and twice divorced. But at his death, his widow was unable to inherit her husband's property, for Raylan's diary revealed what the Russian secret servicemen who had been hunting him for nearly fifteen years had known: he was in fact a woman named Taletsky. Becoming Nicolai de Raylan had been an integral part of a convoluted plan to blackmail Taletsky's wealthy mother, who, apparently, had been less than honest about her parentage. This spurious scheme went somewhat awry, but Taletsky fille managed to get Taletsky mère imprisoned – for contravening an obscure Russian law about concealing a boy's sex to avoid compulsory military service – and then fled the country before a medical examination to determine her sex could be carried out.

Fear of what a medical examination might reveal was the undoing of New York politician and businessman Murray Hall, whose death in 1901 stunned his colleagues, his neighbours and, especially, his adopted daughter, Minnie.

Hall had run an employment agency on Sixth Avenue, served as a member of the General Committee of Tammany Hall and was a good friend of State Senator Bernard 'Barney' Martin. He was known as a mean poker player at the finest gentlemen's clubs, such as the Iroquois, and enjoyed whisky, wine and big black cigars. He was a well-read man and regularly bought books from the store run by C.S. Pratt on Sixth Avenue. 'He seemed to me to be a modest little man,' recalled Mr Pratt, 'but occasionally he showed an irascible temper. He would never talk about himself and shunned garrulous and inquisitive companions.'[32]

One subject Hall was not keen to discuss was his first wife, who was with him when he originally moved to New York in 1876. Their neighbours on Sixth Avenue said this wife complained to them that her husband was making her life miserable – 'he flirted with clients and paid altogether too much attention to other women'.[33]

No one paid too much attention when the first Mrs Hall suddenly disappeared after about three years, and by the time Murray moved to his last residence on Sixth Avenue, he had remarried. Celia Lin, the second Mrs Hall, also complained to neighbours about her bon vivant of a husband, saying he was too attentive to other women. Soon after this, the Halls adopted their daughter; the truth about where this child came from went with Mr and Mrs Hall to their respective graves – Celia died three years before her husband.

But there was another reason why Murray Hall kept many people at arm's length – particularly the family physician, Dr Gallagher. He didn't want anyone to find out that he was suffering from breast cancer – which would, of course, have meant them discovering he had breasts. Instead of going for treatment for his illness, Hall began buying medical textbooks from Mr Pratt's bookstore, in a futile attempt to keep the truth about his body a secret. Death finally betrayed him, and Dr Gallagher had to announce to Murray Hall's political friends and his daughter that he was not the man they all believed him to be.

*It didn't seem to matter. Senator Martin still regarded his old
friend with affection and respect.*

*Suspect he was a woman? Never. He dressed like a man
and talked like a very sensible one. He never sought
political preferment for himself, but often said a good word
that helped along a deserving friend. Why, when the
County Democracy was in the heyday of its glory, Murray
Hall was one of the bright stars in that particular
constellation. He used to hobnob with the big guns of the
County Democracy and I knew he cut quite some figure as
a politician. He was a good fellow and kept a good line on
the voters of the district. He knew most everybody and most
everybody knew him.*[34]

*The Senator was right – everyone had known good old Murray
Hall. But he was wrong, too: none of them had known the woman
who became Murray Hall, or where she came from, or even her real
age. Perhaps, like Handsome Harry, she had simply wrapped herself up in a package and thrown it into a river.*

In her nineteenth year, Valerie Barker could be considered a complete package. After she had been 'finished' at
the convent school and had her formal 'coming out' ball,
she did all that was expected of young women of her age
and background: she threw herself into the county social
life. She spent a great deal of time riding her mare, stabled
at a nearby farm. The farmer remembered that 'She always
groomed it herself. For hours she used to ride on the
common and she would jump anything she came across.
I never saw her have a fall, and she was frightened of
nothing.'[35]

Valerie herself described her life as mostly comprising

Valerie Barker in her teens, getting ready to 'do
things that would get her noticed'

'hunting all day and dancing all night', but 'with no
thought of romance in my heart' – despite receiving, she
claimed, several proposals of marriage.[36] At a Royal
Artillery ball, she became friendly with a young subaltern
in the Oxford and Buckinghamshire Light Infantry, with
whom she went to dances and played golf. 'I was thrilled by
it all,' she would recall, 'not that there was any flirtation,
love-making or clandestine kisses. The curious mingling of

the boy and girl in me continued.'[37] More serious overtures came from an older man, who Valerie would only ever refer to as 'Major Stewart'. Eighteen years her senior, he professed, she claimed, undying love for her and expressed a desire to marry her. She admitted that the mystery major 'had a strange appeal for me', but any plans for a wedding were put on hold.[38]

Though married life may not have entirely appealed to her at that time, wearing a touch of uniform – for which she was to develop quite a taste – did. She became an assistant scout mistress of the First Guildford Troop, helping the 'rather sergeant-major type of lady' who ran it. This was a perfectly respectable, unambitious activity with which to occupy her time and, with the example of Olave Baden-Powell to follow, now a family tradition. Except Valerie seemed to be rather keen to subvert tradition – one troop member remembered her as '. . . a regular tomboy. Her grievance was that she had been born a girl. Over and over again we heard her say, "Why was I not born a boy?"'[39]

But she would soon have cause to be glad that she wasn't. With the ruling families of Europe preparing to go to war with each other – and destroy some ten million lives in the process – Valerie Barker, like so many women of her generation, wouldn't have to wait much longer for her next uniform.

Or her next marriage proposal.

2

~~~~❀~~~~

War and Pearce

*There are so few gentlemen about – and don't women just
love that?*

Peggy Shaw, November 2000

Japan, 1914

*Ichizo Kobayashi, businessman and founder of the Hankyu
Railways, decides to establish a new theatrical troupe that com-
bines Western and traditional Japanese theatrical and musical
forms. In a little spa town called Takarazuka, he will build his
first theatre and a school where his players will train.*

*Kobayashi decides his new troupe will consist entirely of young
women, who will play both male and female roles. Takarazuka productions will be grandiose, glitzy, colourful musical shows – later,
they will include adaptations of Western musicals and films, like*
Gone With the Wind. *Takarazuka will promote a highly idealised
image of love and romance. Those chosen to play the 'young men'
have their hair cropped short and are taught how to walk, speak
and sing like men.*

*To the millions of Japanese women who will flock to see them,
these glamorous 'men-women' will represent all they wish for in an
ideal husband: courtesy, romance, sensitivity – perfect heroes and
gentlemen.*

It has nothing to do with the reality of their lives. The Takarazuka girls are dream men.

When Britain declared war on Germany, on 4 August 1914, Valerie Barker was enjoying a holiday with some family friends on the Isle of Wight. She returned home a few days later to find life changing apace.

Barbed wire was being placed along the south-coast beaches, seafront lights were being switched off and civilians given instructions on what action to take if enemy troops invaded. The army was requisitioning private vehicles and farm horses for military use. The patriotic spirit and sense of duty and self-sacrifice were embodied in an advertisement showing a British bull volunteering to be made into Bovril for the troops serving at the front – a prophetically suitable symbol for the slaughter about to ensue.

Women were being urged to 'Do your duty! Send your men today to join our Glorious Army!' At this point, there was no question of England's women joining the army or any other military service, though many, like Valerie Barker, were eager to play their part in the war effort. 'For the first time there surged over me the wish that I had been born a man,' she said.[1]

Still, there was plenty of perfectly respectable work to be carried out by patriotic young women eager to emulate their menfolk and serve their Empire. The British School of Motoring had been quick to spot this, and had no hesitation in taking advantage: 'Ladies, Learn to Drive. It is easy and inexpensive to learn . . . BSM pupils are driving for Government Departments, Trade and Commerce and Red Cross Ambulances.' Valerie Barker had no need of the BSM and its lessons: 'I had learnt to drive cars at home,' she said. 'I taught myself. One day my mother wanted this car from the garage and so I fetched it. It was the first time I had ever driven a car and I got it round to the front door with nothing worse than a smashed rear lamp.'[2]

However, her first war work was of a more conventionally feminine sort than driving vehicles into foreign parts: she signed up to become a member of the Voluntary Aid Detachment – VAD – attached to St Hilda's Hospital, Haslemere. The VAD was a vast corps of volunteer nurses, managed under the auspices of the Red Cross and the St John Ambulance Brigade. It had been in existence since 1910, but from early 1914 a register had been kept of those who were willing to serve overseas.

In many ways, the unpaid work carried out by the VADs was the most arduous undertaken by women during the war. Mostly middle- and upper-class women, they were pitched from their cosseted, sheltered existence into a world of gassed, maimed and shellshocked men doing battle with wounds, amputations and lice. The VAD shifts were long – from 7.30 a.m. to 8 p.m. As well as nursing wounded soldiers, they drove ambulances of the First Aid Nursing Yeomanry, and stories soon began circulating about a new disease that was apparently running rampant amongst the drivers. It was rumoured that 'khaki fever' had broken out, with many of the women drivers, most of whom were single, having sex with the troops and thus ensuring the soldiers had some pleasant memory to take with them as they were sent up the line to the slaughter. Whether 'khaki fever' really was having this effect or not, the social impact of so many unmarried women and men coming into contact with each other in a manner hitherto unknown was being felt elsewhere within the Empire. At the beginning of the war, contraceptives were almost impossible to obtain outside London or other major cities; by 1919, they were being sold in every village chemist.

The willingness of women from the privileged classes to volunteer themselves for war work, including VAD duty, was much admired by their men. 'This instinct to do something on the part of idle young women, or half-idle, is satisfactory to behold,' said Arnold Bennett,[3] although there was another school of thought that believed fashionable society women got 'a thrill . . . through seeing their portraits in paper . . . with a caption saying they had become "ardent war workers somewhere in France"'.[4] Enid Bagnold, author of *National Velvet*, worked as a VAD at the Royal Herbert Hospital, Woolwich, and kept a diary of her time there. She observed that, just as any other service during a time of crisis, the VADs developed their own particular *esprit de corps*: 'I see already manifested in them the ardent longing to be alike.'[5]

In the early stages of the war, the Government did not appear over-keen to widen the parameters of such women's lives by more than a dutifully minimal measure, especially if it meant women wandering into traditional 'male' territory. When Elsie Inglis, a Scottish doctor, offered to form a women's ambulance unit, a War Office official told her, 'My good lady, go home and sit still.'[6]

But the women of Britain refused to sit still. 'Sex has nothing to do with patriotism, with the spirit of service,' raged Emmeline Pankhurst. 'Women are just as eager to work for the nation as men are.'[7] In March 1915, the Government bowed as much to practical and economic necessity as to public pressure, and the Board of Trade set up the Register of Women for War Service. It was not enough: in July 1915, 40,000 women marched through

London under the banner 'We demand the right to service'.

For Valerie Barker, too, the confines of traditional women's war work had begun to pall: 'As the news of the fighting overseas came through I felt an urge to do something more vigorous,' she said.[8] But her sex was against her.

The first Military Service Act, passed in January 1916, decreed that all single men aged between eighteen and forty-one were 'deemed to have enlisted'; four months later, a second Act made the same claim of married men.

And the call to arms heard by an increasingly frustrated Valerie Barker was also heard some 12,000 miles away, in the far-flung reaches of the Empire, where young men in Australia were heeding the call to serve and protect the country from which many of them had originated. The decision made by two of those young men to return to Europe and fight for the 'old country' was to have fateful consequences for them – and for the woman in whose life they would both play a pivotal part.

Insurance clerk Harold Arkell Smith was born to British parents in the small town of Waratah, Australia. He was thirty-six when he enlisted in the Australian Imperial Forces on 9 December 1915, a tall, dark, well-built fellow, whose only previous experience of arms was the nine years he had spent practising at rifle clubs. However, within weeks of enlisting, he had been made a corporal; by the time he set sail for Plymouth from Sydney aboard the *Ceramic* as part of the 20th Battalion, 16th Reinforcements, he had been promoted to sergeant. The 20th Battalion arrived in England on 21 November 1916 but was not sent into France until May 1917.

Civil servant Ernest Walter Pearce Crouch was forty, of medium build and not quite six feet tall when he enlisted to serve in the AIF at Enogerra, Queensland, on 23 March 1916. Ruggedly attractive and soft-spoken, he was an Englishman by birth, born in Woodford, Essex. In England, Pearce Crouch had served in the London Scottish Volunteers for three years and his estranged wife, Amelia Jane, still lived at 6 Kings Gate, Red Lion Square. After enlisting, he was posted to the Pioneer Battalion and left Melbourne for England on 6 June 1916. There, he was assigned to the Grenade School at Lyndhurst before being posted to France in November 1916. He returned to England and, now a corporal, helped set up the AIF depot at Tidworth, before joining the Officers Cadet Battalion in Cambridge.

Arkell Smith and Pearce Crouch were just two of the 330,000 Australian men and women – affectionately known as 'The Diggers' – who were sent overseas for military service during the war. A Berlin journalist described the Australian troops as 'good workmen, fearful fighters and hard as steel'.[9] The winter of 1916–17 in France was the coldest for thirty-six years, and most of the Australians saw snow for the first time that year. As well as the bitter cold, they found they had to share their trenches with lice, which were particularly partial to feet. Sodden socks discarded on the ground could be seen to move around. As they suffered from the flies and the lice and the wet and the cold, and saw their compatriots slaughtered by the thousands, the Diggers could only dream of the sunshine half a world away and a better life back home: a decent job, maybe their own ranch, and a wife to share it all with. It didn't really matter what they did – any work was better than this.

*

Valerie Barker would always maintain that her most satis-
fying war work came by chance, in 1915. By now, her father
had sold most of their horses and replaced them with a car.
Valerie was walking the family dogs at Rodborough
Common, where a large contingent of the Canadian Army
was encamped. Here, she would claim, she came upon a
Canadian trooper trying in vain to break in a particularly
unruly horse and ended up doing it for him. She was
promptly offered a job working with the Canadians, training their horses. When they left for the front, Valerie was
offered an appointment as second-in-command of the
Bristol Remount Depot, responsible for breaking in new
horses for overseas service. Many such depots had been
established in the south of England, mostly servicing
Australian and Canadian troops. Here, striding about in
her khaki breeches, tunic, cap and riding boots, surrounded by her beloved horses and with about thirty or
forty men in her charge, she was in her element.

Occasionally this idyllic existence was interrupted, when
Valerie was required to take horses from Avonmouth to
Dieppe to replace those killed or wounded on the front
line. General Douglas Haig, commander-in-chief on the
Western Front, would later claim that the Allied Forces
won the war because they had a better supply of horses.

When the Bristol job came to an end, Valerie Barker
found a position at a hunting stable near Shrewsbury,
where most of the staff were women, including the gardener, who became a good friend. When the gardener
decided to leave, Valerie did the same, and by early 1918
was working on an estate – looking after the horses – in
Kent, at Meopham, near Rochester, deep in the heart of
Dickens country.

Nearby was Cobham Hall, the ancestral seat of the Earl

of Darnley; in 1883, the Earl of Darnley was better known as the Honourable Ivor Bligh, once captain of the England cricket team. During the war, Cobham Hall was used as a convalescent home for wounded Australian officers. Just down the road was the Leather Bottle tavern, one of Dickens's favourite pubs, immortalised by him in *The Pickwick Papers*. Many of the Australian soldiers staying at Cobham Hall had become regulars at the pub.

One of them was Harold Arkell Smith.

In February that year, Arkell Smith had been taken seriously ill with acute gastric enteritis and trench fever – a legacy from the lice – and admitted to the Red Cross hospital in Boulogne. He was transferred to the London General Hospital in Wandsworth and spent a month there before being sent to Cobham Hall to complete his recuperation. He had finished his stint in the war as a lieutenant, with three medals to show for his service: a 1914/15 Star, a British War Medal and a Victory Medal.

After meeting Valerie Barker in the Leather Bottle one evening, Arkell Smith became a frequent visitor at her lodgings in Meopham. Sixteen years her senior, he became 'a very devoted suitor and did his best to overcome his rough and ready manner'. He told her that, back in Australia, he owned his own ranch, and danced visions of an idyllic life in the outdoors before her. 'That the ranch existed only in his imagination was one of the disillusionments to come later,' Valerie admitted.[10] But for the time being, she went along with whatever Arkell Smith's fantasies presented to her; and before long, he was asking her to marry him and start a new life with him in Australia.

Valerie's parents were not thrilled by the prospect of their daughter's marriage – they considered her to be too young, especially when it meant such an upheaval. But

Valerie was determined: 'I wanted to go to Australia, where I thought there was always sunshine and, above all things, horses. Besides, I thought I loved him.'[11] Mr and Mrs Barker buried their objections and Arkell Smith bought his fiancée an opal engagement ring – although, given this particular gemstone's reputation for bringing bad luck, perhaps it wasn't the most auspicious symbol with which to officially mark their relationship.

And so Lieutenant Harold Arkell Smith and Lillias Irma Valerie Barker were married at 2.30 p.m., on Saturday 27 April 1918, at St John's Church, Milford, near Godalming in Surrey. As it transpired, it would not be the bride's last such ceremony, but it would be the most straightforward. She wore 'a trim, pale, dovegrey coat and skirt, and a hat with a saucy feather';[12] the groom wore his uniform. The signing of the register was witnessed by Valerie's maternal aunt, Constance Eastwood, and by Stuart Neame, a family friend who had performed the same duty when Thomas Barker had married his Lillias.

The new Mr and Mrs Arkell Smith set off for their honeymoon in London, where they were booked into a big West End hotel. 'I had no misgivings when I set out,' recalled Valerie, but these soon developed when, after having dinner together, her husband disappeared without warning. 'It was near midnight when he returned, reeking of whisky fumes,' his bride would claim. 'I had expected, as any woman would on her honeymoon, tenderness and love. I found neither – only violence. I felt a sudden revulsion against Harold's clumsy love-making. It shocked me.'[13]

Whether this version of events was the whole story, what couldn't be questioned was that, within six weeks of her wedding, Valerie Arkell Smith had fled the marital bed

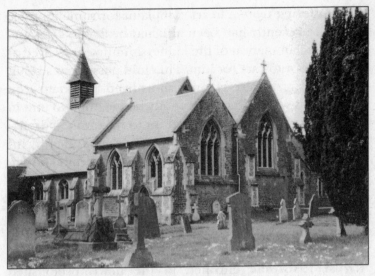

St John's Church, Milford, Surrey

and returned to her parents' home, seemingly appalled by what her role as a wife appeared to entail.

As a married woman, she felt unable to ask her father about such delicate matters and turned to her mother for advice and comfort. Valerie would remember 'sitting on the end of my mother's bed and asking her certain questions. But she refused to answer me and told me that I had made my own bed.'[14] Be that as it may, the newlywed Mrs Arkell Smith was not going to lie in it, and although she would later say that her husband made several attempts to effect a reconciliation, she returned to live permanently at Kennel Moor. Arkell Smith was sent back to rejoin his unit, now stationed at Sutton-Veny, but was soon back in a military hospital again, suffering from influenza, and was subsequently declared unfit for active service.

By now, Thomas Barker was not a well man at all: he had

been suffering from a heart complaint for some months, and more recently had been afflicted by Bright's disease, causing inflammation of the kidneys. A nurse now lived at Kennel Moor to care for him. That July, possibly as a result of Valerie's disastrous and short-lived marriage, he updated his will so that the annuity bequeathed to him in *his* father's will would be passed on to his own children – seventy per cent to his son, and the remainder to his daughter. Just as his father had done for him, Thomas Barker ensured that they would have a modest monthly income for the rest of their natural lives.

After the disappointment and disillusionment caused by her marriage, Valerie Arkell Smith decided to return to what she had been best at: serving her country. On 26 August 1918, she enrolled in the newly established Women's Royal Air Force (WRAF) and became Mrs L. I. Valerie Smith, No. 17218, Motor Transport Driver (General Duties).

From early 1917, women had been employed by the Royal Flying Corps, through the Women's Auxiliary Air Corps, for duties in non-combat areas behind enemy lines in France. But it was not until 1 April 1918, with the war in its final stages, that a separate WRAF was established, with the object of 'enabling them to assist in the war by releasing men for duty at home and overseas'. Under its first director, Chief Superintendent Lady Gertrude Crawford WRAF, numbers had swollen to 15,433 by 1 August 1918.

Whereas the ranks of the WAAC were filled mainly with working-class women, the WRAF drew most of its recruits from the upper classes. Conventional wisdom also declared that the WRAF's 'decidedly ornamental' uniform was considered to be the smartest of the women's services. The one thing that all of them, including the Women's Land

Army, had in common was that their uniforms took away most of their wearers' femininity at a stroke and gave them the outward appearance of men. 'So comfortable did women find their two-legged dress that some land girls preferred to wear their breeches when off duty,' observed Mrs C. S. Peel. Women attached to the RFC and, subsequently, the WRAF also liked to give each other male nicknames, like 'Billy' or 'Mickey'. It made them feel like 'one of the boys'. It was nice to be one of the boys.

In April 1917, Gertrude Macdonald was arrested in Liverpool for 'masquerading in male attire'. She was convicted in July and sentenced to fourteen days' imprisonment 'for wearing His Majesty's uniform without permission'.[15]

The same month, sixteen-year-old Harry Eric Taylor was brought before the West London Police Court and charged with obtaining food and lodgings by false pretences. He was remanded and taken to Brixton prison.

When Harry returned to court for his trial, dressed in a blue serge suit and a man's coat, he told magistrate Boyd that his real name was Ethel Taylor. Furthermore, the court was told that

> *the prisoner, dressed as a man, obtained food and lodgings at Ferber Street, Hammersmith, representing that she was a chauffeur to a captain in the RNA. She left her lodgings the next morning, taking away with her half-a-crown and a photograph of the landlady's daughter. Afterwards she was found trying to obtain lodgings in the next street by similar statements.[16]*

The bemused magistrate, at a loss as to what to do with Taylor, ordered that the prisoner continue to be remanded while further enquiries were made.

Nine months later, eighteen-year-old Charles Brian Capon, a wireworker by profession, was seeking new employment at the Lambeth Recruiting Office in Brixton when the staff there decided to call the police. The officer, Sergeant Dixon, approached the young man who had been causing the staff concern. Charles Capon showed his military protection certificate to the officer, who then asked him a question. 'I did it for a bit of daring,' Capon told him. 'My mother is seriously ill. I thought I could earn more money.'[17]

The question Sergeant Dixon had asked Capon was why was he wearing men's clothing.

Ellen Harriet Capon, of Camden Hill Road, Upper Norwood, was subsequently brought before the Lambeth Police Court on Saturday 19 January 1918, charged with 'masquerading in male attire'. She told the court that, since she was sixteen, she had been employed as a male worker at a factory. She also admitted that she had been '"walking out" with a young woman' and produced a letter to confirm this. Sergeant Dixon then revealed that, after making some enquiries, he had ascertained that 'members of the prisoner's family were aware of what she was doing. She had done well towards her parents in respect of the money she had earned.'[18]

Magistrate Leycester said that he wanted to talk to the prisoner's father. As for the prisoner herself, he demanded to know, 'What are you going to do now, Capon? You cannot go on as you have been doing.'

'I shall work on the land now,' she told him. Land girls, she knew, were allowed to wear trousers without any problems.[19]

Women enrolled into the WRAF through their local labour exchange or recruitment office. As well as filling in numerous forms and undergoing various medical tests, they also had to submit testimonials from people who had known them for a minimum of two years.

A WRAF training depot was set up at RAF Halton camp, though few recruits were actually sent there to begin with. The service had been established in such a higgledy-piggledy fashion that little provision had been made for proper accommodation for the newly enrolled WRAF, and so initially they were encouraged to live at home, from where lorries would collect them each day and take them to their bases for duty. Apart from the lack of accommodation, the standard of food was also bad, and it took until the autumn of 1918 before proper WRAF depots were opened to get women accepted, kitted out and properly trained. WRAF drivers like Valerie Arkell Smith were trained at Number 1 Mechanical Transport (MT) Depot School of Instruction, Hurst Park.

As a driver on general duties, Valerie Arkell Smith was paid thirty-eight shillings a week. Her job involved transporting anything that was required of her, be it food, farm animals or coffins. Qualified drivers on special duty, including ambulance and van drivers, earned an extra seven shillings a week. According to the WRAF's second director, Commandant Dame Helen Gwynne-Vaughan, the work carried out by drivers 'was often isolated and responsible . . . In many places the women drivers washed, cleaned, greased and did the running repairs.'[20]

WRAF members who lived at home were termed 'immobiles' and were paid an extra fourteen shillings a week for their keep, while 'mobile' members lived on camp. Although Valerie had enrolled as an immobile, she was eventually put on mobile service, stationed at Old Sarum. Here, the WRAFs slept in dormitory huts, eight women to a room, and several rooms in each hut. Reveille was at 6.30 a.m., with breakfast at 8 o'clock, followed by the arrival of the immobiles, roll-call and orders for the day. A portion of the day was also set aside for drill and training. The only jewellery WRAFs were allowed to wear was a wedding ring, and their hair had to be concealed under their caps, which were worn all day – even at mealtimes. Supper was at 5.30 p.m., after which they had free time, which was often spent playing hockey, netball or cricket, or attending dances and concert parties. Their day ended with the evening roll-call at 9 p.m., and lights-out at 10 o'clock. Pay-day was Friday, and they were allowed only one day off a fortnight.

Valerie Arkell Smith and her fellow WRAFs had hardly had time to adjust to their regimented way of life when Germany surrendered to the Allies and the Armistice was signed on 11 November. The WRAF was disbanded and the almost-new recruits like Valerie were demobbed, although it would be another year before the last women would leave the service.

Valerie's war years had considerably altered her: the carefree young debutante of four years earlier had been replaced by an embittered, disillusioned wife, estranged from a husband who had not lived up to her expectations of what a gentleman should be. He was certainly nothing like the kindly, courteous man her father had always been.

And now she had lost them both.

Thomas Barker died at Kennel Moor on 1 October 1918, aged sixty-three, and was buried in Milford Cemetery. The epitaph on the unostentatious stone cross that marked his grave read: *He was a simple gentleman.*

His widow left Kennel Moor and moved to an apartment in London with her son. Valerie, however, decided to stay in the West Country, near to where she had been stationed. She had spent some of her fortnightly days off in the town of Warminster, and it was there, after being demobbed from the WRAF, that she went to help run a tea shop. Even

Grave of Thomas Barker, Milford Cemetery,
Surrey

though the war was over, there were still plenty of troops in
the area, many of them Australians, and the tea shop in
Warminster was used to serving plenty of these overseas
visitors. One of the regular customers was Ernest Pearce
Crouch.

Pearce Crouch had had a less eventful war than the
Arkell Smiths. As part of the Australian Employment
Company of the AIF, he had been posted to France for a
brief spell in November 1916 before returning to England.

Then, for seventeen days in December, he had gone
AWOL – absent without leave – but received no worse than
a reprimand and the loss of seventeen days' pay. Like
Valerie's husband, Pearce Crouch had ended the war with
a 1914/15 Star, a British War Medal and a Victory Medal to
his name. He was given a medical discharge because of
neuritis – a painful inflammation of the nerves – in his
right hip, a condition which the army doctors decided had
been made worse by his time in service. Pearce Crouch was
officially demobilised on 24 April 1919. Harold Arkell
Smith returned to Australia on 10 March; he would eventually become a successful small businessman in Sydney.
He never saw his estranged wife again or maintained any
sort of contact with her. They were never divorced, or even
legally separated. Both of them had got very little out of
their marriage; all that Harold left his wife were a few
medals and his surname. Neither seemed as though they
could ever be much use to her.

After becoming acquainted at the tea shop, Valerie and
Pearce Crouch were soon meeting regularly. They
exchanged stories about their war service and discovered
that he had once been stationed at the same camp as
Arkell Smith. Valerie was aware from the outset that her
new suitor was, like her, in no position to marry again in
the near future: 'He told me he had been married for ten
or fifteen years but had not lived with his wife for some
years, and thought he could get a divorce.'[21] But none of
this seemed to matter to her at the time: 'He was a charming companion and, maybe after my experience with
Arkell Smith, the courtesy and gentleness of Pearce
Crouch provided such a contrast that I was caught on the
rebound. I fell head over heels in love with him.'[22]

Valerie and Pearce Crouch were living at Walton Bridge,

Shepperton, when he was offered a job in the advertising department in the Paris office of *The Times*. He asked Valerie to join him there and live with him as his wife; she didn't need asking a second time. Pearce Crouch duly applied for a passport, and, on the application form, asked that his wife's name be added to it.

Her name, he said, was Valerie Pearce Crouch.

3

◦◦✠◦◦

Hail Guest, We Know Not What Thou Art[1]

It's not about one thing, it's about who people want to be . . . when I put on that suit and strap down my breasts, I'm just totally comfortable. I know how to move, I know what to say, I know how to act.

Peggy Shaw, November 2000

The new couple who called themselves Mr and Mrs Pearce Crouch arrived in France in early July 1919; they went to live in Enghien-les-Bains, on the outskirts of Paris, where, according to Valerie, 'We had a little house and were ideally happy.'[2] It was a particularly memorable time to be in that city, and the year or so they spent in France would see life change irrevocably, for the newly liberated French citizens as well as the newly liberated Valerie Pearce Crouch.

The reconstruction of a war-scarred and torn France was still underway in earnest, as was retribution: those believed to have been 'aiding the enemy', and profiteers accused of selling military supplies, were being arrested. In a twelve-month period, the War Damages Courts paid out two billion francs to French farmers, manufacturers and private property owners. On some weekends, the Pearce Crouches visited battle sites and saw for themselves the few yards of mud that thousands had died to gain.

The country's economy was as damaged as its landscape. The *Presse de Paris*, the newspaper that boasted the world's largest daily circulation – five million – closed that year. As the cost of living rose, the government faced a vote of no-confidence and, before Christmas, a general election.

The same month the Pearce Crouches arrived in the city, another war veteran brought his bride to Paris for their honeymoon. Major Denys and Mrs Violet Trefusis were booked into the Ritz hotel where, unusually for a honeymoon, Mrs Trefusis had a tryst with the person she was really in love with: Vita Sackville-West, in France with her husband, the diplomat Harold Nicolson, who was attending the Peace Conference at Versailles. Less than a year before, just after Germany surrendered, the two women had met up in Paris. There, Vita became 'Julian', a male alter ego she had already tried and tested in England, and it was this Julian who impetuously accompanied Violet in the streets, in the cafés and to the opera, disregarding the possible dangers they faced.

Not long after the Trefusis's abortive honeymoon, Vita Sackville-West returned to her home at Long Barn in Kent, and promptly sacked her children's nanny. What malfeasance had this servant committed? Had she been violent to the little boys in her charge? Neglected them? Sold them into white slavery?

It was none of these things. Her 'crime' was to dress in one of Harold Nicolson's suits and take her charges for a walk around the village.

Nicolson asked his wife whether 'vice, drink or foolishness' had been behind this escapade; she said she put it down to 'mere animal high spirits'.[3] Whatever it was, Vita was adamant: the woman had to go. It was one thing for her to put on a suit and become Julian and walk the streets of Paris with her lover – but quite another for her servants to get a taste of how the other half lived. If a woman was going to do that sort of thing, she had to be a gentleman about it.

That July, hundreds of thousands of Parisians watched the victory parade to celebrate Germany's signing of the Versailles treaty; throughout the country, their compatriots threw themselves into the all-night festivities that marked the 'National Fête'. At the same time, the defeated Field-Marshall von Hindenburg sent out an ominous warning that 'The German people will rise again.'

But at least Valerie Pearce Crouch had something to celebrate: she discovered that, as she delicately put it, 'As a result of my love for Pearce I was going to have a baby.' The fact that she and Pearce Crouch were not legally married couldn't dull her joy: 'When I knew I was going to become a mother I was almost delirious with delight. I prayed that it would be a boy,' she said.[4]

On 27 February 1920, her prayers were answered: her son was born. 'It seemed to me then that he was all that was wanted to complete our happiness,' his mother said, 'although by then I had begun to realise that my husband was not quite the man I had thought him to be.'[5] The little boy's parents did not register his birth in France. His mother called him Tony.

The proud parents didn't appear to make many friends during their time in Paris, but Mlle Girodet, the letting agent for their house in Enghien, had good cause to remember her tenants:

> Mrs Pearce Crouch had a mania for affecting masculine attire, and particularly for wearing men's heavy boots. She was very musical and had a remarkable voice. She told me she had been connected with the British Air Force during the war, and I gained the impression that she had actually done some flying. She also said that she had worked as a nurse and, if I remember rightly, told me that she had Italian blood in her veins, one of her grandparents having been of Italian origin.[6]

By late 1920, the *Times*' owner, Lord Northcliffe, in the face of falling sales, was keen to cut costs and warned his staff at home and abroad that 'it may be necessary to greatly reduce their numbers'.[7] It was not an idle threat: numbers *were* reduced, and one Paris employee whose number came up was Ernest Pearce Crouch.

The family returned to England in November 1920 and rented a house in Hook, Surrey, not far from where Tom Barker, Valerie's brother, was living. The loss of Pearce Crouch's job couldn't have come at a worse time, as Valerie was now expecting another addition to their ranks. On 15 June 1921, a daughter was born.

Her mother called her Betty.

Now with two children to support, the pressure was on Pearce Crouch. 'My husband used to go to town every day to look for work,' said his wife, but the prospects did not look good.[8] It must all have seemed so unfair: here was a man who had served country and Empire, travelling thousands of miles to do so, and whose health had suffered as a result. Now, less than five years after his demobilisation, he was struggling to support his family in a country where there were simply too many heroes – and where its politicians seemed more concerned with controlling the behaviour of some of its women than solving the economic problems of its men.

In August 1921, an abortive attempt was made to criminalise lesbianism. It came with the introduction of the Criminal Law Amendment Bill: the main purpose of this legislation was to raise the age of consent to sixteen and to increase punishment for brothel-keepers. But an amendment was added to the Bill that, if passed, would outlaw 'any act of gross indecency between female persons'.[9] This amendment was sponsored by Tory MP Frederick MacQuisten; other prominent supporters included Howard Gritten and Sir Ernest Wild. Why was such a law needed? Frederick MacQuisten explained to the Commons:

> These moral weaknesses date back to the very
> origin of history, and when they grow and become
> prevalent in any nation or in any country, it is the
> beginning of the nation's downfall.
> The falling away of feminine morality was, to a
> large extent, the cause of the destruction of the
> early Grecian civilisation and still more the cause of
> the downfall of the Roman Empire. One cannot in a
> public assembly go into the details: it is a matter for
> medical science and for neurologists. Only tonight I
> was speaking with a man . . . who told me how his
> home had been ruined by the wiles of one aban-
> doned female, who had pursued his wife . . . this
> horrid grossness of homosexual immorality should

also be grappled with . . . this is the far more deep-seated evil.[10]

Wild agreed with his fellow supporters. Such sexual behaviour between women, he said:

> debauches young girls, and it produces . . . insanity. I can quite understand that many members of this House may hesitate to believe such things do take place. I have the authority of one of the greatest of our nerve specialists who has told me with his own lips that no week passes that some unfortunate girl does not confess to him . . . that she has been tampered with by a member of her own sex.
>
> It would be difficult to recite the various forms of malpractices between women, as it would be impossible to recite them in the House. We do not want to pollute the House with details of these abominations. This vice does exist and it saps the fundamental institutions of society. In the first place, it stops child-birth.

The amendment, Wild concluded, was 'simply an attempt to grapple with a very real evil'.[11]

But the amendment had its detractors, even though they proffered some spurious arguments in order to ensure its defeat. Colonel Wedgewood told the House: 'You cannot make people moral by Act of Parliament . . . How on earth are people to get convictions in a case of this kind?'[12] Colonel J. T. C. Moore-Brabazon was also against enshrining lesbians in law. The 'best method', he proposed, was to 'leave them entirely alone'. He rejected the idea of execution for such women as 'drastic' and claimed that a better alternative would be 'to treat them as lunatics and lock them up for the rest of their lives'.[13] Such was the standard of debate that this amendment engendered.

The vote in favour of the amendment was carried in the Commons by 148 ayes to 53 noes (including Winston Churchill and Nancy Astor), and it duly went forward for consideration in the House of Lords where, on 15 August, its merits and fallacies were discussed.

The Earl of Malmesbury was one of the Bill's most vociferous opponents, arguing that it 'went beyond the scope of the Commons'; furthermore, he claimed that 'the more they advertised these vices the more they would increase', and that by passing such a law, its supporters 'were going to increase the opportunities for blackmail without in the slightest degree decreasing the amount of vice'.[14] Their Lordships duly negatived the amendment and that appeared to be that – for the time being.

Ernest Wild and his allies could do nothing about the women who carried out 'malpractices' with other women, and who sapped 'the fundamental institutions of society' – at least, not in Parliament. But events were unfolding in a small village in West Sussex that would cause supporters and opponents of the failed amendment to unite as they vilified one woman whose behaviour, on the face of it, might have fallen within the remit of the proposed law.

And when the time came to punish such transgressions, the right man for the job would be on hand: Sir Ernest Wild QC.

In the mean time, despite his work experience in Australia and France, Ernest Pearce Crouch was still finding it difficult to get a job. This, coupled with his wife's love of animals and the outdoor life, determined their next move:

they decided to become tenant farmers at Bailiffs Court, an estate in Climping, just outside Littlehampton in West Sussex. 'Our idea was to run the place as a farm and guest house,' Valerie explained.[15]

The origins of Bailiffs Court estate dated back to the Norman invasion of England. Next to the Georgian farmhouse where the Pearce Crouches lived was the tiny ancient chapel. Most of the farming carried out on the estate was the growing of crops, such as wheat, oats and potatoes. During their tenancy, the Pearce Crouches also kept chickens, horses, pigs and a few cows, and, as her father had done before her, Valerie started showing her dogs in local shows. They employed a couple, Mr and Mrs Thompson, to help run the house and look after the

The only known photograph of Valerie with Ernest Pearce Crouch, outside the farmhouse, Bailiffs Court, Sussex

children. Everything appeared to be established for the
family to enjoy their new life in the country.

But photographs taken around this time, showing Mrs
Pearce Crouch and her husband standing outside the
farmhouse with one of their horses, tell the real story.
Happiness appeared to be eluding Valerie once again:

> I worked hard on that farm. I made it pay, but my
> husband did not pull with me. We were gradually
> becoming estranged. He began to slack off in his
> work on the farm. He took to lying in bed late, then
> going drinking.
>
> Maybe I was not too amiable myself, being over-
> tired and upset at his neglect of the farm and of me.
> During the quarrels he would seize me by the hair
> and beat me up. Both Mr and Mrs Thompson were
> witnesses of these violent outbursts.[16]

The state of the Pearce Crouch marriage seemed to
reflect the gradual changes that had taken place generally
in Britain, both during the war and in the years immediately after, and their subsequent effects. The traditional
role of the Victorian paterfamilias was in terminal decline:
as so many families had lost the head of their household by
1918, this was hardly surprising. Coinciding with this was
an increase in middle- and upper-class female economic
independence, sparked off by women being employed to
do 'war work'. The returning soldiers came home to find
wives and sweethearts who had had a taste of financial freedom and who had discovered that they could cope
perfectly well without their menfolk.

In the last two years, Ernest Pearce Crouch had lost his
prized job in Paris, been forced to return to England and

was unable to find another decent job. The farm had been his wife's idea, and while he had no real taste for the life, she seemed to be in her element amongst the animals. She had become very much her own woman – and she didn't even really look like a woman any more.

Valerie admitted there was some truth in this: 'I used to wear men's clothing about the farm and for farm work, but everyone knew I was a woman,' she said.[17] Instead of skirts, she was wearing shorts and khaki shirts – to this, she gradually added a man's collar and tie, and then a man's hat. One of her neighbours in Climping, however, thought there was more to Mrs Pearce Crouch's image than met the eye:

> During the day she would walk up and down the village street in breeches and a pullover, with a cigarette between her lips. After she had been here a few months we heard strange stories of her parades in the evening along the lanes adjoining her house. We actually saw her sauntering along one of these lanes in a dinner suit, smoking a cigar.[18]

Pearce Crouch, perhaps unable to cope with the feeling that his masculine dominance had been undermined by everything that had happened since the war, took to drinking and violence – the sort of predictable behaviour that led Edwardian social reformer Edward Carpenter to despairingly dub his own sex 'man the ungrown'.

As her legal marriage had been ended by one form of violence, so Valerie Pearce Crouch's common-law union was being destroyed by another. And as she had when her first husband had filled her with revulsion, Valerie sought parental advice: 'I did not like his treatment of me and I told my mother what was happening. She, of course, knew all about the irregular manner of our association, but she was so fascinated by Pearce Crouch that she always took his part.' Once again, her mother was failing to support her or advise her on her marital problems, just as she had after Valerie had been so traumatised by her wedding-night experiences with Harold Arkell Smith.

But anything else would probably have been expecting a little too much of Lillias's strained relationship with her daughter. Since her husband's death, she had been living in a flat in central London – at 1M Hyde Park Mansions, Chapel Street, near the Edgware Road. She shared the flat with her companion, Mirabel Elcho, and her maid, Kathleen Wells. Lillias hadn't seen a great deal of her daughter in recent years, but Valerie was a constant cause for concern – as she was for Lillias's sister, Constance Eastwood, who had been a witness at her niece's wedding but who hadn't seen her since Thomas Barker's funeral. It later emerged that 'on more than one occasion, there were differences between her [Constance] and her sister, Mrs Barker, about Mrs Smith's behaviour and finally her name was never mentioned between them'.[19]

For whatever reason, Lillias Barker simply couldn't match the close bond that her late husband had enjoyed with their daughter. She seemed unable to come to terms with the unconventional way of life Valerie was choosing, and her disapproval drove a permanent wedge between the two women. Now, after the disastrous marriage with one Australian soldier and an 'illicit' relationship with a second with whom she had had two children, her daughter, for whom she and Thomas had had such high hopes, appeared to have ruined her life irretrievably.

Lillias in any case was in no condition to offer any real

solace or hope – six years before, she had been diagnosed with Parkinson's Disease. Almost symbolically, as her daughter's 'marriage' deteriorated, so did her own health, and in the last few days of her life she suffered from dementia.

She died on 26 September 1923, aged just fifty-five; her daughter, who had caused her so much anxiety, registered the death the next day. Lillias was not buried with her husband; she had left instructions that she was to be cremated. Her jewellery was to be sold and the proceeds placed in trust for her daughter, who would receive a monthly income of £9 for life from the trust funds administered by Royal Exchange Assurance. Her brother Tom would also receive an annuity.

The inheritance from her mother's will did not make an immediate difference to Valerie Pearce Crouch's situation. She soldiered on, running the farm in Climping while relations with her husband deteriorated even further.

But by now she had a special friend: Elfrida Emma Haward. When the two women met in 1922, Elfrida was twenty-six and unmarried. Valerie often used to drive to Littlehampton in her pony and trap, delivering cases of eggs and butter from the farm. Elfrida's father, Edgar, ran a chemist's shop in the town at 15 High Street, where his daughter would serve behind the counter. In 1913, Haward's had become one of the first 'prescription' chemists in West Sussex, issuing medicines to people with National Health insurance. Elfrida lived with her father and her mother, Sarah, in a flat at 8a Beach Road. 'I thought her a very charming girl and a good pal, and used to visit her and her parents at their flat,' said Valerie.[20]

The two women would discuss Pearce Crouch, and Valerie would bitterly lament about what a disappointment he had turned out to be – drunken, violent and lazy, not at all a suitable role model for her son, she insisted. Elfrida gave her friend her spare front-door key, so she could escape to Littlehampton and stay at the flat if things got too much for her to bear at the farm.

And according to Valerie, things *were* getting too much for her. 'For some reason my husband was jealous of Miss Haward and used to disapprove of my seeing her,' she said. 'Things were getting so bad with me at home that I felt I should have to take some action.'[21]

This sounded drastic: what might this 'action' be? Sometimes actions could speak louder than words.

WOMEN'S STRANGE PACT
Plot to Kill Husbands and Live Together

The trial was concluded at Berlin of two young women, Mrs Klein and Mrs Rebbe, aged twenty-three and twenty-five respectively, who were charged with having killed their husbands in order that they might live together.

Mrs Klein was found guilty of the murder, but in view of extenuating circumstances was sentenced to four years' imprisonment. Mrs Rebbe, who was found guilty of attempting to murder her husband, was sent to prison for eighteen months.

Mrs Klein bought arsenic at a drug store on the pretence that her house was infested with rats, and shortly afterwards her husband died. She told the medical attendants that her husband was an habitual drunkard, and they gave her a death certificate that his death was due to alcoholic poisoning.

When the body was examined later, large quantities of arsenic were found. Mrs Klein was arrested,

and in her house were found 500 love letters from
Mrs Rebbe, disclosing an agreement between the
two women to kill their husbands.

At the opening of the case the judge said it was
the most amazing criminal case that had ever been
brought before him.[22]

Well, that was one option. And if Valerie Pearce Crouch
had glanced at this story, it might have appealed. After all,
she claimed that her own husband was an 'habitual drunkard' – surely that would qualify as 'extenuating
circumstances' – and it was known that he had a violent
temper. And there were always plenty of rats to be found
on the farm, so buying some arsenic to get rid of them
wouldn't arouse too many suspicions.

A violent solution to her problems must have seemed
terribly tempting at times. But salvation would have to
come in a different fashion – of her own design.

In the mean time, Pearce Crouch's behaviour was following its familiar pattern, and his wife appeared to be
reaching breaking point.

One night there was a terrible row at home and at 2
a.m. I mounted my bicycle and cycled to the Haward
flat. I told Miss Haward what had happened and
spent the rest of the night in a spare room there.
Next morning my husband came and there was a
scene. Pearce . . . stormed into the room, raving at
me, and seized me by the hair. We calmed him down
and he left.[23]

Badly shaken by what had happened, she spent several
days in Littlehampton Cottage Hospital, while Elfrida was

sent by her parents to stay with some relatives in Durham
to keep her from getting caught in any more of the Pearce
Crouch crossfire. Valerie was given her friend's address,
so she could write to her.

The dreadful events at Beach Road had finally made
Valerie accept that not only must her second 'marriage'
be brought to an end, but so must her entire way of life.
'Once and for all I would break with Pearce Crouch and
fight my own way through life without two children,' she
decided.[24] But it wouldn't be enough to break with the
man she had two children with – she would also break
with the woman who had been the mother of those children. There would be no more Mrs Arkell Smith, no
more Mrs Pearce Crouch. It was the end for them too.
Valerie had decided: for her, the future would not be
female:

> I felt that as a woman I was helpless. For months I
> had been turning it over in my mind. It was too vast
> to be tackled lightly, and I had gone into every possi-
> ble aspect. It was not undertaken lightly. Yet, having
> once decided on the venture, nothing could have
> been easier to put into execution. Nearly the whole
> of my life since childhood had been spent as a man.
> I had dressed as a man because I found a man's
> clothes more comfortable and convenient for the
> work I was doing. I had lived a man's life among
> men, becoming almost accepted as a man, although
> I was recognised as a woman. I had grown accus-
> tomed to the way men thought, talked and acted.
>   I would be able to screen myself against all the
> tortures, miseries and difficulties of the past, and
> work out my own salvation. No man should ever

come into my life again. No man should have it in
his power to break and ruin me.[25]

These rather melodramatic statements, as innocuous as
they might seem viewed from a distance of many years, are
actually quite staggering – if they were indeed the genuine
reasons that lay behind Valerie Barker's extraordinary
decision. Her unsatisfactory marriages, to men she said
were violent, drunk and feckless, would have seemed good
enough reason to turn her back on the life she felt trapped
in. And, surely, any parent would understand the need to
support and provide for a child, which, she would claim
repeatedly over the years, was the overriding reason for
her 'masquerade'. But Valerie Barker also ensured that
she chose a new life and role for herself that she could
enjoy to the full – the sort of life denied to her as a woman.
When declaring her elaborate and daring plan to escape
from the 'miseries' she said she had endured, it seems
obvious that she was undertaking this for more than just
mere financial pragmatism. And, with supreme irony, in
choosing to stop being a 'helpless' woman and escape
from the 'power' any man might have over her, she was
showing that, for all her previous acquiescence to
Edwardian tradition, she was a thoroughly modern
woman.

Needless to say, such a metamorphosis of sex as that
I contemplated could not take place without a great
deal of preparation. Nor could it be accomplished
without somebody being in the secret . . . I decided
to let the Thompsons, who helped me at the farm,
in on my secret. Mrs Thompson was shocked . . .
'You are piling up a store of trouble for yourself and

I dread to think what the future may hold,' she protested.[26]

There was one other person who had to be in on the secret: Valerie's beloved friend Elfrida Haward. If Elfrida's nerves had been upset by Ernest Pearce Crouch turning up on her doorstep and assaulting her best friend, then what she was about to learn was surely enough to give her a breakdown.

I told Miss Haward that I was not what she thought I was; I told her that I was a man who had been injured in the war; that I was really a man acting as a woman for family reasons. I made some excuse about it being my mother's wish, and she believed it.[27]

Incredibly, some of this would have had a ring of truth about it. Many ex-soldiers had offered 'war wounds' as the reason why they were unable to have sex with their wives or fiancées. In many cases, the real explanation was less noble – by succumbing to outbreaks of 'khaki fever' and playing away in foreign fields, they had contracted some sort of venereal disease.

The existence of Valerie's two children was more problematic, but she had an explanation for this, too: while still living as a man, she had had her son with her first wife, who had died, while her daughter was really Pearce Crouch's, with his wife from whom he was now separated. She had met him during the war and they had 'decided to throw in our lot together and run the farm; he as a man, myself as his "wife". It had not worked out, and I was now resuming life as a man.'[28]

Elfrida would always maintain that she had believed her friend's bizarre story, from start to finish. 'Even though I had known her as a woman it was easy to accept her statement that she was a man,' she said. 'Everything about her suggested that she was really a man. Her figure, manner, handwriting, interests – every conceivable thing was masculine.'[29]

But Elfrida's friend was a very different man from the sort Valerie had married as a woman. Both of her husbands had been disappointments to her, and certainly didn't match her expectations of what gentlemen should be. So it made sense that she would try to be a better man than either of them had ever been: a gentleman, a hard worker, a real war hero and the sort of father a son could look up to.

Like 'Handsome Harry', Valerie would become a man 'because it enabled her to get a living and because the masquerade appealed to her romantic nature'. In doing so, she would, according to the writer Sara Maitland, be unwittingly doing what professional male impersonators like Vesta Tilley had been doing on stage for many years: 'They all impersonated the "beau idéal" of their own societies – the soldier, the artist, the dandy . . . they were all aping the male norm that was also male aspiration.'[30]

As far as Valerie was concerned, she believed there were

far more openings for a man, far more spheres a man can tackle . . . even when the work is exactly the same, a man is always paid more. Much is talked about so-called sex-equality, but women are still underpaid for the work they do.

My occupations had been varied enough, but they had always been a man's occupations. I had no

qualifications for secretarial or other office work, no
qualifications for factory work. Nor did I in any way
desire them. But for work in the world of motoring
or aviation, for work on a farm or among animals,
for other work of a masculine nature, I was experienced and fully qualified.[31]

Valerie returned to Bailiffs Court and told her husband
that he had to leave the farm within twenty-four hours or
she would notify the police about the assault at Beach
Road. He complied without too much fuss, although there
was one condition: he would take their daughter with him.
Valerie had vowed to fight her 'own way through life
without two children'. But this wasn't quite as it sounded.
Pearce Crouch suggested to her that their daughter should
be adopted by some Australian friends of his.

He followed up with a phone call in which he
accused me of having time only for our son. It was
not true that I had never cared much about my little
daughter, but there was a vestige of truth in what
Pearce said about the difference in my feelings. I
could not help but feel that my child might have a
better chance in life than if I kept her with me.
    It was a wrench, parting with her, but in the
circumstances I thought it the best thing to do,
particularly as I had satisfied myself that she would
be well looked after.[32]

It would be unfair to suggest that Valerie gave up her
daughter as easily as her few comments on this emotional
subject might indicate. But it is entirely possible that she
might have felt more comfortable with the prospect of

raising a boy – after all, she had virtually been raised as one herself.

In practical terms, handing over a child in the manner described was simple enough; it was an informal arrangement – there would be no official adoption procedure until 1927. Thus Valerie Pearce Crouch was able to give up her daughter to strangers, and the little girl could, and did, disappear without a trace. Her natural mother would always refer to her as 'Betty', but her name did not appear on any register of births, under 'Pearce Crouch', 'Arkell Smith' or 'Barker'. It was as if she had never existed.

For Valerie, it seemed, the most important thing was her son, Tony. Now, with only him to worry about, she could concentrate on getting into character, ready for the big day. She set about arranging to sell off what she could from the farm's assets so she would have some income in the immediate future. Then there were the physical aspects of her new identity and life: 'For weeks I had trained myself, even to the extent of deepening my voice,' she explained. 'A continuous chain of cigarettes helped to coarsen my voice. I had also tried to roughen the skin of my face, and had started shaving to help.'[33]

But perhaps even more important than the physiological aspects of this metamorphosis were the psychological and social factors. For Valerie Barker, the convent-educated debutante, daughter of an independent and much-respected gentleman, the identity of an ordinary working man would not suffice; she wanted to follow in her father's footsteps and be a proper gentleman – living in a smart hotel, dressing and behaving like a decorated officer of the Great War.

William Makepeace Thackeray gave a lecture in 1860 in

which he pondered, 'What is it to be a gentleman? Is it to be honest, to be gentle, to be generous, to be wise and, possessing all these qualities, to exercise them in the most graceful outward manner? Ought a gentleman to be a loyal son, a true husband and honest father? Ought his life to be decent – his bills paid – his tastes to be high and elegant – his aims in life lofty and noble?'[34]

Thomas Barker's daughter would have answered 'yes' to every single one of Thackeray's questions, and her aims for herself were certainly lofty. '"Do it big!" That was the advice I gave myself, once my mind was made up,' she declared. 'Far better to appear somebody important. People would not dare to challenge my identity, and more opportunities would present themselves.'[35]

From a man's outfitters in Littlehampton she bought some plus fours, socks and brogue shoes. Amongst her few bibelots were Pearce Crouch's war medals, the 1914 Star, the British War Medal and the Victory Medal – these, too, would have a place in her new life.

On 15 October, she prepared to leave Bailiffs Court for the last time. 'I put on my plus fours, packed a few essentials into a case and strapped them to my bicycle.' The suitcase bore her original initials, 'V.B.'. 'With an old raincoat on and a tweed cap stuck in my pocket, I mounted the bicycle and made for a station a few miles away where nobody would know me. It would not matter if people in this neighbourhood saw me: they were used to my dressing in that fashion.'[36] This might well have been the case – but it must have mattered to her that her plan didn't fall at the first hurdle.

She cycled to Ford station, about a mile and a half north of Climping; once there, she unstrapped her case and left the bicycle in the cloakroom.

Mrs Valerie Pearce Crouch at Bailiffs Court, waiting
to 'take some action'

In the train I brushed my hair, put my cap on at a
rakish angle as befitted a sporting baronet and
waited for Brighton to come . . . I got into a taxi at
Brighton Station and asked for the Grand. At the
hotel I paid off my driver and tried to look as casual
as I could as I walked through the crowd of people
in the entrance lounge . . . though outwardly calm, I
was far from being so as I asked the clerk for the

room 'reserved for Sir Victor Barker'. The next second a tremendous burden was taken off my mind. Instead of what I feared, a harsh reception from the hotel authorities, all was politeness and servility. Arrangements were made for the 'remaining luggage' I talked vaguely about, and I was shown to my room.[37]

Mrs Arkell Smith and Mrs Pearce Crouch had checked out – and Victor Barker had arrived.

4

The Curious Mingling

Brighton has, from time to time ... been the scene of many peculiar romances.

Sussex County Magazine, 1953

The Brighton that Victor Barker decided would be the ideal place in which to begin his new life was not the glittering Regency town of yesteryear. The years immediately after the First World War were not the resort's best: unemployment and poverty were rife, and much of the housing was run-down and overcrowded. Poor diet nourished diseases such as tuberculosis and rickets. But, despite the somewhat depressed air of the town, there was still plenty to enjoy for those who had the means. According to the then Vicar of Hove, people in Brighton 'dabbled in excitements and revelled in sex'.[1] And if excitements and sex could be had anywhere, they could be had at the Grand Hotel.

With 150 bedrooms on nine floors, the Grand Hotel was the last word in provincial opulence. Built in 1864, it had acquired a reputation to vie with the finest hotels in London. It was one of the first in the country to have lifts, electric lights and external fire escapes. For its privileged residents in 1923, there were many entertainments for them to revel in.

For threepence they could stroll around the nearby West Pier. In the town's twelve cinemas and five theatres, they could be entertained by films such as *When Husbands Deceive* and 'the piquant sex problem play', *Woman to Woman*. They could be serenaded by musical attractions like Ouida MacDermott and her troupe, and applaud her most popular song, 'I'm a Dreamer', in which she lamented of her fantasy man, 'He's ideal but then he isn't real.' Every Sunday, military bands played on the Western Lawn bandstand, and anybody who was anybody went dancing at Sherry's, Brighton's top ballroom.

For Victor Barker, it felt like coming home.

After being shown to his room and unpacking the few 'essentials' he had brought with him, he decided to make sure he really had 'put it over': 'I washed, then lit a cigarette and strolled downstairs. There was nobody in the hotel I knew, and I spent half an hour or so in the lounge watching my fellow guests. Then, not possessing any dress clothes, I left the hotel to have supper in some nearby restaurant.'[2] The next morning, he headed for a gentleman's outfitters.

My purchases included two or three suits, including a dress suit for the evening wear, and a supply of shirts, collars, ties, underwear, hats and the like. With this wardrobe I felt ready to face the world. I put them into a couple of suitcases: they formed the rest of the luggage about which I had spoken at the hotel the previous day. After a few days I had settled down to my new life and felt completely at home in it.

I knew that sooner or later I should have to get a job in order to live and support my son. For the time being, however, I was bent on establishing myself in the role I had adopted.[3]

His choice of new name was quite simple: '"Barker" I had chosen, as it was the family name . . . Victor was a Christian name that had always exercised some appeal. As for the title, my family boasted several distinguished members and I might as well add a baronet to it.'[4] It was also a highly symbolic name: 'Victor', meaning 'conqueror' – it was the name for a winner.

For the time being, money was no problem: the proceeds from the sale of the farm's assets and Lillias Barker's jewellery ensured that. Thus was Sir Victor Barker DSO able to establish himself in Brighton with some conviction, while his three-year-old son was being cared for at another hotel, though by whom, he never cared to reveal.

Meanwhile, Victor was enjoying life on the Grand scale:

The manager, staff and guests all accepted me without question. In lounge and bar I was greeted as a good fellow. I smoked and drank with the male guests, and paid little courtly attentions to the womenfolk. As the weeks slipped by, I began to experience a sense of exhilaration that I was 'getting away with it'. I discovered that boldness was the best way to allay suspicion and, as time went on, I became more and more daring.

The first time I dined at the hotel I called the waiter over and slipped a fiver into his hand. 'I shall be staying here for some time and I'd like you to see that I have every attention,' I told him. After that, I had but to lift a finger to have eager waiters flock around.[5]

It wasn't only the hotel's staff who were impressed by the new guest; he also became a popular figure amongst the residents. He was invited to take part in tennis and swimming parties and went for early morning swims in the hotel's pool. According to one member of staff, 'Sir Victor never missed his early morning bathing. He was a good horseman and, after his swim, would have a horse brought round from the mews and have a ride over the Downs before breakfast.'[6] One of his fellow residents remembered Barker as something of a raconteur: 'Sir Victor used to say that he got shrapnel in the head and in the body . . . generally his stories were of a character to command attention and amazement.'[7]

For his correspondence, Victor took to using his father's

Sir Victor Barker, resident of the
Grand Hotel, Brighton

notepaper, embossed with the Barker family crest: a half wyvern – a dragon with a pointed wing and elevated tail – vomiting flames. This crest had been granted to his great-grandfather James Barker, and was subsequently used by his grandfather James and great-uncles Thomas and William.

Valerie Pearce Crouch always believed Victor Barker was the sort of man she could grow into – and she did. This fellow was the sort of chap that Thomas Barker would have approved of – a man he would have been proud to call his son. A credit to his family name: heroic, courteous, suave – a real gentleman, down to the tips of his polished shoes.

A man's man – and a ladies' man.

Which was what Elfrida Haward believed she saw.

The day after Victor had moved into the Grand Hotel, Elfrida joined him there; she became known to staff and other guests as Victor's 'sweetheart'. 'I did not deny it, as it suited my purpose,' he said. 'If they believed that I was [her] fiancé they would not be likely to suspect that I was a woman.'[8]

However, he did admit that, although he was convinced his fiancée believed he was a man, 'I think she had some doubt as to my being a baronet. I explained that I had dropped the title while living on my farm, but had assumed it again in the hope that it might help me to get a job. I don't think she swallowed this tale, though she never said much.'[9]

Why would she? To Elfrida, this tall, imposing gentle-man was:

young, extraordinarily handsome, beautifully dressed, with perfect manners and tremendous, compelling charm. He paid me compliments and

attentions of the kind that other men had paid me –
that is, he took me out in his car, he bought me
flowers and chocolates, he told me how much he
cared for me. He behaved, in fact, as if he were
deeply in love.

He was always thoughtful and considerate towards
other people. With me he was ideally kind, and a
marvellous cavalier – the kind of companion that
every girl dreams about. In a masculine way he was
gentle; so reliable, so ready with the small attentions
that make any engagement happy. He never forgot
to buy the flowers that matched my frock, the scent
that suited my mood, just the right chocolates or
cigarettes. He could command attention in a
restaurant and order just the right dinner, he could
get a taxicab in a theatre crowd. These are little
things but they mean a lot to a woman.[10]

Elfrida took to calling him 'Bill', explaining:

It is such a manly name – so forceful and
masculine – that I christened him that. It suited him
beautifully.

I remember his hands. No one who ever saw them
would forget them. They were beautiful hands, the
kind that Velasquez painted – lissom, slender, with
the smoothest knuckles I have ever seen. One only
sees such hands once in a lifetime, on a surgeon or a
sculptor. The fingers tapered in the most perfect
manner. They were the hands of a sensitive genius.[11]

Genius or not, Victor's rather lavish lifestyle and
impulses worried his sweetheart: 'He could never go any-

where without a taxicab and if we went to the theatre he could only enjoy a play from the most expensive seats. In clothes, in amusements, in food and drink, in every way he was extravagant.' However, she believed that she managed to curb some of his more flamboyant urges. 'My influence was a restraint on the undisciplined side of his character,' she claimed. 'With me his good qualities – and there were many – came to the front.'[12]

There was, however, one unresolved matter which threatened to put a damper on this burgeoning romance. Elfrida's parents did not yet know that the gentleman who was courting their daughter with such élan was Mrs Pearce Crouch, the woman from Climping who'd often driven over from her farm to visit Elfrida; the one with the brutish husband.

The Hawards had to be presented with some explanation as to how the person they had known as a woman who had lived in terror of her husband, and taken refuge at their home, was now a military hero, living the life of Riley in Brighton and wooing their daughter. They were offered the same explanation that Barker had offered their daughter. 'At first their utter amazement was only natural,' he said. 'But gradually they accepted the idea and adjusted their minds to this strange new state of affairs.'[13]

However, once they had taken this unlikely tale at face value, their concern quickly turned to their daughter's reputation. After all, when this young man had supposedly been a young woman, he had spent the night with Elfrida in her bedroom. Now, that young woman, who had been a young man all along, was living with their daughter in the same room at the Grand.

People were starting to talk. It just wouldn't do. Victor Barker must do the decent thing – he must marry their daughter.

Being a gentleman, Victor could see how it must have looked from their point of view. 'Those kindly, and properly conventional, parents emphasised the possibility of scandal,' said their future son-in-law. 'I have never been dead to the tragedy which was presented to them in this unique situation.'[14] But however much empathy Barker claimed to have for the Hawards, he always blamed them for being so adamant that he must marry their daughter, thus laying a legal minefield that he would surely trip up in at some point in the future.

He seemed not entirely averse to the idea of marriage, and nor was Elfrida – 'We were fond of each other,' said Victor. But his given reasons for favouring a wedding appeared to be somewhat different from those of his fiancée: 'To my shame, I was influenced by the thought that with a wife at my side the likelihood of any suspicion as to my sex arising would fade ever further into the background.'[15] This might have been the case. It is also entirely possible that, as Valerie faded and Victor emerged more fully, he genuinely felt moved to make some sort of public commitment to Elfrida. But at the time he was offering these reasons for his actions, his explanation ensured that no one could vilify Victor Barker, as they had done poor Edward de Lacy Evans, for having 'the insane desire of marrying women'.

Despite her parents' misgivings about their prospective son-in-law, Elfrida Haward would have been well aware that, in marrying Sir Victor Barker DSO, she would be marrying 'up'. Her father might have been a respectable chemist, but within the echelons of the British class system, he was regarded as 'trade' – lower middle class, middle at best. A tall, handsome, decorated war hero and gentleman of independent means was a real catch – and definitely a cut above the sort of men a chemist's daughter from Littlehampton would expect to be courted by.

Despite the unorthodox circumstances in which their relationship had flourished, it seemed a good match, the tradesman's daughter and the knighted military man. But according to Elfrida, there was still one major problem:

> My father and mother did not care for him. My mother had an instinctive dislike of him, in spite of the fact that he made an effort to please her and did everything he could to charm her, just as any young man does for the mother of the girl he loves.
>
> My parents would not settle a sum of money on me when I married, in spite of the fact that they had always intended to do so, because they did not care for him or trust him. They said they would give me anything I wanted myself, if I asked for it, but they would not fix a yearly sum. They were influenced in this decision purely by their distrust of Bill.[16]

Nonetheless, despite this atmosphere of mistrust and caution, preparations for the wedding went ahead. Even here, though, there were disagreements between the prospective groom and the Hawards: he favoured a quiet registry office ceremony but they insisted on a proper church wedding, and Victor Barker was too much of a gentleman to refuse them. St Peter's Church, the parish church of Brighton, was booked for the wedding, but as the Hawards wanted the marriage to take place as soon as possible, to ensure their daughter's honour would not suffer, there wasn't time for the customary reading of the banns on three consecutive Sundays.

Victor and Elfrida would have to get a marriage licence.

To obtain this, at least one of the couple had to live in the diocese in which they intended to get married. A sworn affidavit, or 'allegation', then had to be made by one party, stating that no impediment to the marriage existed. It was also necessary for evidence to be produced that both parties were aged twenty-one or over.

Brighton was part of the Diocese of Chichester, and so, on 10 November, four days before the wedding, Victor Barker went to the West Sussex town and in the presence of one of the Bishop's staff 'made oath that he believeth that there is no impediment of any kindred or alliance or of any other lawful Cause, or any suit commenced in any Ecclesiastical Court to bar or hinder the proceeding of the said Matrimony according to the Tenor of such Licence'. He signed it, 'Victor Barker'.[17]

Of course there *was* an impediment – more than one, in fact. And while Elfrida Emma Haward could produce an authentic birth certificate with her name on it, Victor Barker could not. Still, such obstacles could easily be overcome with forged credentials and a little lying under oath. Whatever means he used, it worked: he left Chichester with the licence.

Four days later, Victor Barker departed from the Grand Hotel on his way to St Peter's. Before he left, he gave one of the hotel staff a generous tip and said, 'Wish me luck.' If ever a groom needed luck, this one would. Still, at least by getting married in Brighton, he would be, as the song went, 'following in father's footsteps . . . he's just in front with a big fine gal, so I thought I'd have one as well'.[18]

On the afternoon of 14 November 1923, Victor Barker, independent bachelor, twenty-nine, and Elfrida Emma Haward, twenty-seven-year-old spinster, were married in St Peter's Church, Brighton, witnessed by the bride's parents,

Edgar and Sarah. When it came to the signing of the register, Barker gave his father's forenames as 'Francis Thomas William'. The ceremony had to be performed by the St Peter's curate, Laurence Hard; in a macabre twist of fate, the vicar, the Revd Dormer, who had been scheduled to carry out the wedding, had collapsed and died in the street that morning while running for a bus. Some years later, the groom pondered, 'Perhaps we should have regarded this as an inauspicious omen.'[19]

The new Mr and Mrs Barker and the Hawards returned to the Grand Hotel for a modest reception, with the bride serving the wedding cake and pouring out the tea herself. Afterwards, the Hawards returned to Littlehampton and left their newly married daughter and son-in-law to begin their honeymoon.

What actually occurred on that honeymoon would, in years to come, be the subject of much conjecture and speculation – and, possibly, a cause of perjury. When it suited her, Elfrida Haward would declare, 'I am prepared to take my oath that everything proceeded in an entirely normal manner. My honeymoon was a perfectly normal one.'[20] Her husband, though, appeared to contradict her when, quite vociferously, he would say: 'Never have I had unnatural instincts, never have I in the slightest been a sexual pervert.'[21] Both of them would stick to their stories; both of them believed they were telling the truth. Neither would be believed.

With the honeymoon over, Barker and his new wife 'settled down to married life together in the best of spirits'. Everything between them appeared, as Elfrida's favourite phrase put it, perfectly normal. Barker was often overheard calling Elfrida 'dear' and 'darling', and she seemed

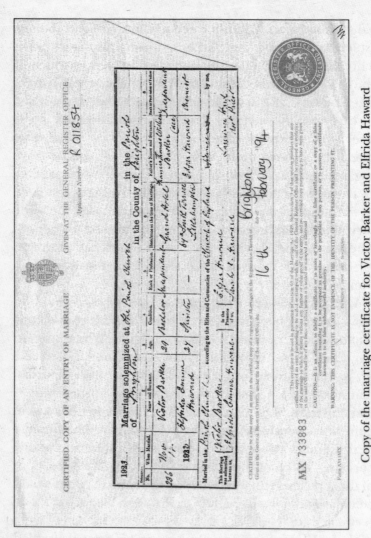

Copy of the marriage certificate for Victor Barker and Elfrida Haward

suitably enamoured with her husband, as anyone would expect a young bride to be. 'A husband that loves you like the dearest of girl friends can't have much the matter with him' – that was what the girl who had fallen in love with

'Handsome Harry' had been told by her mother, and the new Mrs Barker couldn't see much the matter with her own 'Harry'.

While he was busy enjoying life at the Grand and preparing for his wedding, Barker had arranged for his little son to be looked after by a nanny at another Brighton hotel. But with the wedding and honeymoon over, he brought him to the Grand to introduce him to his new 'mummy' and show him off to the other guests. 'Slowly, gradually, he was taught to call me "Daddy", to regard me as his father. It hurt. It hurt a great deal at first.'[22] According to Elfrida, 'Bill adored his little boy. He begged me to give him a mother's care and love . . . it was not difficult to be a mother to him, because he was the sweetest little fellow imaginable, only rather delicate.'[23] She knew the little boy as 'Tim'.

That Christmas, the hotel held a children's fancy dress party. Barker's son took first prize for his Dick Whittington costume. The Barkers enjoyed their first Christmas together, joining in with all the festivities that the hotel had arranged for its guests.

One of the people Victor met at the Grand was Margot Grenville, founder of the Brighton Repertory Company. Featuring a mixture of professional and amateur thespians, the company presented a different play each week; their first performance took place on Monday 17 December 1923, at the newly renovated St Margaret's Hall (renamed the Little Vic) in Cannon Place. Barker went to see some of Brighton Rep's earliest productions and, growing more confident in the real-life role he was playing, fancied taking on some less demanding parts. He signed up for Grenville's company, and was paid a salary of ten shillings a week. 'It was a wonderful training ground,' he said. 'I played every sort of men's role from juvenile lead to heavy father. I was billed as Sir Victor Barker, though I like to think the title was not responsible for the good notices I got.'[24]

Throughout April and May 1924, Sir Victor Barker – or 'Barder', as he was mistakenly called in his first review – was part of the regular cast in the Little Vic's productions. He made his first appearance in a revival of Congreve's *The Way of the World*, playing a supporting character called Petulant. He played several minor roles when, somewhat ambitiously, the Little Vic company presented no fewer than four one-act plays every evening for a week, including Chekhov's *The Proposal.*

My Aunt the Duchess was a musical farce, set in a small village, with an unlikely plot involving a titled lady's sculptor nephew attempting to pass off real people as statues, and featuring songs with unwittingly apt titles, such as 'The Duchess Must Not Know' and 'Colonel Hotstuff'. This outlandish little show earned Victor the best review of his theatrical career: 'The characters were remarkably well played all round . . . Mr Eric Norma as a black man and Mr Victor Barker as the Colonel were responsible for most of the fun, and both were excellent.'[25]

Victor went from playing one titled gentleman to another in the next production, H. V. Esmond's comedy *When We Were 21*, where he took the role of Sir Horace Plumley. This character went by the nickname of 'Waddles', and the name stuck, with Barker soon becoming affectionately known as Waddles to the rest of the company.

Another comedy, *Uncle Ned* by Douglas Murray, featured Victor giving 'quite an amusing study of the character of Dawkins (a butler)'. His swansong at the Little Vic was as 'a

young man about town' in John Galsworthy's *The Fugitive* –
a drama dealing with 'the problems of incompatibility of
temperament and divorce', featuring a husband who 'is
all for keeping of appearances in spite of the fact that he
has no affection for the woman he has married'.[26]

Unfortunately, just as Victor Barker seemed to have
found his niche, his money was beginning to run out. Life
on a Grand scale had to cease and he would have to find a
respectable occupation with which to support his wife and
son. He decided to open an antiques and second-hand furniture shop in Andover, Hampshire, not a million miles
away from where Valerie Arkell Smith had served in the
WRAF. Here, Barker decided to promote himself – from
this time on, he was 'Captain Sir Victor Barker'. He had visiting cards printed, bearing the legend 'Sir Victor Barker,
Bart.'.

Once the shop in East Street was up and running, he
hired some female servants and, briefly, a governess for his
young son. He also bought a .32 Webley pistol and
obtained a certificate for it from Hampshire police.

Life in Andover seemed to suit him: he sang in the local
choir, joined the village cricket club and, in his plus fours,
became a familiar figure in the Star and Garter pub, where
he often popped in for a whisky and soda. But some of the
locals were a little suspicious of their new resident. One
woman said: 'When Captain Barker and his family came to
Andover speculation was very rife as to why these ostensibly
cultured folk should choose this type of place.'[27] The local
tailor noticed that 'When I first measured him for a suit I
was struck by the fact that his shape seemed all wrong for
a man.' And Jack Bevan, secretary of the cricket club,
observed that Barker 'used to bowl and throw in a funny
way, just like a girl'.[28]

It wasn't only his bowling that was a little wide of the crease; when it came to knowledge of antiques, he was stumped. Within a few months, the business foundered and the Barkers were on the move again, though not far away from Andover. They settled into a bungalow in Sarsons Lane, in Weyhill, where Barker was able to indulge his love of horses again by riding regularly with the Tidworth hunt. He kept two hunters and even hired a groom for them. 'He was very fond of hunting,' said the groom, 'but could not master an Arab horse he owned.' He seemed to have other difficulties, too – W. J. Yorke Scarlett, Master of the Tidworth Foxhounds, said, 'We noticed he rode very badly, but he explained that that was due to shrapnel wounds received during the war.'[29]

Barker was still keeping up with all of his social activities in Andover. One of the shopkeepers there said, 'We believed Captain Barker to be a man of means. He often drove his wife into the town from Weyhill for shopping. I remember his appearance at a carnival dance at the drill hall, when he wore evening dress and medal ribbons.'[30]

The groom and the Arab horses and the saloon car Barker had surrounded himself with all looked very impressive, and certainly were not beyond the reasonable expectations of a gentleman of his type. Unfortunately, they were beyond what this particular gentleman could realistically afford. He had left some bad debts behind him in Andover. One of his officer acquaintances, a Colonel St Leger, had lent him some money to get the antiques shop off the ground, and he still owed the Colonel £457.

Barker's profligacy was also having an impact on his marriage. At first his wife had little to complain about:

His temper was good, on the whole. We were both

rather fiery, and he sometimes said I was dictatorial.
He could blaze up in a passion, but it was soon over.
He could not bear to think he was being managed
or subject to someone else's will. The only troubles
were caused by Bill's extravagant tastes and his
capacity for running into debt. Wherever he went,
he would have the best, whatever it cost.[31]

Like his wife, Victor Barker was beginning to learn the
hard way that he had chosen to become a rather expensive
sort of gentleman.

Victor decided that life in Hampshire had cost him too
much and, encouraged by the modest success he had
enjoyed with Brighton Rep, decided he would try and resurrect his stage career. In order to do so, he chose, like
many actors before and since, to adopt a stage name. For
reasons he never explained, he called himself 'Ivor
Gauntlett'. The new name seemed to fit him like a glove: 'I
think the time I spent as Ivor Gauntlett was the most interesting,' he said. 'I was always moving about the country,
meeting fresh people and seeing fresh sights.'[32]

After leaving Hampshire, the Barkers enjoyed the 'fresh
sights' of Brixton, where they lived in a boarding house
near Lambeth Town Hall, registering as Mr and Mrs
Gauntlett. According to the owner of their lodgings:

When they arrived they were a quiet, unassuming
couple and had stayed for about a fortnight before
letters came addressed to Colonel Sir Victor Barker
DSO. I was mentioning at lunch one day, when all
the boarders were present, that such a letter had
arrived and that I was going to give it back to the
postman, when Mr Gauntlett jumped up and said he

was Sir Victor Barker. He explained that it was not
his wish that his identity should have been
disclosed.[33]

Ivor Gauntlett's first role in a touring production was
playing Douglas Cattermole in a revival of *The Private
Secretary* for a wage of £5 a week. He claimed later that
when the tour reached Edinburgh, a letter arrived at the
theatre for him. It was from a woman whose name he
didn't recognise, but who claimed they had met before.
'Out of curiosity, I kept the appointment,' he said, and
agreed to meet his mystery friend for morning coffee at a
café in Princes Street. 'The writer of the letter proved to be
a woman of uncertain age . . . she suggested further meetings. But I did not comply and so what promised to be "an
affair" was nipped in the bud.'[34]

But the theatrical career of Ivor Gauntlett was not;
instead, his next job gave him a chance to appear with a
true legend of the British stage: the formidable Mrs Patrick
Campbell, for whom George Bernard Shaw had written
the role of Eliza Doolittle in *Pygmalion*.

Since 1922, Mrs Pat had been touring continuously
with her own company, starring in revivals of *The
Thirteenth Chair*, *Magda* and *The Second Mrs Tanqueray*, one
of her greatest successes, at every major provincial theatre
in England and Scotland. Now in the twilight of her distinguished career, there were those who questioned the
wisdom of this endless touring. 'It's tragic that she should
be appearing at this stage of her life in the part that
"made" her in the heyday of her beauty', said Cecil
Beaton, after seeing her in *The Second Mrs Tanqueray* at
Bournemouth's Pier Theatre. 'Poor old thing, she does
look awful now! Repulsive . . . twice as large as any man on

the stage.'[35] Some of the critics did not share Beaton's harsh opinion: 'Is there a more energetic, high-spirited woman in the world than Mrs Patrick Campbell? What is her age? She has no age! She has retained her beauty and an intelligence that makes most men seem like half-wits.'[36]

Mrs Pat could make men feel like half-wits, too – especially the newest players in her company. 'The little word she made famous in *Pygmalion* was mild compared with those she used to flay us into shape,' recalled Ivor Gauntlett. 'She would storm and rave and cast wholesale reflections upon our parentage.'[37]

The triple-bill tour was rigorous, spreading the length and breadth of the country: Brixton to Manchester, Luton to Ipswich, Carlisle to Edinburgh. After Ivor Gauntlett left the company, the indomitable Mrs Pat and her troupe continued their provincial tours until 1927.

Gauntlett's agent soon had another possible touring job for him – one with just a little hint of the exotic about it. He was asked to read for the male lead in a short two-hander that would tour music halls. His leading lady would be Dolores, better known to the world as Jacob Epstein's infamous model.

Born Honorine Lattimore, Dolores claimed to be half-French and the granddaughter of one General Count Fournier. Epstein had first encountered her when she was a singer and dancer at the Cave of the Golden Calf, a nightclub run in a basement in Heddon Street, near Regent Street. The Cave was run by Madame Frida Strindberg, a former mistress of Augustus John; Epstein had decorated the club for her.

Epstein made his first study of Dolores in 1921. In the summer of 1922, she moved in with him and his wife

Margaret. She was the model for one of his most famous carvings, *Rema*, and the bronze *The Weeping Woman*; he also made four heads of her. In the studio, Epstein said, 'she was the devoted model, never allowing anything to interfere with posing, taking it seriously; a religious rite'.[38]

Being an Epstein model was not as desirable as it sounded. His previous model, Kathleen Garman, had also been his mistress. One day Kathleen was summoned to the Epsteins' home in Guilford Street by Margaret to discuss her husband's affair – whereupon Margaret produced a gun and shot her. Fortunately for Kathleen, Mrs Epstein was no Calamity Jane, and she escaped with a shoulder wound. No charges were brought against Margaret, and she settled for a quiet life, resigned to the fact that she would always have to share her husband's affection with other women, one way or another. She remained in Guilford Street, while Kathleen lived in a small flat in Regent Square, where Epstein would spend Wednesday and Saturday nights.

But Dolores was installed in the Epstein household purely for practical convenience. He was not interested in her sexually, though he did consider her to be extremely beautiful – he described her as 'the High Priestess of Beauty'. The Epsteins treated Dolores well, often taking her away for weekends and to dinner at expensive restaurants.

Within two years, Dolores was a household name amongst art circles, and on Fleet Street. 'Her sang-froid carried her into some strange adventures . . . her endless amours were a boon to journalists,' said Epstein.[39] Aware of her infamy, Epstein was protective towards his muse – 'My head would doubtless have been well and truly turned had not the spiritual spell of the sculptor acted as my shield against the world,' she said.[40] Once, after she had been arrested in Piccadilly for disorderly conduct, she told the magistrate that her employer was away in America and that this 'had disorientated her'. She escaped with a small fine.

'Dolores was a fine dramatic actress, but also a most temperamental creature with a perverse sense of humour,' recalled her leading man. 'In the midst of rehearsals she would break off and say, "Come on Ivor, let's go down to the Café Royal." Men fell for her like a load of bricks. She loved their flattery and enjoyed the wealth they squandered on her.'[41]

Before becoming one of the most celebrated models in the art world, Dolores had been an actress and dancer and, with her modelling days at an end, had decided to try and resurrect her theatrical career with the melodramatic *Harlequin's Lover*. When Ivor Gauntlett auditioned opposite Dolores, he discovered that the sketch ended with the two characters locked in a passionate embrace – a prospect that didn't seem to overly trouble him when the time came.

> I gripped Dolores in my arms and did not spare her.
> I held her to me in a kiss which I knew no man
> could excel. Then, but not before minutes had
> passed, did I break. I was chosen for the part.
>   Dolores took it for granted that everyone admired
> her. As the result of our passionate scenes on the
> stage, Dolores fondly imagined that I, too, was wildly
> in love with her.[42]

Gauntlett always claimed he kept Dolores at arm's length, even though they spent a good deal of time together outside of the show. When a man who genuinely did have designs on the leading lady tried to get Gauntlett sacked from the show, Dolores insisted he should stay. Matters came to a much more melodramatic climax than they ever had on stage when, according to Gauntlett, he confronted Dolores about the way she had flirted with him. With a rush of blood to the head, he pulled his revolver out of his jacket pocket and threatened to shoot first Dolores and then himself – rather an idle threat, since the gun wasn't loaded. Dolores' retort was a paragon of aptness and coolness – 'Don't be silly.'

This little drama was over and the curtain finally came down on Ivor Gauntlett's stage career when he joined the chorus of a national touring production of *The Bamboula*, a musical comedy starring Alison Stewart and Franklyn Tilton. The story involved English dancers getting mistaken for princes and falling in love with princesses, in the fictional country of Corona – 'a musical play of intrinsic merit, fine singing, delightful dancing, saturated in excellent humour'.[43]

The *Bamboula* tour was gruelling, comprising stints at every major provincial theatre in the north of England. Halfway through the tour, the strain of singing in a low register took its toll: Ivor Gauntlett's voice broke down and he had to leave the play. To add to his troubles, he had creditors on his back again – this time Messrs Allports, a men's tailor in Birmingham, who claimed he owed them £40. 13s. for clothes he had purchased from them. Not so, said Victor – his understanding was that the tailor had given him twelve months' credit.

As Ivor Gauntlett, actor, he was an easy person to track down; as Captain Barker, farm manager, less so. In the summer of 1926, he and Elfrida returned to Sussex, where he was to run a farm in Uckfield, for a salary of 38s. 6d. a week. But after three years of loafing, hunting, shopkeeping and acting, the long days and hard work demanded on a farm proved too much for him, and the couple left after just three months, moving in October 1926 to Oakham, Staffordshire, where Victor was to take up the post of manager of the Dundas Dog Kennels; Elfrida would work as a domestic servant for the owner's wife. Mrs Elsie Hughes, a secretary at the kennels, remembered the new manager from his days as Ivor Gauntlett, juvenile lead and chorus boy:

> I had seen him before he came to Dudley. He was playing in *The Private Secretary* at a Birmingham theatre, and immediately he came to the kennels I recognised him. I made this fact known, and he begged me not to disclose it to Mr Millington, the owner of the kennels.[44]

Mrs Hughes kept Barker's secret, but it didn't take a dramatic disclosure to lose him his job – just plain incompetence. Perhaps, after all the luxury of life in Brighton and the glamorous existence of a theatrical career – even a provincial one – the Barkers simply found this work beneath them. According to Mrs Hughes, the Millingtons dismissed the couple after only a month, as neither of them seemed able to do their jobs properly. Barker maintained their departure was due to 'a difference of opinion with the owner'.

The end of the Barkers' employment also spelled the beginning of the end for their marriage.

After the dog débâcle, Barker managed to get a job as a labourer at the Stourbridge Glazed Brick and Tile Works, hard, unskilled and low-paid work which was brought to an end when he contracted chicken pox. He was ill for weeks and it was left to Elfrida to nurse him back to health. But though her husband made a complete recovery, their marriage was on the critical list.

Poor Elfrida. How great her disappointment must have been – her 'gentleman' husband, partly because of his own profligacy, had had to resort to running a farm and a kennels to support her. And as for herself – why, she had been reduced to a rank little better than a skivvy, washing someone else's floor, cooking in someone else's kitchen.

Boarding houses, guest houses, hotels, rented bungalows, other people's farms – it didn't matter where she and her husband had lived, they were always in someone else's home. So much for dreams of Sir Victor ever having an 'ancestral seat' – they didn't even have a room of their own, never mind a proper home. And how would they ever have one, when her husband seemed incapable of ever living within his means?

It was all a far cry from their Grand life in Brighton and her hopes of a normal marriage with the man of her dreams. How did that song by Ouida MacDermott go, the one they used to hear back then? What was that line? 'He's ideal but then he isn't real.' Maybe that was an omen too, like the vicar who dropped dead before he could marry them. Nothing seemed ideal or real any more.

And to make matters worse, she had a rival for her husband's affections, an actress whose identity Elfrida was too discreet to disclose and her husband too cautious to let slip. 'I knew that my rival had red hair but otherwise I knew nothing about her, and after a time I did not care so much,' said the embittered Elfrida.[45]

Barker insisted that he and his new friend were

intellectual companions and nothing more. She was
a real companion to me, giving her friendship and
asking nothing in return. Of course, a censorious
world will never understand what our relationship
was – we were just friends, each living our own life. I
have nothing but the tenderest memories of her.[46]

Never mind a censorious world – a censorious wife wasn't
convinced by her husband's protestations of innocence.

I always knew he was susceptible. He never could see
a woman without paying her compliments, and
saying pretty things to her. In every hotel we ever
stayed at, women had fallen in love with him, and I
was tired of hearing them tell me how attractive he
was, and how lucky I was to be his wife. But I never
thought he would leave me for another woman.[47]

In fact, it was Elfrida, thoroughly disillusioned, who did
the leave-taking. She returned to Littlehampton to tell her
parents that their worst fears about their son-in-law had
been realised. In November 1928, Mr Haward sold his
chemist's shop and the family moved to Mortimer, a village
near Reading in Berkshire. Haward opened the Thornhill
Pharmacy, where his daughter worked alongside him. It
was hardly the life of a lady, but at least she had a secure
home again.

Meanwhile, her estranged husband had moved to
London and taken a small room in Soho's Rupert Street.
He wrote to Elfrida in an attempt to effect a reconcilia-
tion – of sorts:

My Dear

Must you leave me altogether? Would not a separation do?

I know I've no right to ask this and the final settlement must rest with you.

It was you who wanted your freedom but it frightens me to think of being cut off for ever from you.

Of course, if you ever wanted to marry again I would not presume to stand in the way. I still say I cannot live the ordinary married life with you again, but I still care. You must decide what you think best, only let me know soon.

Did you get my letter-card and Tim's letter? He often speaks of you.

Yours, Bill.[48]

But Elfrida was not coming back to him. 'I decided to put him right out of my life,' she said. 'I burnt all his letters and photographs, and began to forget.'[49]

Still, at least Victor had some compensations: he had a

'I cannot live the ordinary married life with you again': Mr and Mrs Barker separate new lady friend – Elfrida's red-headed 'rival' – to keep him company, and, ever hopeful, had decided to embark on another change in career – he had a half-baked notion that he could become a film actor.

Barker believed that he stood more chance of getting film work if he had a portfolio of photographs, showing him in various outfits and poses, to impress producers with. He went to several Soho studios, where he had himself photographed in a number of different uniforms – one or two of them specially hired – proudly wearing his collection of medals. This now included a DSO and a Croix de Guerre.

Head-and-shoulders portraits, profile portraits, full-length portraits, standing to attention; in most of them he stared defiantly at the camera, but without managing to look either entirely confident or happy. And, for once, his behaviour unwittingly appeared to fit a pattern that was consistent with the sexual category many would assume him to be. According to sexologist Magnus Hirschfeld, 'The inclination to be photographed in the costume favoured by them is widespread among transvestites.'[50]

Despite his impressive bulging portfolio, Barker's efforts to break into the film industry came to naught. But his equally impressive collection of uniforms and war decorations would soon be on display in front of an altogether more appreciative audience.

It was just a step to the right.

5

∽◦◦◦◦∽

*An Officer
and a Gentleman*

*For a woman, passing as a gentleman is more difficult . . .
you stand out if you're a gentleman.*

Peggy Shaw, November 2000

Victor Barker gave several different versions of how he
came by his next job. In one, it happened because a letter
meant for somebody else was delivered to his room in
Soho; in another, someone who lived in the same building
as him noticed a letter addressed to 'Captain Victor Barker
DSO' and decided he was just the man they were looking
for.

It hardly matters which version contained the most
truth – the outcome was exactly the same: late in 1926, he
went to work as live-in secretary to Colonel Henry Rippon
Seymour, one of the leading figures in the National
Fascisti, at their offices at 5a Hogarth Road, Earls Court.

And whatever else could be said about this latest twist in
the ever-fluctuating fortunes of Victor Barker, it was not
without some irony; for he had become involved with a

political movement that would just as easily have accepted Valerie Arkell Smith. And, unlike other political parties during the 1920s and 30s, where women were mainly encouraged to make tea, not policies, fascism often gave these women a chance to be, in real terms, politically active, whether it was taking part in pitched street battles with Communists or selling fascist newspapers.

It was one of the most contradictory developments in Britain's socio-political history that many women who had been active suffragettes would later sign up to join Mosley's British Union of Fascists. They included Norah Elam, Mercedes Barrington, Mary Allen and, most notably, Mary Richardson, who had been with Emily Wilding Davison when she threw herself under the King's horse at Epsom during the 1913 Derby. Mary Allen, founder of the Women's Auxiliary Service during World War I, which paved the way for women police officers, joined the BUF and, in 1934, met with Hitler and Goering in Berlin. The Home Office kept a dossier on Allen, describing her as 'Franco's most dangerous agent in Great Britain . . . the most classical example possible for a "Fifth Columnist".'[1] Having fought so hard for female equality, Mary Richardson could see nothing contradictory in her new political affiliations, declaring that 'having regard to my previous political experience, I feel certain that women will play a large part in establishing Fascism in this country'.[2] It was to prove an eerily accurate observation.

The British Fascisti was formed in 1923 by twenty-eight-year-old Rotha Lintorn-Orman, a woman whose solid, upper-middle-class background would have been familiar to Valerie Barker and her family. Lintorn-Orman, the daughter of a military family – her grandfather was a field marshall – was described as 'a forthright spinster . . . with a taste for mannish clothes';[3] she had served in an ambulance unit in Serbia during the First World War and became Commandant of the Motor School, Devonshire House, in charge of Red Cross ambulance drivers.

Lintorn-Orman claimed that the idea for establishing the Fascisti came to her while she was doing some weeding – there would be no reds in her beds, she decided. Forming the Fascisti was the answer because, as she saw it, there was 'a need for an organisation of disinterested patriots, composed of all classes and of all Christian creeds, who would be ready to serve their country in any emergency'.[4]

The Fascisti motto was: 'For King and Country'; it regarded itself as 'the adult growth of the Scout movement' – the movement founded by one of Valerie Barker's distant relatives. Its first president, L. A. Howard, declared: 'We are anti-Socialist, anti-Communist, and anti-Jewish . . . Ours is a broad, national policy of country before self . . . We are out to smash the reds and the pinks.'[5]

The Fascisti's Brighton and Hove Divisional Officer, Richard H. Back, put it another way:

> The British Fascisti is simply a loyalist organisation
> of men and women. It is purely a patriotic move-
> ment having for its objections the protection of His
> Majesty the King and the Empire . . . there is not the
> slightest resemblance in any way to the 'Ku Klux
> Klan' or any other 'terrorist' organisation. The first
> and most important principle is 'Britain for the
> British', aliens of whatever nationality being barred
> from the ranks.[6]

On enrolling, members had to pledge that they would

'render every service in my power to the British Fascisti in their struggle against all treacherous and revolutionary movements now working for the destruction of the Throne and Empire'[7] – which probably covered most possibilities. There was no uniform, but badges bearing the 'For King and Country' motto were provided.

The Fascisti's members were drawn mostly from the lower ranks of the armed forces, but the ruling classes were also much in evidence: they included the Earl of Glasgow and Viscountess Downe, a friend of Queen Mary. The organisation's activities – when they weren't busy spying on Communist Party meetings – included holding Empire Day rallies (5,000 people attended their 1925 event held in Hyde Park) and garden parties and planning All-England Fascist tennis tournaments. In August 1925, BF members assembled on London's Finchley Road to greet the visiting King George V and Queen Mary, and their loyalty was reciprocated by the monarch, who gave them a fascist salute and raised his hat to them.

The house newspaper, *Fascist Bulletin*, contained advertisements offering fascist ties, Christmas cards and cigarettes for sale. Their broad church of activities also included setting up fascist clubs for children, to counter communist and socialist Sunday schools.

Rotha Lintorn-Orman was prone to making wild claims about the Fascisti membership – by the end of 1924, she said its ranks had swollen to 100,000; eighteen months later, the figure was put at 150,000. However, many historians dismissed the Fascisti, and other predecessors of the British Union of Fascists (formed by Oswald Mosley in 1932), as 'totally insignificant . . . each pettier and more irrelevant than the other'. They were regarded as 'antisemitic, intensely patriotic, highly irresponsible, and

embarrassingly adolescent . . . void of experience in political matters, ignorant of the real meaning and purpose of
fascism . . .'[8]

Within a few years of its formation, the British Fascisti
had splintered several times, spawning the National Fascisti
and the British National Fascisti, and the splinters flew
about in a manner that was to prove highly dangerous for
the newly 'promoted' Colonel Barker.

By the beginning of 1926, membership of the National
Fascisti, Victor Barker's 'splinter', stood at a mere 364, and
nobody outside that membership seemed optimistic about
its future. 'That it has led a precarious existence is certain,' observed the *Daily Herald*.

> Its HQ has been stationed at about 12 different
> addresses in five months and it has certainly moved
> four or five times, and not always of its own volition.
> The Fascists seem . . . to be amateurish, rather
> muddle-headed people, lacking any definite sense of
> direction. They pose as super-patriots, a hundred
> per cent British, yet they take their name and inspi-
> ration from a foreign movement utterly un-British in
> its ideas or methods.[9]

In particular, the National Fascisti even seemed to be an
embarrassment to its fellow travellers. Miss Lintorn-Orman
wrote a letter to the Home Office on behalf of her British
Fascisti from their headquarters in Battersea, stating that
'we have no connection whatever with the National
Fascisti . . . who wish to pursue more violent methods than
those favoured by our organisation'.[10] Perhaps she was a
little out of touch with her fellow fascists. It is certainly
true that punch-ups between communist and fascist

factions were common, and often resulted in supporters from one side or another ending up in court. But her own far-right wing could hardly claim to be non-participants in such incidents. In October 1925, four members of the Fascisti hijacked a delivery van belonging to the *Daily Herald*, one of its biggest critics on Fleet Street, and drove it into the railings of a London church. The four culprits were each ordered to be bound over for £100.

One MP became so concerned by the rising tide of violence that he asked the Home Secretary in the Commons 'if he is aware that bodies known as the Fascisti regularly practise military drill and that numbers of them are armed; that such conduct constitutes an offence against the law; and whether he will state why no legal action has been taken in the case of the Fascisti'.[11]

But successive governments were not over-anxious to contain the myriad fascist contingents – some politicians even believed they might serve some sort of secondary purpose. As clashes between left and right progressed onward through the next decade, Prime Minister Stanley Baldwin considered them to provide ideal opportunities by which these two birds could be killed with each other's stones. 'We English hate fascism but we loathe bolshevism as much,' he is alleged to have said. 'So if there is somewhere where fascists and bolsheviks can kill each other, so much the better.'[12]

However, such unseemly behaviour was not to Victor Barker's taste. 'I began to dread these sorties,' he admitted later – though his reasons were purely pragmatic: 'The Reds always went for the colour-bearer. I always had the feeling that during one of these rough-houses, I should have the clothes torn from my back and be revealed as a woman.'[13]

But paradoxically, Barker's time with the Fascisti was probably his most fulfilling as a man. This was the sort of life he had always envisaged for himself: mixing with other officers and gentlemen, serving his King and country, engaging in gentlemen's sports and being able to wear his uniform and medals with pride. He also greatly enjoyed giving boxing and fencing lessons to the younger men of the Fascisti. On several occasions, he also gave them

lessons in Life with a capital L, telling the young fellows of the snares and pitfalls they should avoid. I do not mean that I assembled all the lads in the common room and gave them a set lecture on life, but that I got two or three of them together and talked to them. Particularly did I warn them of the folly of getting mixed up with women . . . this will probably seem very cynical, but you see I knew what I was talking about.[14]

Fascisti President Brigadier-General Blakeney was impressed with his brother officer.

I thought Colonel Barker was a very keen officer. He seemed to take a very deep interest in the movement and was always a keen, patriotic sort of fellow. Whenever there were matters in which it was necessary for stout fellows to take part he was ready for the job. All his efforts were in the interests of the movement, to which he was very much devoted.[15]

But one task which the 'stout fellow' was called upon to carry out in 1926 was to be a source of embarrassment to him – even thirty years after it happened. That year, the

Boxing clever: Colonel Barker, all ready to give
some young chaps 'lessons in life'

Fascist Gazette announced that on Armistice Day, Sunday 14
November, it would 'send a deputation to lay a wreath on
the Cenotaph at 3 p.m. and afterwards hold a meeting at
the Irving Statue behind the National Gallery'.[16] As colour-
bearer, it was Victor Barker's duty to lay the Fascisti's
wreath alongside the other floral tributes. But, apparently,
this was one honour that he would rather have foregone. 'I
felt a surge of horror at the thought of performing this

office, yet could not get out of it,' he said. 'It has always haunted me . . .'[17] He admitted to a sense of shame at posing as a war veteran alongside genuine old soldiers on such a solemn occasion. Nonetheless, cometh the day, cometh the man – and he did his duty.

Once again, it seemed that overzealous patriotism, a sense of duty – and, probably, a characteristic rush of blood to the head – had got the better of any natural caution he might have considered exercising in order to maintain a low profile. Barker was flirting with the danger of exposure – but this time, there was a real risk that he would get caught with his pants down.

On 8 March 1927, at about 5.30 p.m., a group of dissaffected former associates of Barker and Seymour, mostly from the Fascisti's Croydon branch, arrived at 5a Hogarth Road. The men – Giles Edward Eyre, Gilbert Ware and John Overhead – were, according to Barker, 'some of our own folk who had broken away from the national body to form a party of their own'.[18]

In reality, it was a little more complicated than that.

Eyre and his associates believed that Seymour had become 'the self-elected president of the organisation' and that he had 'brought about a complete change in their rules, without the sanction of the general body of members'.[19] In December 1926, they had gone to Hogarth Road and demanded to see what subscriptions and donations were being spent on, and called for 'a general meeting of the members to discuss the matter of the change in the rules'.[20] On this occasion Seymour's detractors were over-ruled by his supporters, and Eyre and his friends were thrown out of the building. However, this only served to fuel their suspicions that Seymour had 'systematically misappropriated the funds of the society'.[21]

When Eyre, Ware and Overhead knocked on the door of 5a, it was answered by Victor Barker. Eyre told Barker that he and his associates wished to see Colonel Seymour in private. The men's manner, coupled with the fact that they were brandishing large sticks, set off Barker's alarm bells and he tried to close the door on them. Instead, they forced the door open, brushed Barker aside and made their way inside the building. Apart from Barker and Seymour, three women were on the premises at the time, one of them busy at a sewing machine making black shirts.

Seymour, who was in an upstairs room, heard a scuffle, followed by a cry – of pain or warning, he couldn't tell – from Barker, and immediately reached for a sword he kept on the wall. When Eyre and the others entered the room, Seymour took a Webley pistol out of his bureau drawer and threatened to shoot the first man who came within a yard of him. The visitors weren't to know the gun wasn't loaded and, faced with the prospect of being shot or stabbed, or both, kept their distance.

In the mean time, Barker had called the police; when they arrived, a full-scale argument was in progress, and Seymour was still holding the gun on his 'intruders'. The police searched the premises and found twenty-six rounds of ammunition; they took possession of these and Seymour's pistol – for which he was unable to produce a certificate. He was promptly arrested and, the next day, appeared at West London Police Court, charged with common assault and possessing a firearm; he pleaded guilty to both charges. On the first, he was fined £5; alter-natively, he would spend a month in prison. However, magistrate Kenneth Marshall directed that the plea of 'guilty' to the second charge be withdrawn – because, it now emerged, the gun that Seymour had wielded was not his: it belonged to his secretary, Victor Barker.

The police had noticed that the firearms certificate which Barker had produced for them was actually for the pistol he had owned when he lived at Weyhill, and therefore did not match the Webley currently in his possession. He was arrested and taken to West London Police Court, charged with 'uttering a forged firearms certificate, knowing it to be forged and with intent to deceive'. He was released on bail, and committed for trial at the Old Bailey.

And so, in a bizarre twist of fate, by trying to protect his superior officer and employer, Victor Barker found himself on the wrong side of the law.

'I thought it was all up then,' he admitted. 'I really expected to get about two years.'[22] It seemed that, in his efforts to be regarded as a patriotic 'man among men', he had somewhat overstepped the mark. Now there was a real danger that his fragile house of cards was about to collapse around him – and what on earth would his Fascisti comrades do or say when they discovered their colour-bearer was of a quite different complexion?

On 15 July 1927, 'Victor Barker, 35, retired Army officer' appeared in front of Judge Atherley-Jones and a jury to face the charges; counsel for the defence was Mr Freke Palmer, and the prosecutor was Mr Percival Clarke. On paper, the case looked straightforward enough; however, nothing could have prepared the assembled throng for what they saw when the prisoner came into the courtroom.

Victor Barker's eyes were swathed in bandages.

Mr Freke Palmer explained to the court that his client 'had previously suffered from temporary blindness owing to war wounds', and that the strain on his nerves, or neurasthenia, caused by the court case 'had brought on the eye trouble again'.[23] If the bandages were a premeditated ploy by Barker to gain the jury's sympathy for a wounded war hero, thus offsetting a guilty verdict and all its repercussions, it worked to perfection. He was found not guilty, and duly discharged.

This closest of close shaves was enough to convince Barker that, perhaps, it was time to move on. 'After that salutary lesson,' he explained, 'I ceased my connection with the Fascists.'[24] But staff at the Director of Public Prosecution's office were not satisfied with the outcome of the trial and, smelling just the slightest whiff of rat, were asking pertinent questions about the defendant. 'Was anything said by the Defence as to his military service?' one of them wanted to know. 'The bandaged eyes seem to me very suspicious,' commented another.[25]

Eventually, one of the civil servants was instructed to 'draft a letter to the War Office giving what we know about Barker and ask if they are in possession of any information as to his identity'.[26] Then Kensington police wrote to the Under-Secretary at the War Office, stating that 'there was a remarkable rumour current in Andover that he was in reality a woman masquerading as a man'. Furthermore, they said that Barker used that name for 'family reasons, owing to some trouble which occurred with a Brother Officer whilst he was serving in the Army'.[27] However, just as both police and prosecutors seemed to be within a whisker of bearding their former suspect, they concluded that 'nothing has transpired to justify the suggestion that he was in reality a woman' and that 'It hardly seems necessary to pursue the case at present.'[28]

As U-turns go, this was quite incredible. It was obvious that someone, somewhere had decided that this was a Pandora's box that they didn't want to be responsible for lifting the lid off. Despite the fact that the Hampshire police did take some action – cancelling Barker's firearms certificate 'as he is no longer regarded as a fit person to be in possession of firearms' – for the time being, the case on Victor Barker was closed, although a sage in the DPP's office predicted, 'We shall probably hear of him again.'[29]

So Colonel Barker took his leave of Colonel Seymour's Fascisti and their Red-bashing, and their creative accounting, and went to lay his burden down by the riverside.

'I went down to Hampton-on-Thames and took lodgings with some people who treated me well. I did nothing there, and spent most of my time on the river – by myself.'[30] He stayed at Maybury Lodge, Thames Street, a house owned by a Mrs C. Fry, and tried to relax; he went swimming in the Thames and even indulged in a little friendly boxing. 'He told me that he was at the War Office,' said Mrs Fry. 'He always insisted that his real name was not Barker, and that the War Office and Scotland Yard were the only people who knew his real identity.'[31]

While staying at Maybury Lodge, Barker paid frequent visits to the Red Lion Hotel; the landlord there remembered him well.

> His appearance was rather unusual. He said that he
> had not been living with his wife for some time.
> Later, a middle-aged woman turned up with him.
> When the woman did not turn up, he used to go to
> telephone her. Once, he asked me to find him a job
> and I told him I didn't know of anything.[32]

Barker eventually explained to the landlord that the

woman was actually his second wife. However, as was now almost second nature to him, he kept the truth about exactly who she was and what part she played in his life well hidden.

But before anyone had the chance to ponder the spurious logic of his story, Victor Barker was able to leave Hampton and return to London. For once, his financial fortunes had taken an upward turn – but in rather tragic circumstances.

Tom Barker, the younger brother who, as a son, had been such a disappointment to his parents, had led a quiet life. He had been running a poultry farm in Chessington, Surrey, bought for him by his mother, where his big sister, 'Val', used to visit him occasionally. His income had been supplemented by the annuity bequeathed to him by his parents.

Poor Tom had never been able to match his sister's physical robustness and put up little resistance when he contracted tuberculosis. He succumbed to this terrible disease on 3 July 1927, dying at his home, Holt Cottage, aged just twenty-eight. He was buried in Milford Cemetery, next to his father – closer in death than they had been in life. In his will, Tom bequeathed £1,000 to his sister Valerie. It was a tidy sum that, Victor Barker decided, would at last enable him to live in the manner to which he felt he should have been rightfully accustomed. In death, as in life, poor Tom Barker would be overshadowed by his sister.

That October, Barker and his mystery 'second wife' moved into a furnished service flat on the ground floor of 8 Hertford Street, in the heart of London's Mayfair, just off Piccadilly and a short walk from Hyde Park, Green Park and Buckingham Palace. The flat was not cheap: there was an annual rent of £295, plus £175 premium and £250

Grave of Tom Barker, Milford Cemetery, Surrey

deposit for fixtures and fittings. However, Colonel Barker was very much at home: the building's other tenants included a number of high-ranking military men, such as Brigadier-General Critchley, Captain Sir Harold Nutting and Colonel Sir Edward Worthington KCVO. Here, he would be able to live amongst his own kind – officers and gentlemen all. Here, his uniforms and his decorations would let him be recognised and respected and accepted.

Barker's confidence was bolstered by being able to put

to good use things that Valerie Barker had witnessed on her visits to France. This, coupled with detailed information about the front-line conditions imparted by Arkell Smith and Pearce Crouch, would give Victor Barker's military make-up verisimilitude – enough, certainly, to convince most of those who met him of his authenticity.

The 'second Mrs Barker' seemed happy enough with her husband's way of life. 'I lived the life of a man about town,' he admitted. 'I took my wife out to theatres, dined at the Monico, and danced at the Piccadilly.'[33] A female tenant at Hertford Street reported:

> I went into their flat several times and regarded him and Mrs Barker as an ideally happy couple. Once, we were talking of life after the war and Barker said, 'I cannot understand it nowadays. Every married couple appears to be discontented and unhappy. We are the only happily married couple left. All the others seem to be indulging in divorce. There will be no divorce for us, will there?', turning to Mrs Barker. She laughed and said, 'No, dear.'[34]

However, not everyone at Hertford Street was convinced by the Colonel. The building's manager, Mr J. W. Thomas, remembered that his tenant would 'cry like a woman when he was having a dispute with his wife'. Thomas also recalled Barker telling 'amazing stories about the war, which I distrusted, as they did not sound convincing to me as an ex-serviceman. Barker had several suits of uniform and was very fond of strolling round Shepherd Market in the full dress of a staff officer and wearing many medals.'[35]

Thomas was also witness on several occasions when Barker's most treasured possession – his son – came to visit his father. 'When his child came from the country to stay with him for weekends, he sent his wife away. He never allowed the wife to see the child and the child called him Daddy.'[36]

But the man who had the closest contact with Barker and son at this time was Mr Wrigley, who served as his valet for nearly a year. According to Wrigley, Barker was

> one of the most charming men one could ever meet and generous to a degree. The boy was devoted to his Daddy. When I used to take him out for walks in the Park he used to prattle to me of his Daddy's war experiences. 'Daddy was one of the first officers to go to the war,' he would say. 'Have you seen the medals the King has given my Daddy?'[37]

Wrigley *had* seen the medals. As Barker's valet, he was privy to his wardrobe and many of his daily routines.

> Each morning he would tell me to have his razors stropped, and I had to take a shaving mug into the bathroom. Always he left a soap-filled shaving brush and the razors lying about as though they had just been used. He used to leave the flat between 9 a.m. and 10 a.m., often in uniform, ostensibly to go to the War Office, and would return in the evening and take Mrs Barker out to dinner. They seldom dined at home.[38]

Barker occasionally went to a barber's in Whitcomb Street to have his hair trimmed and his neck clipped. Proprietor John Bloomfield remembered this customer well:

Several times he asked to be shaved. There was a very slight growth on his chin, and I used to laugh and say, 'You have a face like a woman.' He never seemed in the least embarrassed and used to say, "Some of us men are lucky.'[39]

Barker's 'man about town' wardrobe comprised a mixture of made-to-measure suits and off-the-peg casual wear. 'He had a very extensive wardrobe and several sets of uniform, which he used to wear at different times,' said Wrigley. 'Sometimes he would tell me he was dining at the mess, and would go out in the mess blue uniform of a major in the Lancers. Each of his uniform tunics had the ribbons of the DSO, the Croix de Guerre, a Belgian decoration and the three Great War Medals in correct order.'[40]

Barker was 'very particular about his decorations', but on more than one occasion, Wrigley wondered about these medals.

I recall that I once thought it rather curious that no name appeared on the leather cases containing the medals. Nor was his name inscribed on any of them except the Mons medal. That was inscribed 'Captain V. Barker, 17th Lancers', which I thought strange, as he had told me that he went to France in August 1914, as a second lieutenant, and as such fought at Mons. I wondered why his Star was inscribed 'Captain', but I never asked him.[41]

Any doubts Wrigley may have had about the veracity of Barker's military history were dispelled when they fell into discussion about their exploits.

He told me that when war broke out he was at
Sandhurst. As he was a fluent French linguist he was,
he said, sent to France with the first contingent for
special duties. He talked of having been wounded
several times and he described in detail his hospital
experiences.

I was at Mons myself and for a very long time we
talked of the incidents connected with it. To me it is
amazing that anyone who was not at Mons could
have learned so much concerning minor incidents
of the retreat, and incidents which followed the
Battle of the Marne.[42]

Wrigley was on hand to help Barker prepare when he
had a very special dinner engagement.

One night, he told me to lay out his mess uniform,
as he was dining at Buckingham Palace. He dressed
that night with the greatest of care and, as he left
the flat at about 7 o'clock in a taxicab, he asked me
the time, and when I told him he said, 'Oh, I am
early. Tell the taxi-driver to take me round the Park
before going to the Palace. When he returned that
night he had a double whisky and soda before going
to bed, and told me he had had a wonderful time at
the Palace and that the King had offered to decorate
him with the Order of the British Empire.

'I did not want any more decorations,' he said,
'and so I begged to be excused the honour. The
King gave me these instead' – and he showed me a
pair of gold cufflinks with the Royal monogram
engraved on them. After that he always wore those
links.[43]

Barker remembered this incident rather differently: 'It is quite true that I had a pair of sleeve links with the King's monogram on them, but I never said I went to Buckingham Palace to receive them,' he said. 'They belonged to a relative of mine, killed early in the war, who did receive them from the King.'[44]

Barker often held dinner parties for officers he had met during his time with the Fascisti. Out of these dinners grew the idea for a new, informal association for Old Contemptibles – it would be called the Fellowship of Mons, named after the battle that took place in Belgium in August 1914, the first between the British Expeditionary Forces and the German Army. He had briefly been a member of a similar organisation, the Mons Club, but, he said, 'inquiries which were made with regard to military service became just a little bit difficult and so I discreetly resigned'.[45]

The answer was obvious: if he formed a club of his own, it was unlikely that the president would check his military background – since he himself would be the club's president. However, he was adamant: 'No one can suggest that I founded the fellowship with any improper motives. I did it to bring a little brightness into the lives of some of those gallant fellows who, after fighting and suffering for their country, have precious little nowadays to cheer them.'[46]

The Fellowship of Mons' inaugural dinner was held on 17 December at Barker's flat, and was attended by fourteen veterans. Barker, the club's elected president, welcomed his guests wearing full officer's dress and all his medals. He had designed and drawn a special menu card for the dinner. 'He made a splendid speech,' said Wrigley, 'telling stories of Mons. He joined in the singing of the songs we used to sing on the march and sang as heartily as any of the fellows.'[47]

One ex-sergeant major considered Barker to be

the finest type of officer and gentleman anyone
could wish to meet. His devotion to his work in connection with and assisting the ex-servicemen, Mons
men in particular, surpassed all understanding. He
was generous to the extreme and was always willing
to come to the assistance, financially or otherwise, of
any ex-serviceman who should be in need of same.[48]

The Fellowship of Mons proved so popular that it
became necessary to hold its meetings at a hotel near the
Strand. 'The Colonel always presided at these functions,'
said Wrigley, 'and the men thought the world of him.'[49]

But, according to Barker, the feeling was not entirely
mutual. Having been accepted by the ex-soldiers as one of
their own, he felt dissatisfied with the calibre of their per-
sonalities:

There was nothing in them. When they were not
talking about women they were thinking about
them, or racing, or perhaps stocks and shares. Their
conversational powers rarely exceeded the ability to
tell a smoking-room story and, as they accepted me
as one of themselves, they did not pick and choose
their words.[50]

Barker's involvement with the Old Contemptibles deep-
ened as the months went on, and that August, when 1,500
of the veterans, accompanied by 'Old Bill' the war bus,
processed from the Embankment to the Cenotaph to hold

their annual commemoration ceremony, Victor Barker marched with them – and was photographed by several national newspapers doing so.

'I met him first when I was attending a meeting of the Old Contemptibles in Peckham,' said Alfred Nathan, landlord of a pub in Great Alie Street in London's East End. 'I served with the Dorsets at Mons and was invited to a social at Peckham, where I was introduced to "Colonel Sir Victor Barker DSO". We discussed old times in France and the Colonel knew, or claimed to know, several of the officers of my regiment. His intimate knowledge of conditions in France, and especially conditions during the retreat, was amazing.'[51]

Colonel Barker's 'intimate knowledge' also impressed other new friends he had met in the bar of the Adelphi Hotel, where he had become a familiar face. One of these acquaintances, Colonel R. Neave, remembered how he first encountered Barker in the bar 'in full staff uniform, wearing the DSO, Mons Star and a number of medals. He entered into conversation with me, told me he had been in the 17th Lancers, and described vividly and clearly the horrors of Mons.'[52]

Barker decided to organise a dinner for the Fellowship of Mons members at the Adelphi. 'All sorts of distinguished people were present,' said Neave, 'and old war songs were sung, Colonel Barker drinking with the best of them, and playing the liveliest role of them all. Later, he appeared in full ceremonial dress as a colonel, sword and all.'[53]

No one present at these events would have thought that their swashbuckling brother-in-arms had a care in the world. But he did, and it was the old, old story: his money was running out.

The expensive flat, the valet's expenses, the lavish dinners, the rounds of drinks at the Adelphi – they had all steadily whittled away at his brother's legacy. He knew that, before too long, he would have to generate some income, if he wanted to maintain the standard of living that he was enjoying so much. But what occupation would befit the type of man he was, the type of man all his friends believed him to be?

The answer appeared logical: since he had moved to Hertford Street, he had enjoyed arranging and hosting dinners, planning menus to suit his guests, and making them feel relaxed and comfortable. So why not try and use those skills in a public capacity and open a restaurant, the kind in which any self-respecting gentleman soldier like himself would feel at home?

In February 1928, Barker saw an advertisement in the *Daily Express* for the leasehold of a café near Leicester Square. It looked ideal, and the following month, he took over the premises at 26 Litchfield Street from a Mrs Roper Johnson, to whom he paid a lump sum deposit and £10 a week rent. The tiny street off Charing Cross Road was home to a number of diverse small businesses – W. E. Brain, safe-makers; dressmaker Millie Martindale; silversmiths Stocker Bros; and the Automatic Perfume Spray Co. Ltd.

The new proprietor was assured that the café's weekly trade averaged about £35 – with overheads only totalling £12–£15 a week, he was confident this latest venture would prove to be one of his most profitable. He decided to change the restaurant's name from 'Johnny's Café' to the slightly classier 'Mascot Café', and opened for business on 12 May. He soon became a familiar figure, strolling up and down the street with his dog, and also at the Marquis of

Granby pub in Cambridge Circus, where he often stopped for a drink. 'I knew the Captain very well,' said the pub manager. 'He was not a person who would talk a lot unless you were more or less in his confidence. He rarely patronised the saloon bar . . . his usual drink was a quartern of whisky.'[54]

Although, under its previous incarnation, the Mascot Café had a reputation as an inexpensive place to dine, Barker was keen to attract the sort of clientele that he was mixing with socially. He used his contacts in the Fellowship of Mons to try and encourage a better class of customer to patronise the Mascot. One of the veterans, an ex-commander in the Royal Navy, organised a lunch at the Mascot for a large group of Old Contemptibles. One of those who attended the lunch remarked that 'rarely had I seen so many distinguised barristers, lawyers and business-men at any charitable function of the sort'.[55]

This ex-officer was one of the few to question the Colonel's credentials. 'I just glanced at Colonel Barker and became convinced that he was never a regular officer in the cavalry. I never met anyone who exhibited so many peculiar and interesting mannerisms.'[56] When he quizzed Barker about his cavalry experiences, however, his suspicions were allayed by what he heard.

Despite the best efforts of his friends and associates, business did not exactly boom at the Mascot, though it wasn't through lack of effort. The loyal Mr Wrigley helped out in the restaurant occasionally, waiting on tables, and remembered Barker 'with shirt-sleeves rolled up doing the cooking, a glass of whisky by his side'.[57] But by September, Barker was asking his valet if he knew where he could lay his hands on £500. 'I introduced him to a money-lender, but the man refused to do any business with him,' said Wrigley.[58]

As a last desperate measure, Barker made use of the late-night licence that had come with the Mascot's lease, but found this wasn't to his taste: 'I had no use for the class of man and woman who began to use the place at night,' he said.[59]

Financial worries were coming back to haunt him and, unbeknownst to him at the time, trouble of another kind was lurking around the corner.

The newsdesk at the *Daily Sketch* had received an anonymous tip-off that it might be worth their while paying a visit to a restaurant near Charing Cross Road. Why? Because there was a Colonel Barker running it who was really a woman. The *Sketch* sent an undercover reporter to investigate the claim; the first time he visited the Mascot, Barker was not on the premises. 'Trade seemed very slack in the little place,' said the reporter. 'It was obviously a struggle for existence.'[60] On his second visit, the reporter was luckier: Barker was there and soon the two men fell into conversation. As usual, Barker was only too happy to talk about his war service and his wounds, and the reporter went away intrigued, but with no hard evidence to support his suspicions.

When he visited the Mascot, Barker was absent once more, although his wife was there this time. When her husband arrived sometime after she had left the café, he struck up another conversation with the reporter and, after a few whiskies, began to relate more tales about his wartime experiences. Somehow the reporter managed to turn the conversation to the subject of Barker's strapping build. Without a moment's hesitation, Barker undid his blue jacket and declared, 'Yes, you will see that I am also a big-made man,' and slapped his chest heavily. 'My waist might be taken for a woman.'[61]

Whatever the *Daily Sketch* and its staff might have suspected, their undercover reporter, in the face of Barker's brazen display, had to admit defeat. Like the Kensington police, the Director of Public Prosecutions and the War

Man about town: every
inch a gentleman

Office staff before him, he could find no evidence to support the anonymous allegation.

However, despite vanquishing Fleet Street, all in all, the café was not proving to be a lucky Mascot for Barker. His skill and judgement as a small businessman had been found wanting, and both he and the business were living well beyond their means. During the four and a half months of the Mascot Café's existence, the takings had amounted to no more than £166 – less than a third of what he had expected – and he now owed Mrs Roper Johnson a tidy sum in back rent. Her patience finally ran out and she filed a summons on him for the money. He went to see a solicitor at the offices of John Hill and Sons and there he made a sworn affidavit in response to the summons. In this signed affidavit, he swore that he was a retired colonel, that he had been in charge of army canteens during the war; and that he had served as a messing officer in the Cavalry for eighteen months. He signed this document as 'Leslie Victor Gauntlett Bligh Barker', a name which merged elements from his past and present: 'Leslie' from his brother's name; 'Gauntlett' from his acting days; and 'Bligh' from the Earl of Darnley, master of Cobham Hall, where Valerie Barker had met her husband.

It didn't really matter which names Victor Barker chose to use: putting his signature to this document was to sign his own 'death' warrant.

Faced with mounting debts, there appeared to be no other solution: the Mascot Café would have to close, Barker would have to get some kind of job, and he would have to leave Hertford Street – and the lifestyle that living there had brought him.

He moved into a small maisonette at 17 Markham Square, Chelsea. 'Barker came with excellent references,' said his new landlord. 'He had an Alsatian dog which he often took out. The woman known as Mrs Barker was here at times, but did not live regularly here. They were an exemplary couple of tenants, very quiet and well-behaved.'[62] On 15 September, Barker started his new position as reception clerk at the Regent Palace Hotel, just off Piccadilly, for a salary of £5 a week. It was a pleasant enough job, which didn't make too many demands on him – and, best of all, it came with a nice, steady wage, without having to work day and night with rolled-up sleeves and worry endlessly about unpaid rent. He could close the door on that chapter of his life and start all over again.

The doors of the Mascot Café had been closed for good the week before and Barker had no reason to return to the premises. If he had, he would have found, pushed through the letterbox, an official-looking document that warranted his urgent attention.

In the wake of Mrs Roper Johnson's action, a bankruptcy court official had called at the Mascot a few days after its closure, to serve a bankruptcy notice and a receiving order on Leslie Victor Gauntlett Bligh Barker, requesting that he be present for a public examination on 24 January 1929, at 11 a.m., at the Bankruptcy Buildings, Carey Street, WC2. Finding no one on the premises, the official posted the document through the door, assuming that the proprietor would find it on his return.

But Victor Barker was now at the point of no return.

∽◦○◦∾

Unlawful Wedded Wife

I do not think a man-woman a pretty character at all.

Samuel Richardson, *Clarissa*, 1747

The passing women I have known have just wanted to pass – they didn't want to be noticed, they just wanted to be one of the millions. They didn't want to make a statement or anything.

Peggy Shaw, November 2000

The bankruptcy court order stayed where it was, on the floor of the abandoned Mascot Café, unopened and unanswered. In due course, a warrant was issued for the arrest of 'Colonel Leslie Ivor Victor Bligh Barker' (sic), for contempt of court in failing to appear for public examination in bankruptcy and 'for not having filed a statement of affairs or surrendered to the proceedings'.[1]

Bailiff James Glover was ordered to go to the Regent Palace Hotel where, his colleagues had ascertained, the man cited in the warrant was now working. Glover's instructions were to arrest this man and take him to Brixton prison.

After Glover and his charge left the hotel on 28 February, the hotel manager decided to open Victor Barker's locker – in it, he found some men's dress clothes, an eyebrow pencil, a well-used powder puff, a few safety pins, two pieces of ribbon and a razor.

After the taxi had deposited its passengers at the gates of Brixton prison, the arrested man was taken into a reception room where several others were sitting. 'Here was a motley collection of men,' observed Barker. 'Some were obviously perfect sahibs, but others were the lowest of the low. We were all bunched together and given a mug of cocoa and a double bun.'[2]

After their light refreshment, the new prisoners were told to undress and get ready to be examined by Brixton's medical officer, Dr Francis Herbert Brisby. One by one, as his name was called, each man went into the doctor's room, stripped to the waist.

When 'Victor Barker' was called out, he was still wearing his singlet. As soon as he entered the room, an officer snapped at him, 'What do you mean by keeping that vest on? Take it off at once!'[3] But Barker would not comply: instead, he asked if he could speak to the doctor in private. The officer left the room, and then, hesitatingly, Barker told Dr Brisby what his subsequent medical examination would confirm: that he wasn't their kind of man. He pleaded with Brisby to pass him through this admission procedure and save him from his secret being revealed. The doctor politely refused the request, and was able to report that 'During my examination of her, I saw no signs of malformation of external genitalia and her breasts were fully developed and pendulous.'[4]

Barker was given the rest of his clothes to put back on and the Governor of Brixton rang Deputy-Governor Mary Size at Holloway Prison – one of his new prisoners had turned out to be a woman, he told her, and so was being sent to her at Holloway without delay.

There was little that could faze Size, the former governor of Borstal who had trained under her formidable predecessor, Lilian Barker, and had become the first female deputy-governor of Holloway in 1927. She was used to admitting all sorts of prisoners within those walls – not only from London, but from sixteen counties throughout Britain. But when she went to the reception ward to meet her newest prisoner, she was perplexed:

> I saw two men – one an extremely handsome, well-groomed gentleman in a dress suit, the other, a plain-looking man in ordinary clothes. I looked from one to the other and, feeling somewhat perplexed, asked, 'Which of you two is the prisoner?' . . . the man in ordinary dress stepped forward and, pointing to the man in the dress suit, said, 'Madam, this is the prisoner.'

The prisoner didn't have many possessions on him, but he was asked to hand them over. 'My cigarettes were taken away and my small flask confiscated. I asked to drink the contents but was refused.'[5]

According to Mary Size, her new inmate, denied a drop of Dutch courage, 'was in a state of nervous tension when she arrived, and appeared to be very concerned about her woman friend and her small son. She was placed in hospital, where she recovered from the shock in a few days.'[6]

In the hospital, Barker gave a statement to his solicitor Adrian de Fleury – he signed it as 'Lillias Irma Valerie Arkell Smith (known as Leslie Ivor Gauntlett Bligh Barker)'.

It was nearly a week after the arrest at the Regent Palace Hotel before the news reached the papers. *The Times* ran a small piece, under the heading 'Woman's Masquerade as a Man', but referred to the prisoner only as 'Colonel/Captain Barker'. That was enough: sensing a good story, the newshounds of every major British newspaper were let loose on the streets of London, sniffing out a trail of evidence that would lead to their prey, who was currently unavailable for comment in Holloway prison.

The *Daily Herald* was one of the quickest off the mark, and managed to produce a very detailed outline of Barker's activities, under the headline: 'Exploits of "Man-Woman"'. The *Evening News* wasn't far behind, as it revealed: 'New Stories of the Amazing Masquerade. Woman "Captain's" Tales of Army Life. "How We Fought at Mons: A Job at the War Office"'.[7]

One civil servant in the Director of Public Prosecutions' office must have found it hard to hide his glee – for he had seen the prediction he made eighteen months before thoroughly vindicated: 'I thought this mysterious individual would turn up again,' he reminded colleagues.[8]

The wheels in a number of government departments were starting to turn, as they began exchanging information about this Barker fellow. The War Office and the Director of Public Prosecutions started to pass files back and forth to each other immediately they heard the name mentioned.

The Under Secretary of State at the War Office had received a letter from a Mr T. H. Griffiths, the Managing Director of Hampton & Sons Ltd, a draper's in Pall Mall East, from whom the said Colonel Barker had bought new curtains in May 1928 as part of the Mascot Café's refurbishment. Mr Griffiths wrote that: 'It is indeed a curious fact that upon the usual Trade Enquiry being made, we were informed that Colonel Victor Barker was at that time Equerry to the Prince of Wales, and this fact doubtless influenced us in granting him credit.'[9] What was more curious was that, between 1917 and 1929, the only equerries to serve the Prince of Wales were Captain Lord Claud Hamilton and Captain Piers Legh, information that could easily have been verified. So much for the efficacy of Hampton's 'usual Trade Enquiry' process – snobbery seemed to carry more weight than accuracy.

While the many government departments were carrying out their investigations, the *Daily Herald* had picked up on the possibility that the law was not being followed to the letter: '"Captain Barker" Conundrum – Is She Lawfully Detained?'[10] The 'conundrum', the story explained, was that the prisoner, who was being held at a women's prison, had been arrested as a man, which meant that, technically, he – or she – was in custody unlawfully.

Barker's lawyers had also spotted this legal loophole and were keen to exploit it to secure their client's freedom. On Friday 8 March, Mr Freke Palmer applied for his client to be bailed from Holloway. He made application in front of a bankruptcy judge sitting in chambers for the release of 'Colonel Leslie Ivor Victor Bligh Barker', on the grounds that all information in connection with the bankruptcy had now been supplied, and thus Barker had 'purged the offence'. The judge agreed with Freke Palmer and ordered

'The Man-Woman': a *Sunday Dispatch* artist's
'impression' of the prisoner in Holloway, March 1929

that the prisoner should be released from Holloway forth-
with.

This news was conveyed to Barker, whose delight at
impending liberty soon turned to anger. 'She was very
indignant when I explained that she would not be allowed
to leave the prison clothed as a man,' said Mary Size. 'She
insisted that she would wear her male clothing and no
other.'[11] The Deputy-Governor was adamant: no woman
would leave her prison dressed as a man. This was all very
well; but as she soon realised, size, in this case, *was*

important. 'The Colonel was a powerfully built woman, whose measurements far exceeded any outsize garments I had in stock,' she said. Size sent out for some clothes that would fit this most unique of prisoners, and the next day Barker was handed a parcel of incongruous women's clothes, comprising a grey tweed coat and skirt, striped silk blouse, silk stockings and a velour hat.

This only served to make an already bizarre situation verge on the farcical. 'So long was it since I had worn feminine garments that I had forgotten how to put them on,' said Barker. 'I remember how the woman officer giggled as she watched me, all fingers and thumbs, trying to get into my new outfit.'[12]

Barker was released from Holloway at around 4 p.m. on 9 March, dressed in the women's clothes he had been forced to wear; he attempted to use the velour hat to conceal his face from the pack of photographers who were trying to get a snap of the former prisoner with the 'manly stride and Eton-cropped hair'. The pack of reporters had been joined outside the prison's main gates by over a thousand people – 'nearly all women', one reporter noted – all hoping to get a peek at this figure they had read so much about in their daily newspapers. Mounted police had to be brought in to control the crowd.

Unfortunately for the onlookers, they were all waiting in the wrong place: Barker was allowed to leave by an alternative exit through a staff gate at the back of the prison. Accompanied by Size, he had to make his way along some waste ground in adjacent Dalmeny Avenue and then climb into the garden of the prison hostel, from which he would finally take his leave.

During this 'great escape', Mary Size couldn't help but be impressed by Barker's strength and gentlemanly manners: 'The Colonel vaulted over the wall with the greatest ease. I climbed up the side of the wall and when I reached the top she grabbed me and lifted me to the ground.'[13] Despite all these best-laid plans, however, they discovered that some photographers had positioned themselves in houses opposite the hostel and thus were able to get a few shots of the prisoner, albeit with his face hidden.

Now that the truth about Barker was being unravelled, everyone who had ever met him was becoming terribly wise after the event.

The loyal valet, Mr Wrigley, had been buttonholed by the press, who were only too eager to tell him the truth about his former employer and extract a telling quote. Wrigley did not let them down: 'What! The Captain a woman! Impossible, impossible. The news shocks me'; though he also admitted, 'I could never quite weigh the man up.'[14]

A barmaid at the Marquis of Granby told reporters that she had always suggested to people that Barker was a woman: 'I don't know why but I always had that feeling'; while a female tenant at Hertford Street claimed: 'I always thought Barker a strange sort of man.'[15] An assistant who worked at the dairy shop opposite the Mascot Café described how:

> Only quite recently I said to my friend, 'I am sure he
> is a woman dressed up.' He seemed so effeminate
> with his refined features. We used to see him every
> day up and down the street, and he was always very
> well groomed. He walked with a little stoop forward
> and accounted for it by saying he had been shot
> through the stomach in the war, and had to wear a
> belt.[16]

Mrs Hughes, the secretary at the Dundas Dog Kennels, claimed, 'I always had doubts about the captain. I never questioned his sex, but I did not credit the stories he told.'[17]

'The Londoner' diarist in the *Evening News* tried to get in on the act:

> Now that I have taken a good look at the portrait . . .
> I can see plainly that the Colonel is a woman . . . I
> might despise those others who took the Colonel for
> a male warrior. But we can make excuses for them.
> How many men have you known who might, dressed
> as women, pass muster as women? Now that I look
> back, I can remember many of them.

The diarist also realised that physical fear might have been a deterrent to anyone thinking of challenging Barker. 'How should anybody dare to stop a six-foot Colonel and call him a woman in a fancy dress?'[18]

The *News of the World* was having a field day with the story, and published its own version of the 'Life Story of "Man-Woman"; Secrets of Six Years' Masquerade; Amazing Impersonation; The Bewildered "Bride".' An editorial called what Barker had done 'a masterpiece of sex impersonation . . . crowned by an unprecedented exploit – the wooing and wedding of another woman . . . '[19] But it got it right by saying: 'Had it not been for a clash with the law, the masquerade might have still remained undiscovered . . . So widespread and diverse are the ramifications of her adventurous and colourful career that the unravelling of the threads created a romance almost without parallel in the history of sex impersonation or in the annals of imaginative literature.'[20]

Novelist Francis King, then a teenager living with the
aunt and uncle who were his guardians, read the Sunday
scandal sheet's version of events and tried to ask them
about it in more detail – especially the question that was on
everyone's lips: 'How could the Colonel's "wife" not have
realised that something was missing?' King's enquiries got
him no further than being told he 'should not have been
reading the *News of the World*'.[21]

And so the column inches continued to fill up with
seemingly endless stories about the adventures of the
'man-woman' and the repercussions of the revelations.
Anthony Praga in the *Sunday Express* wrote a column about
'The Romance and Tragedy of Women Masqueraders'.

> If there is one remarkable thing about women who
> masquerade as men, it is this – they are nearly always
> under a military obsession . . . Every kind of
> romance, every kind of heroism, every degree of
> tragedy or farce, nobility or squalor, has been repre-
> sented by such women. They form an endless chain
> of abnormality that stretches from our own day into
> remote time . . . they present an intensely interesting
> psychological drama, a mystery of inexplicable
> change – the mystery of spiritual hermaphrodism.[22]

Barker took great exception to being called 'abnormal'.
'It is all so horrible,' he told the *Sunday Dispatch*. 'Why
don't the public believe me when I say that for the last six
years I have led an honourable and straightforward life?'[23]
As far as he was concerned, he had always behaved like the
gentleman he was – why couldn't everyone understand
that? Didn't they recognise a gentleman when they saw
one? Didn't they see one when they looked at him? After

six years, that was what he saw when he looked in the mirror.

Barker was being either deliberately obtuse or appallingly naïve. Whichever it was, he was certainly misjudging the public mood. Did he honestly believe that the average British citizen of 1929 would consider it 'honourable' for a married woman to leave her husband, live with an undivorced man and have two children by him, then take on several male identities and go through a church wedding with a woman who, as she steadfastly maintained, believed she was marrying the man of her dreams? Did he really think that his activities and occupations would be regarded by them as 'straightforward', especially as several of those activities and occupations had led him into debt, into the law courts and, eventually, into prison?

After all, what hope could he possibly have of gaining any understanding or sympathy from traditionally hostile parties when he couldn't even count on getting support from those who, quite reasonably, he might have expected to? There was at that moment in Britain one woman who had seen herself branded as 'abnormal' and her work as 'obscene', and had endured several court cases where more than her reputation had been on trial. Surely Radclyffe Hall, the now infamous author of the banned novel *The Well of Loneliness*, had some sympathy for Barker's plight?

Perhaps 'sympathy' isn't quite the right word.

'I would like to see her drawn and quartered,' was Hall's verdict on Barker. She told her friend and agent Audrey Heath that she considered Barker to be 'a mad pervert of the most undesirable type, with her mock war medals, wounds, etc.; and then after having married the woman if she doesn't go and desert her! Her exposure at the moment is unfortunate indeed and will give a handle to endless people.' Hall considered that Barker's antics would set back the cause closest to her own heart – 'some sort of marriage for the invert'.[24]

Support for Barker did come, however, from an unlikely source – one of the former members of the Fellowship of Mons said, 'Although he has revealed her identity, which has come as a great surprise to all of us, I assure you she is a great loss to the ex-servicemen she came in contact with. We still maintain and have the greatest respect and admiration for her, now as ever.'[25]

The local press in Brighton were beginning to respond to the news of the stranger who had once been in their midst, with stories about 'Brighton and the Man-Woman'. An editorial in the *Evening Argus* said: 'The public mind is not satisfied with the extraordinary incident as it at present stands. There are obvious difficulties in discussing it. But very many people in Brighton and Sussex would welcome some kind of official statement on this peculiar case.'[26]

And it wasn't just people in Brighton and Sussex who were seeking 'official statements': police officers investigating the case in London and Berkshire would have been delighted to get some co-operation from the leading figures in what was rapidly becoming a farcical farrago.

Occasionally, the police resorted to straw-clutching: they contacted Mr S. P. Vivien, the Registrar-General of Jersey, to see if there was any hint of a previous marriage there – presumably unaware that even Barker couldn't have pulled off a same-sex marriage whilst still a toddler. 'The case does not come within the sphere of my department,' Mr Vivien reported back to them. 'I have no recollection of any similar "marriage" between two women having taken place by a superintendent-registrar's licence or certificate, but had such a marriage taken place it would have been the duty of this department to make inquiries with a view to any necessary action.'[27]

The police had managed to track down Ernest Pearce Crouch, who had spent the last six years living and working alternately in Britain and France; he politely declined to give them a full statement.

Meanwhile, in Mortimer Common, Berkshire, Elfrida Haward had been helping the police with their enquiries – in her own way. She was defensively vague about nearly everything she was asked about and clammed up when pressed for details of her marriage: 'It is so long ago that it is difficult to remember,' she told the officers. Her main concerns seemed to be the inconvenience the situation was causing her and the unwelcome publicity that was now threatening to overwhelm her and her parents. 'I have been worried by newspaper reporters,' she explained. 'Will this be published in the newspapers? How long will this take?'[28]

Her concern about what would be reported in the press was curious, as she had already been putting her side of the story to any reporter who waved a notebook in her direction – and taking great care to present herself as the wronged heroine, deceived by the man she loved and trusted. To the *News of the World* she wailed:

> I cannot understand it all. I am at my wits' end.
> What have I done to deserve this? It is a terrible
> position for a woman to be in. I trusted Victor more
> than anybody in the world. It appears now that my
> trust was misplaced – and that is the greatest tragedy
> of all. What can I do now? I never imagined that my

> husband was anything but the person he always
> appeared to be. I can never forgive this deception
> and the horrible experience which has been forced
> upon me.[29]

The police could understand this: after all, if what she
said was true, she had been deceived in the most unimag-
inable way and now the glare of publicity threatened to
exacerbate her embarrassment and distress. But they could
not understand what happened next: in a development
that almost beggared belief, Colonel Barker sold his story
to a Sunday newspaper – and so did his wife.

The prosecutors were incredulous: Trevor Bigham in
the DPP's office wryly noted that 'It rather looks as if in
future we shall have to make use of press agents if we are to
get statements of facts from witnesses in criminal cases!'[30]

On Sunday 10 March, the *Sunday Dispatch* published the
first of four instalments of 'The Man-Woman – "My Story"'.
The paper also devoted several pages to photographs,
showing 'The Man-Woman's Life in Special Pictures'. The
photographs had obviously been supplied by Victor Barker
himself: they showed a young Valerie Barker at school in
Belgium, and astride a horse at Kennel Moor; and, finally,
Victor Barker, an upright, sturdy figure, resplendent in full
dress uniform and sporting his set of medals.

Throughout the four instalments, Barker (assisted by
his Fleet Street 'ghost') emphasised the same point, over
and over again – 'Judge me how you will, I say with all sin-
cerity that what I have done has been solely for my boy.'[31]
He didn't refer to his son by name but proudly boasted
that

> He is such a manly youngster. He has never known

me as his mother, but as his father, and I think he
regarded me as a very gallant one at that. The
stories that were told him of my war exploits were
not so much vainglory but with the set purpose of
giving him a manly example to follow. There will be
people who will say I was wrong in this too.[32]

Having lived as both a man and a woman, Barker was
able to give the world the benefit of his experiences by
sharing his opinions of the two sexes. Neither, it seemed,
had left him overly impressed.

I put myself so thoroughly into the role of a man
that honestly I believe that now I have both the
man's and the woman's outlook on life; on the great
question of sex, having lived so long as a man with
men I know their point of view thoroughly, and as
a woman I know the other – and honestly I am
disgusted with both.[33]

The majority of men, he said bitterly,

talk of nothing but women and their conquests,
while the extent of their conversation is 'What'll you
have?' As for women, they have been truly described
as 'gold diggers'; they want all they can get without
the obligation of giving in return. They squeal if
they have to pay. I may have been unfortunate
in the women I met – those I came across in the
'profession' [acting] were for the most part empty,
brainless creatures, although here and there there
were real womanly women whom it was an honour
to know.

Being a woman myself I was perhaps harsh in my judgement, but it is difficult to express the loathing and contempt I felt as I watched some of them preen and trick themselves out to capture the attention of some man. As for men seen by a man from a woman's point of view, I think they are little better than women. Some men will never learn how to treat women. I think perhaps one of the main reasons why neither my wife nor any of my other women friends suspected my sex was because I knew just how to treat them.[34]

Barker addressed a question that the *Dispatch*'s editor knew his readers would want answered: 'What did it feel like to be a man?'

To that there can only be one answer, and that is that a man seems to have the better and easier time. There is, I am certain, more opportunity for a man in the world than a woman – that is why I became a man.

I believe that, similarly placed, I would do much the same again. I do not mean that I would deliberately do those things which I now realise were wrong, but they were done in foolishness and not with any wrong intent.[35]

Finally, in a last-ditch attempt to gain some public sympathy, he suddenly dropped his masculinity in favour of a more typically feminine façade, and declared, 'I am waiting, a lonely woman, for whatever may befall me. Is there no one who will help me? No one who will give me a chance to make good? I am frightened to be seen in public and yet I must make a peepshow of myself unless I can pay my debts and go away where I shall not be known.' He added, for good measure, that 'Trousers make a wonderful difference in the outlook on life. I know that dressed as a man I did not, as I do now I am wearing skirts again, feel hopeless and helpless.'[36]

Hopeless and helpless appeared to be how Elfrida wished the world to regard her in her version of events published in the *Sunday Express*, defiantly entitled 'My Story: By the Man-Woman's Wife: Mrs Barker Reveals the Truth'. 'I have nothing whatever to be ashamed of – nothing to regret having done,' she declared.[37]

This woman who had been so wronged and so embarrassed by being thrust into the public eye allowed the paper to publish a half-page photograph of herself, plus part of the letter that 'Bill' had written to her after they had separated. This in itself was something of a revelation – for in it Victor referred to his son as 'Tim', not 'Tony'. His stepmother called him 'Tim', too. 'Tim was so fond of me that he never thought of me as a stepmother,' she said. 'He called me "Mummy" and was, I think, fonder of me than "Daddy". Bill always said he was deeply grateful to me for my care of Tim.'

Now, Elfrida revealed, she had discovered what a wonderful thing hindsight was. She told the *Express*:

I was never given any real explanation of why 'Sir Victor Barker' had thought it necessary to go to the length of posing as a married woman and living with a husband just for the purpose of covering up his identity. Looking back over the matter now, I can see how foolish I was not to realise it was a far-fetched story, but doubts never entered my head at the time.

In order to emphasise how much she had been misled, she was a little economical with the truth regarding her courtship with Barker: 'He was persistent,' she claimed. 'He courted me for two years before I finally gave in and promised to marry him.'[38] This was a claim that would never stand up in court, and when the time came, Elfrida decided to drop it from her 'defence'.

However, she persisted in portraying herself as the innocent, unwitting victim of the piece, and her husband as the villain:

> I hope no other woman will ever know the torture I
> have been through. I hope it will never fall to the lot
> of another helpless and unsuspecting person to have
> to go through the days of agony and incredulous
> bewilderment that have been my fortune this week.
> It could not have been more of a shock to any
> woman in the world than it was to me to find myself
> utterly deluded, utterly alone in experience, in a
> position that made my name known to every man
> and woman in the country. It is terrible, incredible,
> hideous. I shall, of course, consult a solicitor to find
> out what my legal position is.[39]

By now, everyone was considering their legal position, even the bankruptcy court officials. They had to publish an amended notice in the *London Gazette* on 15 March, to substitute an earlier notice published on 23 November 1928, regarding 'Arkell Smith, L. I. V. . . . commonly known as L. I. V. Gauntlett Bligh Barker, petition filed 5/10/28, order 19/11/28'. The Director of Public Prosecutions' department was also exploring the possibility that there might be sufficient grounds to charge Barker with an offence under Section 156(a) of the Army Act, stemming from his impersonation of an officer and wearing medals which had not been awarded to him. Finally, the DPP's department were able to pull a charge out of the jumble of evidence they had amassed, and on 15 March, at around 12.15 p.m., Inspector Walter Burmby called at 17 Markham Square.

The door was answered by Victor Barker, dressed in light-coloured flannel trousers, light shirt and dark jacket. Burmby ascertained that this was the person he was looking for and proceeded to serve a summons under Section 1 of the Perjury Act, 1911, alleging that the person otherwise known as Lilias Irma Valerie Arkell Smith had committed

> wilful and corrupt perjury in an affidavit sworn
> before Mr C. V. Hill, solicitor and commissioner for
> oaths, at 126 Seymour Place, Marylebone on June
> 29, 1928, in connexion with an action in the King's
> Bench Division of the High Court, between Edith
> Maud Roper Johnson (plaintiff) and Victor Barker
> (defendant), in which affidavit she swore that she
> was truly named Leslie Ivor Gauntlett Bligh Barker.[40]

An astonished Barker replied, 'I had not the slightest idea I was committing perjury.'[41]

On 27 March, wearing a grey coat and skirt, with a black felt hat with the brim turned down and, in a rather camp touch, a large fur boa, he appeared before Marylebone Police Court. The fur, it turned out, had a practical purpose: he could easily hide his face behind it. The building was packed, as were the corridors, as several hundred people queued vainly to get a seat. The case had come before magistrate Mr Hay Halkett; appearing for the prosecution was Mr C. Wallace, with Mr F. Freke Palmer representing the defendant.

Before official proceedings got underway, Mr Freke Palmer asked the magistrate to grant permission for his client to remain seated throughout the hearing, and also drew his attention to the fact that it was illegal for anyone to take photographs or make sketches of the defendant. 'There have been many photographs of the defendant appearing in the Press,' he said, as a result of which his client's life 'has been made practically impossible by these photos and sketches'.[42] The magistrate allowed the defendant to stay seated, and reminded those present in the court that no visual images of the defendant could be made.

Outlining the prosecution's case, Mr Wallace said that the alleged perjury was contained in a paragraph in the sworn affidavit made in response to Mrs Roper Johnson's High Court action, in which the defendant had stated: 'I have had experience in the catering and refreshment business. During the War I was in charge of Army canteens and during the time I was in the Cavalry I acted as messing officer in various messes to which I was attached for about 18 months.'[43]

So far as they had been able to discover, Wallace continued, no one of the name of Victor Barker had been in the Cavalry or any other arm of the Service since 1913 up to the present day. He outlined the events leading up to the defendant's subsequent arrest on 28 February, after failing to attend the public examination. Bailiff James Glover gave evidence in connection with these events, as did Charles V. Hill, the solicitor who had drawn up the affidavit in question. Mr Wallace asked him if he was able to recognise the defendant known as 'Leslie I. V. G. B. Barker'. Mr Hill said he could not. Noticing that Barker's head was still bowed down low, Mr Hay Halkett interjected, 'No one could recognise the defendant as she is now.'[44]

In his client's defence, Mr Freke Palmer declared, 'There has been a great deal of publicity in this matter, because a woman had been bold enough and has succeeded in earning her living as a man when she found that she could not do it as a woman.' He stated that there was no law against a woman dressing as a man and that it would be nothing short of persecution to prosecute his client 'because she had called herself a man and given her maiden name in the affidavit', and that 'it did not matter a brass button whether the defendant called herself Barker, a man, or called herself Mary Smith, crossing sweeper, so far as the material particulars were concerned. She had been known as Barker for some time and she used the name by which she was known.'[45]

The magistrate agreed with Freke Palmer, although he thought there was still a case to answer, albeit not a very strong one.

And then Barker's worst fears were realised: Wallace said he would ask the magistrate to hear evidence and commit the defendant for trial for an offence under Section 3 (b) of the Perjury Act, 1911, for 'knowingly and wilfully causing a false statement to be entered in a register of marriage'. Wallace then proceeded to tell the court details of the wedding that had taken place on 14 November 1923 at St Peter's Church, Brighton.

Dr Brisby, the medical officer at Brixton prison who had examined Barker, gave evidence next. Then came the moment that everyone in the court – except for the defendant – had been waiting for.

Barker had been quietly weeping into his fur through-out the hearing and became markedly more distressed when the second charge came to be considered. Elfrida Haward had been called to give evidence in regard to this allegation, and Barker broke down completely when he saw his estranged wife. Compared to her distraught husband, now clad in his incongruous female attire, Elfrida cut a small, neat figure in her smart cloche hat. She was asked if she could recognise the defendant in court. Since the weeping figure was still keeping his head down, Elfrida said she could not. Then, in a moment of painful melo-drama, she was asked to leave the witness box and approach the defendant. When she did so, Barker raised his head and looked at his wife. No one could possibly guess what was going through their minds, though one reporter made a stab, describing this moment as a 'tense silence'.

Elfrida returned to the witness box and admitted that she had known the accused as Mrs Pearce Crouch in Littlehampton, and that this person had told her she was really a man.

'Did you believe that?' Mr Wallace asked her.

'Yes,' said Elfrida.

'Was she dressed as a man when she told you that?'

'Yes.'

'Did you . . . go through a form of marriage with the defendant?'

'Yes.'[46]

At this point a copy of the marriage certificate was pro-duced and shown to the magistrate.

Now Mr Freke Palmer cross-examined Elfrida about Ernest Pearce Crouch and his violent behaviour towards his wife, before submitting to the court that 'as two persons of the same sex could not marry there had been no marriage, and therefore no offence'. Mr Hay Halkett wasn't having any of this: 'That would be a *reductio ad absurdum*,' he told Freke Palmer. 'It would cut at the very root of marriage. I think it would be a false statement and a very material one.'[47]

Freke Palmer declared that his client would be pleading 'not guilty' to both summonses.

The perjury charge was dropped but when, as Mrs Lillias Irma Valerie Arkell Smith, Barker was formally charged with 'wilfully causing to be made a false entry relating to marriage', his reaction was not that of a six-foot army officer: he fainted. Those clothes must have had quite an effect.

Barker was granted £50 bail and his trial at the Central Criminal Court was set for 24 April. He was helped from the courtroom, in great distress, an emotion which could only be exacerbated when he learned which Old Bailey judge would preside over this case which centred around a marriage between two women.

It would be Sir Ernest Wild, Recorder of London, the same Ernest Wild who, in August 1921, had been such an outspoken supporter of the failed attempt to make illegal 'any act of gross indecency between female persons'; who had declined to 'pollute the House' by disclosing the various forms of malpractices between women; and who regarded any such practices as 'a very real evil'.

Despite his years as an MP, politics had never really been the forte of Ernest Wild: it was always the law. Born in East Anglia on New Year's Day 1869, Wild had made his name, while still a young man, as defence counsel in murder cases, many of them prominent. He entered Parliament in 1910, as Conservative MP for North West Ham, but, as one political pundit observed, 'though his voice was often heard, it cannot be said that he made any mark in the House'.[48] During World War I he served as a Special Constable, and he belonged to the Freemasons.

An ardent fan of Kipling, Wild was an aspiring playwright and poet himself. In 1893, he had written an operetta, *The Help*, and a slim volume, *The Lamp of Destiny and Other Poems*, was published in 1918. He was especially fond of composing heavily sentimental verses that extolled a view of women that was distinctly Victorian:

> *Let her be fair*
> *With silken hair*
> *Rippling in waves of gold,*
> *Child of the Snow-king*
> *Rapture invoking,*
> *Seventeen winters old:*
> *Eyes azure-tinted,*
> *Rosebuds imprinted*
> *On lips and dimpled cheek,*
> *Form supple, slender,*
> *Needing defender,*
> *Womanly, wayward, weak.*[49]

Little wonder, then, that he was firmly opposed to female jurors, especially in cases where the defendants were homosexual. 'Women can forgive the greatest injuries which men can do them,' he explained.[50]

For no apparent reason, Wild once had himself photographed in costume posing as Napoleon, with his wife as the Empress Josephine. It appeared that the desire to masquerade as an important military figure was more widespread than had been supposed.

In 1922, he was appointed Recorder of London and bestrode the Old Bailey like the old-fashioned legal colossus he was widely regarded to be by his peers. 'When Wild's wild, he's bloody wild,' observed one fellow jurist. When passing judgment, 'his sentences marked a healthy reaction from the sentimentality which, in its sympathy for the prisoner, forgets the wrongs of the victim'.[51]

This, then, was the eminent jurist chosen to pass judgment in a case where the subject of exactly who had been the victim would remain a matter of conjecture for decades. A man who regarded all women as 'wayward' and 'weak' and preferred them 'supple, slender . . . needing defender'; a politician who believed that sexual contact between women 'debauches young girls, and produces . . . insanity'.

Victor Barker was neither supple nor slender, but would most certainly be in need of a doughty defender when he was brought before such a man.

If the news that Recorder Wild was going to be the judge he would have to face wasn't inauspicious enough, Barker must have feared the worst when he learned who the prosecuting counsel was to be – Percival Clarke, the very same prosecutor he had faced when brought to trial on the false firearms certificate charge in 1927.

Then, as if matters weren't already grim enough, came another bizarre twist to the tale. On Saturday 20 April 1929, Sir Herbert Austin, the much-respected and long-serving Clerk of the Central Criminal Court, shot himself in his office at the Old Bailey. It was reported that 'for some time Sir Herbert had worn a strained expression and that more recently he had not been quite his normal self'.[52]

Come the morning of Wednesday 24 April, and reporters outside the Old Bailey took note of the 'large number of people queuing outside the Court hoping to obtain admission, the majority being women'. At the head of the queue was 'a woman in a rich fur coat, who sat on a folding chair which she had brought with her'.[53]

By the time the defendant was due to enter the dock, the court was packed to its capacity. The drama began when the Clerk of Arraigns barked out, 'Lillias Irma Valerie Arkell Smith – surrender!' All eyes were on the 'tall, broad-shouldered, upstanding figure' who walked up from the cells below the courtroom. Everyone wanted to get a good look at what this particular defendant was wearing, and they were not disappointed: they could see a collar and tie under a fawn raincoat; there was a red rose in the lapel of the coat and, lower down, heavy boots and golf socks. It was all topped off with a 'black "billy cock" hat', which, according to the *News of the World* reporter, gave the appearance of 'a country farmer, accustomed to horses, big and rather ungainly'.[54] Another journalist agreed that the figure 'was almost entirely masculine in looks', while another noted: 'Her face was the face of a handsome man. Her face was expressionless.'[55]

From the dock, the 'country farmer' looked round and saw 'people of every class and type, rich and poor, all come to feast their eyes, and ready, even hoping, for all the thrilling, prurient details of my married life that they eagerly hoped would come out'.[56]

When the two charges were read out, the defendant pleaded 'not guilty' to the first, and 'guilty' to the second. His fate was now in the hands of his defence team, Sir Henry Curtis Bennett KC and Anthony Hawke.

But first came Percival Clarke. He opened the case by

outlining the key events of the defendant's life, including the 1927 case, which brought an embarrassing admission from the prosecuting counsel.

Recorder Wild wanted to know, 'She stood her trial in this Court as a man?'

'Yes. Not a soul in Court – I prosecuted her on that occasion – was aware that there was other than a man in the dock.'[57]

Clarke continued with his saga, laying before the court the bare details of the marriage that took place between Barker and Haward. Recorder Wild appeared to have some difficulty grasping this point: 'Do I understand that these two women were living together as man and wife from 1923?' he asked Clarke. When the prosecutor confirmed that this was the case, Wild said he would want to know more about 'this travesty of marriage'.

Clarke concluded his opening statements with an unequivocal condemnation of what Barker had done. 'I submit that these facts show that this person has a total disregard for the truth or for the sanctity of an oath,' he declared. 'Whenever it is convenient to her she swears to matters which may or may not be material and which are quite untrue.' Then he made a rather curious statement. 'The matter, moreover, goes further than that. If she wanted to marry another woman she could have gone through a ceremony in a Register Office. There is no justification for her abusing the Church to go through this ceremony.'[58]

Appealing to the traditional views of women he knew this particular judge held, Clarke hammered home his final argument: 'Your Lordship will appreciate how important it is that marriage registers should not be falsified. That is an aspect of the case which is of considerable gravity.'[59]

Then it was the turn of Sir Henry Curtis Bennett, who proceeded to present his own version of his client's life, placing particular emphasis on her two unhappy relationships, with Arkell Smith and Pearce Crouch, both of whom he portrayed as very heavy drinkers. He described her life with Pearce Crouch, the birth of their two children and what had transpired when that relationship fell apart, claiming that:

> No one hearing that history can have anything but sympathy for the defendant and admiration for the way in which, through great difficulties, she had been able to face the world by earning her own livelihood.
>
> Before this form of marriage had been gone through, she had lived in the same room, and it is idle, I suggest, that one should be asked to believe that Miss Haward did not know perfectly well that she was, in fact, living with a woman.[60]

Once again, Recorder Wild requested some clarification on this matter: 'You say they lived together as man and wife? I shall want to know all about that.' However, true to his character, he suggested to Curtis Bennett that he did not want 'anything prurient to be stated in court, anything that ought to be said might be put in writing'.

The defence, though, objected to this, and Wild spelled it out for them: 'I shall want to know whether they lived together under the normal relations of man and wife.'

'I shall be able to tell your Lordship all about that,' Sir Henry Curtis Bennett assured him.[61]

And so into the witness box came Elfrida Haward, who

Henry Curtis Bennett would attempt to get to talk 'all about that'.

She entered the courtroom, appearing rather nervous and agitated; ever the gentleman, Recorder Wild asked if she wanted to be seated, but she declined. She avoided making any eye contact with the defendant. Answering Curtis Bennett's questions, she confirmed that, yes, she had known the defendant as Mrs Pearce Crouch, and, yes, she believed her then to be a woman.

'Did she tell you she had been seriously wounded in the war?' Curtis Bennett asked. Elfrida said yes, and that she had been told the wounds were abdominal.[62]

Then the sensitive subject of the marriage was broached. Elfrida confirmed that she had followed Victor Barker to the Grand Hotel the day after he moved in, and lived with him there.

'Living there as apparently husband and wife?' asked Curtis Bennett.

'Yes.'

'Did you sleep in the same room and bed?'

'Yes,' came the reply.[63]

Then, before the question that was on the tip of everyone's tongues could be asked, Elfrida suddenly came over all unnecessary. She turned rather pale and looked as though she was about to faint; an usher quickly gave her a seat and the court waited for her to recover.

Obviously thrown by this, Henry Curtis Bennett drew back from putting the question he had been on the verge of asking. Instead, he enquired of Elfrida, 'Did your father then, believing the defendant to be a man, insist that there should be a marriage?'

Oh yes, she confirmed. 'He was very upset and wanted us to marry.'

Recorder Wild had some questions for the 'bewildered bride': 'You told him you had been living with this apparent man?'

She did.

'You first met this person apparently as a woman, and he told you he was a man?'

He did. And yes, Barker had courted her as a man and she had believed he was a man.

'When did you learn that she was a woman?' Wild demanded.

'Not until I saw it in the newspapers,' Elfrida replied.

'Were you sleeping in the same room?'

'Yes.'

'You never knew from first to last?'

Elfrida was adamant: 'Never, after she told me she was a man.'

'How did he keep up the deception with you?'

'I do not know.' Everything, she said, appeared to be 'perfectly normal'.

'He appeared to behave as a husband would behave to a wife?'

'So far as I know.'[64]

Wild now handed back to Curtis Bennett, who, seizing the opportunity created by the judge's line of questioning, asked Elfrida: 'After the form of marriage did you always occupy the same bed?' The implication was clear – if the couple had always slept together, it must have been impossible for Elfrida not to realise the truth.

But she had the perfect answer: 'Not always,' she said.[65]

Despite her nervousness, it appeared as though the defence couldn't make a dent in Elfrida's story. The cross-examination of this witness was over and she was free to leave the witness box. Whatever embarrassment and discomfort she might have felt when giving her evidence, she would have left knowing how fortunate she had really been – for she had managed to avoid revealing in public what she had told the police in private.

> During the honeymoon at Brighton sexual relations occurred and Miss Haward thought that everything was perfectly normal. After the honeymoon, sexual intercourse did not take place again. Miss Haward explained that she had been brought up very strictly by her parents, was not strongly sexed and had little knowledge of physiology . . . she is now of the opinion that artificial means were employed . . . '[66]

Perhaps realising that things were not going the defence's way, Henry Curtis Bennett made a clumsy attempt at pleading mitigating circumstances on his client's behalf: 'This sort of thing does not repeat itself frequently. I do not think such people exist. It is only one in millions who could live as a man and deceive people.' His client, he suggested, was 'more sinned against than sinning. She took the very stupid course of believing that she could earn more money and get employment easier as a man than as a woman. Once having taken the step she had to carry it through or lose her employment. May I again refer to what she has suffered owing to the great interest which the public has taken and is taking in her when she is going through the great ordeal of her life.'

'One might almost use the words "prurient interest",' interjected the judge.

'Yes, my Lord,' Curtis Bennett concurred. 'It is astonishing that the misery of this woman can be made a sort of entertainment by people who increase her wretchedness

'Utterly deluded' – Elfrida Haward sells an image of
herself, in happier times, to the *Sunday Express*;
everyone is amused

by coming here to stare at her. She has lost her employment. She has suffered all this publicity. Has she not been
punished enough?'[67]

Recorder Wild agreed with the defence that the case
was of 'an unprecedented and very peculiar character'.
He found himself, as he would say, on the horns of a

dilemma: 'Supposing I pass a light sentence, others may do the same thing? If this sort of thing were repeated it would be very bad.'[68]

Wild wanted some time to think about what he should do. Sentencing, he said, would be postponed until 2 p.m. the next day. Then he would show who had the whip hand.

We were driving through Rottingdean today and turned into Whipping Post Lane. I'd never really taken much notice of that name before, but today – perhaps because I was thinking of you – its meaning made an impact on me for the first time. 'Whipping Post Lane' – obviously a public punishment site had once been situated on or near this place. It was a common penalty in the eighteenth century: the convicted would be sentenced to one or, sometimes, several floggings, often in addition to a prison sentence with hard labour.

And I thought of you, contemplating your possible punishment, seventy years before. And in thinking of you, I thought of other punishments meted out to those whose 'crime' had been little different from yours. And I wondered: did you think of them at all? Did you know about them? Did you remember how the judicial system had made an example of so many of them, and fear that a similar fate awaited you? That you were to be the latest whipping boy? And where would your whipping post be?

Mary Hamilton had four of them, in Taunton, Glastonbury, Wells and Shepton Mallet. In September 1746, she was arrested in Glastonbury, and accused of posing as a Dr Charles or George Hamilton and also marrying Mary Price two months earlier. It was thought she may have had as many as fourteen previous wives. There was no law which covered her crimes; the nearest charge available came under the Vagrancy Act, so that she was prosecuted 'for having by false and deceitful practices endeavoured to impose on His Majesty's subjects' and tried at Taunton.

Finding her guilty, it was declared that 'The he, she, prisoner at the bar is an uncommon notorious cheat; and we, the Court do sentence her or him, whichever he or she may be, to be imprisoned six months, and during that time, to be whipped in the towns of Taunton, Glastonbury, Wells and Shepton Mallet.' But even that wasn't enough: all four floggings were carried out during the winter months, just to give the punishment a nice little touch of malice. It was nothing personal, of course. Henry Fielding, in The Female Husband, *declared: 'it is to be hoped that this example will be sufficient to deter all others from the commission of any such foul and unnatural crimes . . . for unnatural affections are equally vicious and equally detestable in both sexes . . .'[69]*

So while I was thinking about whipping posts today, Mary Hamilton was in my thoughts. So, too, was Sister Benedetta Carlini, an abbess in Renaissance Italy. She was convicted of forcing younger nuns to have sex with her by impersonating a male angel called Splenditello.

Benedetta spent the last forty years of her life in solitary confinement within the walls of the abbey, fed on bread and water and allowed out only to attend Mass – or to be flogged.

And Recorder Wild said, 'Supposing I pass a light sentence, others may do the same thing? If this sort of thing were repeated it would be very bad.'

We should spare a thought for Ann Marrow, too. In July 1777, she was found guilty of 'going in men's cloaths [sic], and personating a man in marriage, with three different women . . . and defrauding them of their money and effects'.[70] She was sentenced to be pilloried at Charing Cross and given three months' imprisonment. Being pilloried meant the prisoner was locked in a wooden frame so that public abuse of all sorts could be heaped upon them. Ann Marrow was pelted with stones and anything else that came to the hands of the mob who came to punish her. They were mostly women, too, and such was the brutality of their bombardment that she was blinded by the assault.

By 1688, Cornelia Gerrits van Breugel and Elisabeth Boleyn had been living together in Leiden for a year. They decided they wanted to solemnise their relationship, so Elisabeth went shopping and bought some men's clothes for Cornelia, who would be the 'groom'. And so it was that Cornelius Brugh, bachelor, married Elisabeth Boleyn, spinster, in the Reformed Church of Amsterdam, and then returned to Leiden to live as man and wife. But after two and a half years, Cornelius became weary of his attire and his male identity, and discarded them both so he could become Cornelia again. It wasn't too long before neighbours noticed that the young newlyweds were no longer the couple they had been, and the authorities were notified. The two women were arrested, tried and convicted, and those whom God had joined together, by man were put asunder: they were sent into exile for twelve years and forbidden to live together again.

I try and think what that really meant. Forbidden. Together. Again.

But in 1908, Xavier Mayne, author of The Inter-Sexes, *wrote: 'Before we loathe the homosexual as anarchist against Nature, as renegade toward religion, as pariah in society, as monster in immorality, as criminal in law, let us feel sure that we have considered well whatever the complex mystery of Life presents as his defence . . .'*[71]

And I thought about Elizabeth Johnson, a maidservant in Massachussetts. In 1642, she was whipped and fined for 'unseemly practices' with another maid.

And I thought of how Roman-born Giovanni Bordoni had served his master well. As body-footman to the Governor of Angiari in the 1740s – he came highly recommended by the

*Governor's brother, the canon of Santa Maria in Transtavero –
Giovanni's duties required him to be as handy in the kitchen as he
was with a pen, comb and razor. And he was. However,
Giovanni's many amatory adventures did not please his master,
and matters came to a head when he eloped to Rome with a young
lady, pursued by members of the Governor's household.*

*In fact, Giovanni's success with young women had begun
when, as fourteen-year-old Catherine Vizzani, she was already
'continually romping with her own Sex'.[72] For two years, she had
a passionate affair with a certain Margaret, until they were discovered by Margaret's father. Catherine fled from Rome and
became Giovanni Bordoni.*

*When Giovanni surrendered to the Governor's chaplain, he
ordered one of his servants to shoot him; the resulting thigh wound
turned septic, and Giovanni died in a convent hospital, aged
twenty-five, 'killed for an Amour with a young Lady'. On her
deathbed, Catherine removed the 'leathern Contrivance, of a cilin-
drical figure, which was fastened below the Abdomen, and had
been the chief Instrument of her detestable Imposture . . . and
laid it under her Pillow'.[73] When some of the hospital staff took it
apart, they found it was stuffed with old rags.*

*Catherine's body was dissected by Dr Giovanni Bianchi, who
concluded that 'her seducing at least two young Women to run
away from their Uncle, were flagrant Instances of a libidinous
Disposition; Proceedings incompatible with any virtuous Principle,
or so much as Decency'.[74]*

*I thought of how Belgian-born Georges Maresco had served his
country well. During World War I, after escaping from German
custody, he worked for the Belgian Intelligence Service. In peace-
time, Georges became something of a ladies' man, popular in cafés
and dance halls. But in 1920 he was struck down by a mystery
wasting disease and became blind and partially paralysed. After
visiting a shrine, Georges pronounced himself cured, and had a*

brand new set of stigmata on his hands and feet into the bargain. While the Church accepted this as a bona fide miracle, they decided that Georges should be refused the Holy Sacraments.

During the course of the miraculous events, it was discovered that the stigmata weren't Georges' only distinguishing features – for he was really Berthe Mrazek, former nurse and lion-tamer. The Church insisted Berthe give up her male identity, which she refused to do, and the authorities decided to keep her imprisoned to ascertain her state of sanity, although no formal charges were brought against her. Female admirers sent numerous floral tributes to Berthe, much to the consternation of her gaolers.

Catherina Linck had served several countries well in the early eighteenth century. She had fought for the Hanoverian, Royal Prussian, Royal Polish and Hessian armies. Sometimes she was Anastasius Beuerlein, sometimes Peter Wannich. But when she married Catherina Muhlhahn in Halberstadt in 1717, her wife knew her as Catherina Margaretha Linck.

The bride's mother never approved of the marriage, and she it was who unfrocked her son-in-law, ripping off his trousers to reveal a Vizzani-like 'leathern Contrivance', subsequently produced in evidence against Linck. Both Catherinas were put on trial for sodomy.

But, protested Linck, both Muhlhahn mother and daughter had always known she was a woman. Why, her wife had seen her naked and had even removed the 'contrivance' on occasion. Muhlhahn denied any such knowledge, denied that she hadn't known the truth about her husband.

Linck was sentenced to be hanged; Muhlhahn was given three years' imprisonment, to be followed by banishment from Germany.

But Recorder Wild said, 'Supposing I pass a light sentence, others may do the same thing? If this sort of thing were repeated it would be very bad.'

And Justice Jonathan Crabtree said a deterrent was needed 'in these days of sexual openness and lesbianism and bisexuality', as justification for the six-year prison sentence he meted out.[75]

The prisoner before Justice Crabtree on 21 September 1991 was nineteen-year-old Jennifer Lynn Saunders, who was found guilty of two counts of indecent assault against two young women, aged seventeen and fifteen, despite the fact that both had consented to sex with her. In court, they swore it was not Jennifer they had consented to have sex with, but 'Jimmy'. 'When I discovered he was a woman, I felt dirty,' said one of them.[76] *But Saunders maintained that 'Jimmy' was created to protect their relationship from the wrath of his girlfriend's parents.*

In the end, Jimmy couldn't protect Jennifer, and she became a whipping boy, pilloried by the trial judge: 'What you did was for all practical purposes rape. You have blighted their lives . . . you have called into question their whole sexual identity.'[77]

'Hanging's Too Good For It,' said the father of 'one of evil gender-bender Jennifer Saunders' victims'.[78]

Nine months later, the Court of Appeal reduced Saunders' sentence to two years' probation, but did not overturn her conviction. Appeal judge Lord Justice Staughton said he doubted whether the original sentence 'would have any deterrent effect'.

There are crimes, there are victims and there is punishment. Whipping posts. Whipping boys. Pilloried. Forbidden. It can all be contained in one sentence. Yours.

On Thursday 25 April 1929, the final act of this popular drama was played out at the Old Bailey. Recorder Wild had had time to consider the appropriate sentence, but he was not going to waste the opportunity he had been given to pass judgment, not only on the crimes committed by the defendant who now stood before him, but on what those crimes represented.

> He [Barker's defence lawyer] has put it to me that
> you were on the horns of a dilemma. He put it . . .
> that you took Miss Haward to a hotel in Brighton a
> month before you conducted this alleged marriage,
> and there you lived together as man and wife. He
> put it also that her father, discovering these relations
> between you, insisted on your marrying her.
>   In my judgement, you were on no such horns. You
> had merely to show that you were a woman.[79]

Then Wild made a quite extraordinary and unexpected statement that must have given Barker and his lawyers some semblance of hope. Although he said he had been impressed with the evidence of Elfrida Haward, he added that 'Without expressing any view as to the truth or falsity of Miss Haward's evidence, I am assuming in your favour that Miss Haward must have known before the alleged marriage that you were a woman.'[80]

Wild also made reference to the publicity the case had received, a point made by defence counsel, and said that he would 'mitigate the sentence because of the not unnatural, if somewhat morbid, interest that this case had apparently aroused'. But he sounded a more ominous noted by adding, 'That interest I can well understand. It is part of the punishment of your perverted conduct.'[81]

He concluded:

> I have considered and carefully pondered on
> everything which can be said in your favour, and
> the result at which I have arrived is this.

You are an unprincipled, mendacious and unscrupulous adventuress.

You have, in the case before me, profaned the House of God, you have outraged the decencies of

'An unprincipled, mendacious and
unscrupulous adventuress'

Nature, and you have broken the law of man. You have falsified a marriage register and set an evil example which, were you to go unpunished, others might follow.

So grave in the eye of the law is the offence which you have committed that the maximum penalty for it is seven years' penal servitude.

In all the circumstances of this case, showing all the leniency I can, I pass on you a sentence of nine months' imprisonment in the second division.[82]

The prisoner was seen to slump back in his seat, and start to cry. Then, regaining some composure, he slowly stood up and, a gentleman to the last, bowed slowly to the judge. A female warder led the way back down the stairs. The courtroom began to empty, and the reporters rushed off to file their stories.

It was all over: there was nothing more to see. They had all had their tuppenceworth.

7

⊷⊙⊷

Punishment
Like a Man

Now gone to gaol, for to bewail,
Is prigging Tommy Mary.

Anon., 'Tommy Mary Walker'

**I went through the world as a man. It did something
different to me – and what happened was that I felt very
isolated and scared.**

Peggy Shaw, November 2000

The case of Colonel Barker appeared to be closed, but interest in his fate had spread far and wide: Inspector Burmby received a letter at Scotland Yard from a Miss H. Seutermeister, of Baarn, Holland, voicing her concern: 'I think, nevertheless the peculiar conditions of her case, Mrs Smith very sympathetic and am in sorrow about her life during the first time after leaving the prison. I should like to know how I could help her. Please, will you tell me if she has friends enough to help her forth?'[1] Inspector Burmby duly referred Miss Seutermeister's enquiry to Mr Freke Palmer.

Elsewhere, silence on the subject fell over a certain country house in West Sussex. Visitors to the Bailiffs Court estate knew better than to discuss the house's former tenant in front of their hostess, Lady Moyne.

But it was still the topic of many a conversation in public bars, across garden fences, in the streets, as people talked and laughed about Colonel Barker. In the Worcestershire town of Evesham, forty-two-year-old William Sidney Holtom discussed it with his old friend, Mrs Oughton, whose son-in-law he used to work with. 'He said he was very interested in the Colonel Barker case and frequently expressed indignation about the masquerade,' she said.[2]

William had also chatted with his neighbours about the case outside his house while proudly cuddling his eighteen-month-old son, little William, and, later, over a beer with his mates at the Evesham Labour Club. The Club Secretary knew him as a regular patron. 'He never was actively interested in politics. He used to come oftentimes with his wife and sit always in the same corner of the room. He would puff at an old clay pipe all the evening. He smoked twist, too.'[3]

Another club member recalled that:

He was of the regular navvy type. He had a great shock of black hair, which dipped on to his forehead like an unruly curl, and he always wore a muffler and navvy's trousers tied round with string. He used to come in on Sundays for his pint before dinner.

He took a normal man's interest in sports – particularly football. He also played dominoes in the club. He joined the fishing club, and paid into a fund for the outing, but just before the trip he asked for his money back. He said his wife was unwell.[4]

However, Holtom hadn't been able to afford to spend too much time with his mates at the club in recent months, not since he'd had to give up his regular job as a timber haulier's carter just over a year ago. His best workmate, Haines, had been crushed under the wheels of a horse-drawn wagon that Holtom had been driving, and after that, according to a former neighbour, 'His nerves went to pieces.' Since then, Holtom had taken odd jobs, working for a market gardener, and mending boots at the three-storey cottage he shared with his wife Mabel, their six-year-old daughter Doris, toddler William and Mr and Mrs William Smith, their lodgers of three months. Holtom seemed happy enough doing this sort of work, but, just lately, hadn't been feeling too well.

He refused to see the doctor. It would soon blow over.

The police who had been working on the Barker case had come to the same conclusion. In the wake of the trial, their only concern was to see if any other charges could or should be brought against anyone else involved. Elfrida Haward was an obvious candidate – her apparent duplicity before and during the trial had been a source of frustration for them. However, in the end, they decided not to pursue possible charges of perjury and obstructing the police in their enquiries, and allowed her to fade back into the safety of obscurity, with what remained of her reputation.

But there were still some possible hairs to split, if they could be bothered. During their investigations, the police had discovered that Colonel Barker wasn't the only man who had made false declarations concerning the lady purporting to be his wife. Their correspondence with the Passport Office revealed that, in June 1919, when Ernest Pearce Crouch applied for his passport to enable him to leave for Paris, he had 'falsely represented the woman Arkell Smith to be his wife'.[5] This was pointed out to the Passport Office by Scotland Yard, but they decided no further action was to be taken in this matter. They had got their man – there was no need to pursue another.

Meanwhile, at Holloway prison, their man was having trouble becoming a woman again. After a brief interview with Deputy-Governor Mary Size, she was ordered to strip out of her usual attire and undergo a medical examination. On doctor's orders, she was then taken straight to the prison hospital, in a state of near collapse. Some of the difficulties to be faced were purely practical: there was no prison uniform available on the premises to fit this inmate who weighed in at a flabby 16st 8lb. So, for her first week, she was kept in the hospital until some special clothes had been made to fit her most unorthodox figure.

The prison doctors were concerned about their new patient, who seemed unable to eat or sleep properly and lay in a state of silent inertia. After two weeks, her new uniform was ready to wear and the prisoner formerly known as Colonel Victor Barker had to start adjusting to living as Valerie Arkell Smith.

And now other curious yarns were starting to unravel, their strands tangled with uncommon flotsam and jetsam.

Her name was Mrs Minnie Rebecca Drewett, it had now been established. When the fifty-eight-year-old woman's body was pulled from the Thames near Tower Bridge at the end of March, the police thought they were dealing with a case of a man who had a predisposition for wearing women's attire. Despite the female clothing found on the body, its masculine features and iron-grey moustache gave their theory some verisimilitude.

It wasn't until the body arrived at the mortuary that their error

*was realised: the five-foot-two-inch corpse was that of a woman.
Her skirt and one shoe were missing.*

*The subsequent inquest into Mrs Drewett's death destroyed
another of the police's theories – that she had been working as a
bargeman on the river but had reverted to wearing women's clothes
shortly before her death.*

*During World War I, the 'Woman With Moustache' had served
as a corporal-cook with the Australian Imperial Forces in France.
This soldier's identity had been overturned after he was wounded
and taken to a dressing station in Etaples.*

*Drewett was forced to return to England, and to pick up the
threads of female life. She took to drinking heavily. Her last known
employment was at the White Cross Hotel, Richmond, from where
she had been dismissed for being drunk and abusive.*

*No one could say for certain whether she had meant to fall into
the Thames or whether she had toppled in accidentally, overcome
by drink – and, mercifully, so drunk she was unaware of what was
happening to her. It was obvious she had been painfully aware of
what had happened to her before. Perhaps she had been only too
relieved to bring to an end a way of life that had not been of her
choosing.*

*Meanwhile, in a hospital in Oakland, California, doctors
informed the patient who was suffering from tuberculosis that
they could not save him. From the moment he entered hospital, he
had known the end was near; even if he recovered, it was still the
end of his life. So he decided to tell the doctors what his wife had
known for some time: his real name was not Peter Stratford, as he
had told them, but Deresley Morton.*

At first they didn't get it – until they realised he meant Miss
*Deresley Morton. Not that this really made any difference; Peter
was still going to die and his estranged wife would have to be
informed.*

Elizabeth 'Beth' Stratford, née *Rowland, was living in*

Hollywood at the time of her husband's death on Thursday 2 May 1929. Peter had courted her for two years before they finally married in Kansas City in 1925, where Beth had been working as a secretary. The couple parted not long after the wedding when Peter went to live on the Pacific Coast, where the warm air was better for his ailing lungs. A few months later, they were reunited and settled in Niles, California.

No, insisted Mrs Stratford, during their courtship, and at the time of their marriage, she had been completely unaware of the true sex of her husband. It was only a few months ago, after they had been reunited in Niles, that she had learned the truth, at which time the couple had parted company again and she had left her husband to live in Hollywood and concentrate on writing film scripts. The manager of the hotel in Niles where they had lived remembered them well; he said the couple had actually resided there since 1926, and never appeared to quarrel, but confirmed that, yes, Mrs Stratford had left rather suddenly three months ago. No one knew why, though Mr Stratford had been receiving letters from Los Angeles written by a woman called 'Alma' who apparently shared his belief in the cult religion Sufism.

While Peter's body lay unclaimed, awaiting burial in Potter's Field, Oakland, a search of his room in Niles uncovered a number of letters, a marriage certificate and other personal papers which testified to his literary work, assisting a number of playwrights and authors. It also transpired that Peter had also occasionally supported himself by taking casual labouring work.

But before Peter, there was Deresley Morton. She had come originally from New Zealand, though her father was British. Deresley had arrived in New York in 1909 to seek her fortune in films, and found work there as a writer and literary critic before becoming Peter Stratford. Just after the First World War, Peter decided to make a move and ended up living at the home of Mrs Thomas Nawn, in Hillsdale, near Hackensack, New Jersey. 'Peter came to

*us from New York, saying he wanted a chance to rest,' said Mrs
Nawn's daughter, Gene, herself a writer. 'He seemed ill mentally
and physically, but later brightened up.' Miss Nawn seemed to
know more about what Peter had been doing than most of those
around him: 'He obtained a position with the government medical
forces during the war in New York, and because of his masculine
walk and a voice that bordered on baritone, he was able to conceal
his identity.'*[6]

*No, none of the Nawns had ever suspected that their guest was
anything other than a man, absolutely not.*

No sooner had the prisoner now known as Valerie Arkell
Smith begun to adjust to an alien identity and an alien
way of life than she was forced to attend to an outstanding
legal matter.

On 14 May, the adjourned public examination was
finally heard in the London Bankruptcy Court, which was
packed to capacity. The case was heard by Mr Ferrars
Vyvyan, the Assistant Official Receiver, who subjected
'Lillias Irma Valerie Arkell Smith, better known as
"Colonel Barker"' to a merciless rapid fire of questions.

The court heard business details of the farm at Bailiffs
Court, the antiques shop in Andover, the brief stint at the
Dudley dog kennels and the inheritance from Tom
Barker's will, culminating in the failure of the Mascot Café.

'To what do you attribute your failure?' Vyvyan asked.

Barker replied, 'I failed because of the misrepresenta-
tion of the takings of the café. I worked extremely hard
there, but I could not make it pay.'[7]

After just half an hour, the examination was closed and
a female prison warder tapped her charge on the arm.
They made their exit through a side door.

*

Life inside the bleak walls of Holloway was proving particularly difficult and distasteful for one who had always been a smartly attired, well-groomed gentleman. How was such a man to adapt to the far-from-sanitary conditions of jail and the food which 'might have been calculated to break the strongest spirit, to implant an intense hatred of mankind and of the forces of law and order'?[8]

But it was the monotonous routines and work of prison life that was the most daunting challenge for an inmate whose life had hardly been commonplace. The day began the Holloway way when the morning bell sounded at 6 a.m., and each prisoner had to stack their bed up, and roll and fold their bedding. By 6.30, they would be washed and dressed, then their cells and everything in them had to be thoroughly scrubbed with cold water. Breakfast was at 7 a.m., followed by cell inspection. At 8.30, prisoners went to the chapel for prayers, returning to their cells at 9 a.m. They were allowed an hour's exercise in the yard before going to the workrooms. Lunch was at noon, followed by a ninety-minute break, during which they could write letters or read books from the prison library. Providing their behaviour had been good, prisoners were allowed to write and receive one letter a fortnight, but only one a month if they received a visitor. Work continued until 5 p.m., when supper was taken, and then came lock-up.

Although inmates at Holloway weren't reduced to picking oakum, some of the work they were compelled to do was still mightily tedious. Hemming handkerchiefs ranked high on Barker's list of irritants, though clothing of every description was made in the workrooms.

But she reserved particular resentment for the fact that class had no part to play in prison: in the eyes of the law, everyone really was equal, as 'the scum of womanhood mingled with those who had fallen foul of society, law, order'.[9] This disdain was well hidden by Barker, at least from Mary Size, who believed that 'She worked hard and behaved very well. There was nothing spectacular about her. The attitude she adopted towards the other women was kind and considerate. She helped the teachers in the evening classes to distribute handicraft materials and made herself generally useful.'[10]

Some of the inmates were of more interest to Barker than others, perhaps because their histories had been almost as colourful as hers: Kate 'Ma' Meyrick, hostess of the Forty Three Club, jewel thief Christine Lewis, and two elderly sisters who had specialised in stealing from hotels. But uppermost in her thoughts was her son and the absolute necessity of concealing 'the truth' from him. Concern increased when news came during the summer that the boy had been taken ill with a serious bout of colitis. Although he recovered, his welfare was to be a constant cause of anxiety.

William Sidney Holtom was becoming more worried about his state of health. He had been taken ill at home, and his lodger, William Smith, had offered to help undress him and put him to bed, but Holtom had refused any assistance. That evening, one of Holtom's next-door neighbours popped in to see how he was doing, and it was obvious his condition was deteriorating.

Three days later, Holtom was admitted to the men's ward at Evesham Infirmary, where he was examined by Dr Duncan. To do so, the doctor had to remove the strapping that Holtom had bound around his chest. Shortly afterwards, he was transferred to the women's ward, critically ill with enteric fever, or paratyphoid.

Word soon spread that William Sidney Holtom was not a man's man – or a woman's.

As the local press picked up on the story, Mabel admitted to reporters that, at William's request, they had never gone through any form of marriage ceremony. William was already living with another woman when Mabel had met him, four and a half years before, while on holiday in the Ladywood district of Birmingham. Back then, he was working for his brother at a coal wharf, she said. They had met again in Worcester, where Mabel was in service. She soon found herself in love with William, but was understandably upset when he refused to marry her. However, she did eventually agree to leave Worcester and live with him in Evesham. After the birth of their son, Mabel admitted that 'Our life together was then quite happy and perfectly normal. I had not a worry in the world.' Her husband would take on any sort of work, however menial, to make sure that she and the children never went without. But one thing that made him an especially exceptional husband was that he always had sympathy for the amount of housework she had to do. After a day spent doing the washing, he would tell her, 'I always thought that women's work was the hardest. You must be tired, my girl.'[11]

No, of course, she never suspected that he wasn't a man: 'I believed him to be a man and our life together was perfectly normal. I swear before all that I hold holy and sacred that I never once suspected anything but what my husband was a man. I cannot bring myself to think otherwise.'[12]

It was all perfectly normal – just how Elfrida Haward had described her marriage to Victor Barker.

Yes, said Mabel, her husband was always kind to the children. He was never happier than when he was playing with

them and singing to them or bouncing them on his knee.
But whose children were they?

For Mabel was still, legally, Mrs Williams – she had married William Frederick Williams, a waggoner, on 9 June
1919, in Munsley, Hereford. She had had her daughter
with Williams before leaving him to set up home with
William Holtom. At one point she and Holtom had quar-
relled and separated, which Mabel admitted was 'one of
the blackest times in my life; I felt as if death would be a
relief, for I had grown to love my man'. But the happiness
of their reconciliation was completed with the arrival of
little William. 'He was in seventh heaven when he learned
it was a boy,' said Mabel, insisting, 'I believe him to be the
father.'[13]

But he wasn't.

He was Sarah Holtom, *née* Withers, who had also once
been married, to farm labourer William Holtom, in
Admington, near Stratford-upon-Avon, when she was just
eighteen. After two years, Sarah left the matrimonial
home. 'I had a feeling I should like to be on my own and I
left him,' she said. 'The idea struck me that it would help
me if I dressed as a man, as I did not like the idea of
domestic service. I spent the few shillings I possessed in
buying men's clothing, and then tramped to
Birmingham.'[14]

Sarah had left the matrimonial home with very little but
her husband's name, which she would herself use for the
next twenty years. It was this William Holtom who had
worked as a cowman, timber haulier, navvy, coal heaver
and road mender, who swore like a trooper, was fond of a
drink and a smoke of black twist, had a good singing voice,
but spoke in high-pitched, squeaky tones, and was an affectionate husband and father of an eighteen-month-old son.

While Holtom, now in a private ward to protect him from prying eyes, recovered from his illness, Evesham police were preparing to charge Mabel Beatrice Hinton (sic) with making a false statement to the Registrar of Births and Deaths at Evesham in connection with the registration of the birth of a child – her son – on 16 September 1927, in Evesham, by stating that the boy's father was one William Sidney Holtom. The Evesham Superintendent-Registrar, Henry Gardiner, interviewed

Evesham's Man-Woman – another 'Colonel Barker',
May 1929

Mabel on 8 May regarding the registration of the child. It was then, he said, that Mabel said she had been told that William was a woman and could not possibly be the father of the child. Mr Gardiner said that Mabel had given him the impression of telling the truth.

A month later, she was brought before Evesham Borough Police Court on this charge, by which time Sarah Holtom was well enough to be summonsed to give evidence. She didn't know who the father of the little boy was, she told the court. She had asked the defendant and she had told her she didn't know, either. Had the defendant thought she, Sarah, was a man? No, she didn't think so. She hadn't told Mabel that she was a man or a woman, but she had worked and kept her as would a husband.

Mabel Beatrice Hinton was committed for trial at Birmingham Assizes, and granted bail and legal aid. When she appeared there on 11 July, she pleaded guilty to the charge. The court heard that her estranged husband, William Williams, was willing to take her back, if he could find work where they were not known, and the judge declared that Mabel would be bound over in the sum of £30 'to be of good behaviour for two years'.

The grimness and confinement of prison life, not to mention the enforced existence as a woman for the first time in six years, had started to take its mental toll on Victor Barker as he struggled to live as Valerie Arkell Smith: 'My nerves began to get ragged and it only needed the least thing for me to fly off the handle. One day I became so upset over some trifling incident that I threw a mug of cocoa over a wardress. Then I dashed into my cell in hysterics.'[15]

The distressed prisoner was taken before Deputy-Governor Size, who sentenced her to two days' solitary confinement, one on bread and water only, the second with porridge included. Despite this glitch in her good-behaviour record, the prisoner was duly given a release date of 15 December.

This time, there were no curious crowds of onlookers to observe the departure. Had there been, they would have noticed that it was not merely the Colonel's reputation which had diminished: the man who had entered prison weighing nearly seventeen stone was now nearer thirteen. Nonetheless, this particular prisoner's departure left Mary Size with a lasting memory: 'I shall always remember how, on the morning of her discharge, she stood between the entrance gates of the prison to brace herself before she faced life in the outside world again.'[16]

And the outside world had a new joke to enjoy, in public bars, across garden fences, in the streets.

'What does Colonel Barker's DSO stand for?'

'Dick Shot Off.'

The appearance of this 'virile-looking creature in blouse and short trousers' with 'no breasts, lanky limbs' caused a tremendous shock that winter. There she was, a rather gruff, unpleasant heroine parading about in men's clothing, sharing a house with 'a healthy girl . . . thoroughly feminine' – at one point, they were even seen having dinner together in bed.[17]

In December 1929, the audiences at New York's off-Broadway Garrick Theater watching Thomas Dickinson's play Winter Bound *were the first to see a stage character such as Tony Ambler. Tony's companion, the healthy and feminine Emily, tells him, 'The trouble with you is you're neither a man or a woman. You're a he-woman.'*

8

⊷⊙⊷

*The Honeymoon
is Over*

*It's a different kind of fear to being a woman among men –
it's a very uncomfortable feeling.*

Peggy Shaw, November 2000

Henfield, Sussex ,18 August 1934

*Kennelman John Hill needed to phone a friend that evening, so at
about 7.30 p.m., he made his way to the telephone box by the
Station Hotel. When he got there, he found it was already occupied, so he had to wait his turn – Henfield only had one public
call box. Jessie Evans, a local nurse, finished her call and cycled
away from the box, failing to notice that she had left her purse
behind. Hill was a little more observant and, looking in the purse,
saw that it contained £4. 2s. 9d.*

*Evans had only got about 300 yards down the road when she
realised her mistake and returned to the call box – but both her
purse and the man who had gone in there after her had
vanished. She rang the police; half an hour later, Sergeant
Howard Miller found the man in a nearby pub: 'He had*

obviously had a drink, but was perfectly sober.' Miller asked him if he had seen the missing purse. 'I know nothing about it,' John Hill told him. 'You were seen to enter the call box where the purse was left,' replied Miller. 'I know nothing about it,' insisted Hill. But Miller wasn't satisfied: 'I shall detain you while I make further inquiries,' he told his suspect, and duly cautioned him.[1]

But then Hill murmured, 'It's all right,' and produced the purse from his pocket. When Miller examined it, he found it was empty – at which point Hill handed over the missing money, minus 2s. 9d. He told Sergeant Miller that he had intended to take the purse to the police station in the morning but had 'called in at the local for a drink. If truth be told I had more than one and I forgot all about the purse.'[2]

On 20 August, the police served Hill with a summons, which prompted a dramatic response: the next day, he caught the first train to Victoria. When he arrived, he found police waiting to arrest him. 'If I could have committed suicide, I should have done so that night,' he would say later.[3]

After he was taken back to Sussex, Hill offered a rather implausible explanation to the police: 'I did not mention to you when you served the summons that I had got a job in London to go to. I didn't want to lose the job.'[4]

On 4 September, John Hill appeared before Steyning magistrates, charged with stealing a woman's purse. The defendant was 'dressed in a brown sports coat and grey flannel trousers, a sweater and striped shirt, and narrow starched collar and tie . . . the figure was that of a tall well-built man approaching middle-age'.[5]

Hill's lawyer, Mr Coleman, told the court that there was no case for the defendant to answer on a charge of stealing the purse by finding. The purse, he said, bore no mark of identification and that would be sufficient to exonerate his defendant from any guilty

*intention or motive at the time the purse was found – something
the prosecution had to prove.*

*However, the chairman of the bench was of the opinion that the
case had to go to trial. John Hill pleaded 'not guilty' and reserved
his defence. He was allowed bail and committed for trial at the
West Sussex Quarter Sessions.*

After leaving Holloway prison, Valerie Arkell Smith went to
a friend's flat and changed out of the woman she had
been. The female clothes she was wearing when she left
prison were discarded and she slipped into something
more comfortable – Colonel Barker.

At a meeting with his lawyer, Mr Freke Palmer, Barker
was told his son was well and happy and still unaware of the
court case and its revelations. 'He must not know that you
are really his mother and not his father,' he was told.[6] The
£9 a month annuity Barker received was only enough to
cover his son's boarding school fees, and supporting himself without risking exposure again would prove difficult. It
would be necessary to rummage in the name-bag once
more, and this time he pulled out a name that had previously belonged to the head of the law firm who had
defended him at the Old Bailey.

Armed with a 'safe' identity, he duly wrote off for a variety of jobs, and eventually joined the staff of Catesby's
furniture store on Tottenham Court Road. After six
months, he found himself surplus to requirements and
struggled to find another job. When, in 1930, he became a
car salesman, it looked as though his persistence was going
to pay off.

His optimism proved ill-founded: a female customer
recognised the salesman who had been serving her as

Colonel Barker and promptly informed the showroom manager. Two Scotland Yard detectives duly arrived but, other than confirming that the customer had, indeed, been right, they could do nothing: no offence had been committed. An agreement was reached with the firm's bosses that their notorious employee could continue working for them, at their new showroom in Golders Green, as long as he remained unrecognised – surely one of the most ridiculous contracts of employment ever entered into.

It was also one of the most futile: if Barker and his employers imagined that, after featuring so prominently on the front pages of national newspapers, the image of this man would quickly fade from the collective memory, their hopes were to be dashed once more. When yet another woman customer recognised that the tall, well-built figure attending the cars was the same one she and thousands of other women had pored over in the scandal sheets, it was clearly time to put the brakes on his career in motors.

Barker next earned a little money working as a film extra at Elstree Studios, but the work was irregular. He tried working as a door-to-door salesman, selling cleaning materials, but never cleared more than ten shillings a week profit.

In the summer of 1932, he ended up in Shanklin, on the Isle of Wight, earning £3 a week as assistant to Saga, a seaside fortune-teller. Saga's little hut at the end of Shanklin Pier drew a steady stream of customers eager to have their fortunes told before taking in some of Shanklin's other attractions, which that year included Elsie and Doris Waters, the Royal Italian Circus and Wee Georgie Wood.

To supplement his earnings, Barker also worked as assistant to a diver who went off at the deep end of the pier in an asbestos suit, soaked in petrol and set alight. The assistant's job entailed going round with a collecting box, encouraging people to pay for the privilege of watching a lunatic engage in this pointless and suicidal activity. Both jobs were strictly seasonal, and when the summer came to a close, so did Saga's hut – and it didn't need her to look at her assistant's palm to predict that his situation could only worsen.

He returned to London and, in 1934, wangled a job working as a kennelman, for a meagre fifteen shillings a week – in the West Sussex village of Henfield.

A village which had only one telephone box.

Thirty-nine-year-old John Hill, described as a kennelman, and dressed in grey flannel trousers, a grey sweater and brown jacket, appeared at the West Sussex Quarter Sessions in Chichester on Thursday 27 September 1934, charged with stealing a woman's purse containing £4. 2s. 9d. However, before the trail ensued, clarification was needed regarding a legal technicality.

The bench chairman, Rowland Burrows KC, told the court:

> The prisoner is committed for trial in the name of
> John Hill, and I want to make it quite clear that that
> is not the prisoner's real name; and I want to make
> it clear at the outset that the name we know the
> prisoner by is John Hill. I want to say in the hearing
> of the people that we are going to swear on to the
> jury that, having been committed in the name of
> John Hill, the prisoner will be tried in that name,
> and furthermore for the purpose of this trial, it does

not matter what the sex, occupation, or identity of
the prisoner is.[7]

The prosecutor, Mr Brown, outlined the details of the
case, as previously heard by Steyning magistrates. Then
the defendant was called into the witness box and asked by
his counsel, Mr Pensotti, to give the court his real name. 'Is
it,' he asked, 'Lillias Irma Valerie Barker – I am sorry, I
mean Arkell Smith?'

'Yes,' replied John Hill.[8]

The defendant went on to say that he had had no intention whatsoever of stealing the purse and wanted to either
return it to its rightful owner or, failing that, hand it in to
the police. When asked why he had originally denied all
knowledge of the purse, he replied, 'I got frightened.
There were a great many things which might be discovered
which I did not want to be discovered.'[9]

Mr Pensotti submitted to the jury that this was not just
another ordinary case:

You are not dealing with an ordinary kind of person.
Let there be no misunderstanding about it. You are
dealing with a person who is charged before you as
'John Hill' and who has told you in the witness box
'My name is not John Hill. I am a woman.' You are
dealing with a person who in Henfield had for some
time apparently been masquerading as a man. You
are dealing with a person who had something to
hide, something that that person did not want to
come out, something, perhaps, that she was ashamed
of for the sake of her son, and perhaps for many
other considerations. I ask you to bear that in
mind.[10]

The jury heeded Mr Pensotti's plea and returned a verdict of 'not guilty'. John Hill was discharged.

If he had not been so consumed by his own problems that year, Hill might have noticed the demise of one of Victor's old 'flames'.

Dolores, once the darling of the art world, was found dead in a bleak basement room in Paddington. In 1930, she had decided to sell her memoirs to an American magazine, an act that angered Jacob Epstein. He dismissed her claims about life at Guilford Street as 'packed-full of inventions conceived by the not very scrupulous brains of the scribblers who seized on her notoriety and exploited it'.[11]

In the end, Dolores died in the same manner in which she had lived her last years – alone and largely forgotten.

Nothing had turned out the way it was supposed to.

Colonel Sir Victor Barker DSO was getting a little tired of slumming it as John Hill. Menial, low-paid work had not been part of the grand plan he had devised which would support his son and keep him in the manner to which he had become accustomed, and which befitted a decorated titled gentleman soldier. 'The days when I could attend such functions as the Lord Mayor of London's banquet, the President's Private Reception at the Royal Academy, complete in full dress and decorations, and carry it all off with a swagger were now far behind,' he lamented.[12]

It was probably the most lucid appraisal of his situation he had ever made.

But John Hill was still a name less likely to cause trouble than Colonel Barker, and Hill was able to find other work soon after the Chichester court case. He spent the rest of 1934 and 1935 working as an assistant chef at two large hotels in Cornwall and Devon, followed by a brief spell as

live-in manservant and general factotum to a South
African millionaire. For reasons he never made clear, Hill
didn't last long as a rich man's Man Friday.

By the autumn of 1936, describing himself as a 'widower', he applied for a servant's job in London, working
for a Mrs Adrian Scott at her home at 3 George Street,
Hanover Square. It was there, he said, that

> I learned how really hard a servant's life could be.
> My duties included keeping the various rooms in
> order, cleaning, tidying, and the like. There was a
> dining-room, drawing-room, an office, a waiting-
> room, a bedroom, a bathroom, and flights of stairs
> between them.
>
> Every day between four and five hundred letters
> arrived from all parts of the world, enclosing contri-
> butions large and small for the charity my employer
> was running. On the floor, in nearly every room, in
> the open safe, everywhere this money littered the
> place.[13]

There was an air of dismal inevitability about what happened next. As Hill explained:

> I was hard up, desperately so. I had to have some
> money from somewhere. Debts dating from my
> workless days before I got this job were becoming
> more and more pressing. With all this money about
> in the house the solution seemed obvious. Nothing
> could be easier than to borrow a few pounds, which
> would never be missed, and then replace them at
> some later date when I had saved them out of my
> earnings again.[14]

This cunning plan might well have been carried out flawlessly, except for the fact that Hill didn't take the money from piles that 'littered the place', or from the floor, or the open safe – he went into Mrs Scott's bedroom and took five one-pound notes from her handbag. 'It was probably my lack of experience,' he later offered by way of an explanation. 'An expert thief would have got away with it, for nothing could have been more easy.'[15]

And nothing could have been more easy than for Mrs Scott to discover that this money was missing and call the police. At about 2.15 p.m. on Sunday 14 March, Detective-Sergeant David Smith called at 3 George Street and told Mrs Scott's employee that he was making enquiries about five pounds that had gone missing. 'I don't know anything about it,' protested Hill. 'You can search me if you like. I would like you to as it would then clear me.' He then unbuttoned his waistcoat for the officer, who noticed that he was 'full in the chest'. 'You know who I am?', he asked the policeman.[16]

Indeed he did.

Realising the jig was well and truly up, Hill came clean and admitted taking the money. He showed Smith where he was hiding it, under a newspaper on a shelf in the kitchen. 'I have been taking it for a long time. It is quite easy, as money is lying about all over the place.'[17] Smith cautioned Hill and informed him he was taking him into custody.

John Hill was taken to Marlborough Street Police Court 'wearing men's clothes and a heavy dark blue overcoat' and charged with the theft of five pounds. He was remanded for a week, which he spent in the hospital ward at Holloway prison.

The *News of the World* had been keeping an eye on the

re-emergence of the figure who had provided one of their
best stories eight years before. But now they were merely
content to use him as a yardstick against which to measure
similar stories the paper claimed were 'even more remarkable than the "Col. Barker" story'. For once, their claims
were not without some justification.

'DARBY AND JOAN' WHO WERE NOT –
TWO WOMEN 'WEDDED' FOR FORTY YEARS
DEATH REVEALS THEIR SECRET[18]

*The story came from Paris, where a Ministry of Justice enquiry
had revealed the story of two women who had lived together for
forty years in Juan-les-Pins on the Riviera, where they had been
regarded by neighbours as a 'Darby and Joan' couple.*

*'Darby' was Monsieur Camille Bertin, 'a Frenchman of inde-
pendent means', who had come to the Riviera in 1897,
accompanied by a woman called Hilda Mary Joan Scott, a native
of Cambusling, Glasgow. Bertin had introduced Miss Scott as his
fiancée, and in due course they were married at the local mairie.
Nothing seemed extraordinary – 'Camille' was a name common to
both sexes in France. Within six years of the marriage, the Bertins
had a family of three daughters. The couple were renowned for
lavish entertaining – but it wasn't just the scale of it that people
remembered: 'It was noted as something peculiar that their guests
were always women. Never was a man received at their table.
Furthermore, the three daughters were brought up to avoid the
opposite sex.'[19]*

*Forty years of happiness came to an end when Mme Bertin
died in 1936; her husband followed her less than a year later. His
sudden death resulted in a judicial enquiry; during the course of
this investigation, documents deposited by him with the Bertin
family lawyer revealed the forty-year secret. A sealed letter told how*

the two women had originally met in London: 'Both had had an unfortunate love affair in their teens, and had decided to console each other.'

The biggest secret, however – the origins of the three Bertin daughters – remained just that, for 'Neither the lawyer nor the police can throw any light on this mystery, for, if there was adoption, the records have not been kept. [20] *And the claim that the Bertins' story was 'more remarkable than the "Col. Barker" story' was validated in one respect when it was reported that:*

> *The French law recognises the marriage and the birth registration as perfectly legal because, for purposes of legislation, the only things that carry weight in France are the papers presented by the persons wishing to marry or to register births. Therefore in law there is nothing to show that Camille Bertin was not a man, and that the three children were not born of his union with Miss Scott.* [21]

It had been possible to trace the original birth certificate of Camille Bertin, which allowed a burial certificate to be issued – for Mlle Camille Bertin, whose epitaph made a fitting end to the story: 'But that will not prevent the tombstone recording that the body buried is that of "Monsieur Camille Bertin, beloved husband" of the woman who lies beside him in the name of Mme Camille Bertin. [22]

While *News of the World* readers were learning about the French 'Colonel Barker', the case of R. vs John Hill was heard at Marlborough Street on Monday 22 March. Hill realised his predicament: 'Useless it was to plead that I intended to replace the money soon,' he said. 'Useless to make any excuses at all.'[23]

He pleaded guilty to the charge. But it wasn't to be as

simple as that. Detective-Sergeant Smith decided to outline the defendant's entire personal and employment history, including the marriage to Elfrida and the subsequent trial. 'Drink is the probable cause of her downfall so far as dishonesty is concerned,' he suggested.[24]

The magistrate was intrigued by the defendant's life as a man: 'What is the suggestion why she does this? Is it eccentricity or is there something behind it?' he asked prosecuting counsel Laurence Vine. Vine replied that, yes, the defendant had told him that 'she had a reason for wearing man's attire, but she did not propose at the moment to divulge her reason'.[25]

The magistrate's curiosity had to go unsated, for the time being, and he had to satisfy himself with fining the defendant twenty shillings, and ordering him to pay back the five pounds to Mrs Scott within a month.

So much for the 'obvious solution' to Hill's financial problems – he was in more debt than ever and, in the process, had made a proper show of himself.

FROM A WOMAN TO A MAN
COLONEL BARKER IN PERSON
AND HIS BRIDE ON A GREENLIGHT
HONEYMOON
SERVED IN THE ARMY AND WAS NOT
DISCOVERED TO BE A WOMAN
MARRIED A MAN, NOW ON
A HONEYMOON[26]

Luke Gannon, the impresario behind most of Blackpool's tackiest sideshows, liked to keep posters of his 'acts' at the South Shore home he shared with his wife. Mrs Gannon was something of a local attraction herself, better known as palmist and clairvoyant Madame Kusharney. Gannon had tried his hand at all sorts of occupations, from racing tipster to a salesman peddling 'Rejuvenation Tablets', but he finally found his forte as Blackpool's premier promoter of the peculiar.

True, it was a struggle every year, finding bizarre acts that would keep the crowds amused for the entire Blackpool summer season. But Gannon seemed to have an uncanny knack for discovering the world's queerest flotsam and jetsam, scooping them up and bringing them to Blackpool's seafront.

One exhibit warned of the 'dangers' of masturbation; people paid sixpence to see the 'face of an old bachelor; a confirmed onanist. He became idiotic and rapidly sank into second childhood.'[27] Other regular exhibits featured a series of 'Starving and Freezing Brides', with deprived couples supposedly sealed behind glass. In fact, the participants emerged from their beds after closing time to eat and drink in hearty fashion with their friends.

However, in the 1930s, no one questioned Luke Gannon's reputation for being the 'leading impresario of intersexuality'.[28] And his attraction for the summer of 1937 had quite a reputation himself – 'the most famous inter-sexual character of our time', declared the Mass-Observation project.[29] Yes, decided Luke Gannon, Colonel Barker and his bride would be worthy successors to the act that had been the biggest draw he'd ever promoted in Blackpool: the Rector of Stiffkey, Harold Davidson.

In March 1932, the Revd Harold Davidson, Rector of Stiffkey, a parish on the north Norfolk coast, was put on trial for 'immoral conduct'. During the four-month trial, Davidson's relationships with dozens of young women would come under public and judicial scrutiny. He consistently denied that there was any impropriety in his friendships with these women, but evidence was produced in court to suggest that he had frequently solicited women 'for immoral purposes', and made 'improper suggestions' to a waitress in a Chinese restaurant.

Davidson was convicted and, still supported by his wife and family, immediately lodged an appeal. He went about raising the finance needed for such a costly undertaking in a suitably oddball manner: he sat in a barrel on Blackpool promenade, where over 3,000 people paid to see him.

His wife would claim later that her husband had never meant to be a barrel of laughs – it was all a dreadful mistake. An impostor pretending to be Davidson had apparently approached Luke Gannon, saying he would undertake to fast in a barrel to raise £500 towards funding an enquiry into his case. Posters advertising Gannon's newest attraction had already gone up all over Blackpool when the real ex-rector contacted the promoter and the hoax was rumbled. However, Davidson found Gannon's offer of a fortnight's booking, at £100 a week, one that he simply couldn't refuse, although the nature of the show was altered slightly. Davidson would sleep in his barrel while a woman called Barbara Cockayne would do the actual fasting and, as the posters had it, 'the Rector would watch over Barbara'.[30]

Unfortunately, the show only lasted for a few days before the police fined Gannon and Davidson for causing an obstruction.

To complete his public humiliation, Davidson was officially defrocked by the Bishop of Norwich at Norwich Cathedral in October. Thousands of onlookers cheered the soon-to-be ex-rector as he made his way to the cathedral.

He returned to Blackpool the following summer to become part of another sideshow, somehow persuading his daughter Pamela to join him in his folly. The Davidsons occupied 'fasting cabinets', and, for their amusement, the pleasure-seekers on Blackpool's Central Beach could pay to view them. Yet again, the police decided to intervene, and the 'fasters' were arrested and charged with, of all things, attempted suicide. But this time the ex-rector would have his day in court, and when they were found 'not guilty', he successfully sued Blackpool Corporation and was awarded £382 damages.

Harold Davidson, the ex-Rector of Stiffkey, had learnt his lesson: and the lesson was 'don't become a freak show in Blackpool'. Unfortunately, he hadn't learnt the lesson that said 'don't become a freak show in Skegness'. Perhaps fancying himself as another Daniel, Davidson again agreed to be the cynosure of a seaside show, this time at Skegness Amusement Park, where he was required to sit in a cage with a lion called Freddie. All went well until, on 28 July, Davidson was addressing the holiday-makers who had gathered to view this 'spectacle' when Freddie decided he had had enough of his cellmate and pounced on him.

Davidson was rushed to Skegness Cottage Hospital with his face and neck badly mauled, and died there two days later. As a mark of respect, Luke Gannon put Davidson's old fasting barrel on display on Central Beach, tastefully topped off with a fake 'body'.

But the connection between Davidson and Barker did not end at Blackpool's seafront. In the wake of her husband's untimely death, Mrs Davidson decided it was time to put her side of the story, and sold it to a weekly national publication called *The Leader*, which billed itself as 'The All-Family News Magazine'. Mrs Davidson's tale of woe, loyalty and tragedy was the leading feature throughout August and September. However, as her story was reaching its end, another headline-grabber was taking its place: 'Colonel Barker, the Man-Woman who Hoaxed the World.'[31]

The Leader claimed that it was serialising Colonel Barker's soon-to-be-published autobiography, *A Soldier of Misfortune*. However, no mention was ever made of who was publishing the book. Furthermore, the 'extracts' that ran throughout September and October did not read as though they formed parts of a completed book, and were replete with the same melodramatic, sentimental and self-pitying tones as 'My Story by the Man-Woman' less than ten years before. However, this time, the Colonel's 'life story' was more interesting for what it left out than what it told. The marriage to Arkell Smith was dealt with in less than a paragraph, and the time spent with the Fascisti and the resultant court case was given only slightly more space. The relationship with Elfrida Haward was expressed in the vaguest and blandest possible manner. Much of the story's emphasis was placed on Barker's nine months in prison and his 'romance' with Dolores.

Yet again, the need for money had caused Barker to make a peculiar decision. Writing his 'life story' and having it serialised in a national magazine was hardly conducive to ensuring that his son, supposedly the entire *raison d'être* for his various identities and livelihoods, remained oblivious to the truth about his father. Appearing as a seaside attraction was one thing; but having his photograph appear week after week in *The Leader* seemed to be an incredibly risky and foolhardy thing to do, especially at a time when, unusually for him, he was earning a decent weekly wage.

Was it really only eight years before that Barker's defence lawyer, Sir Henry Curtis Bennett, had made a futile attempt to gain a judge's sympathy for his client by declaring: 'It is astonishing that the misery of this woman can be made a sort of entertainment by people who increase her wretchedness by coming here to stare at her'? Only eight years since, briefly adopting the manner of a meek and mild woman, Barker himself had declared, 'I am frightened to be seen in public and yet I must make a peepshow of myself unless I can pay my debts and go away where I shall not be known'?[32]

Luke Gannon didn't care about misery and wretchedness, but he did care about entertainment and peepshows – and the hunch he'd had about his latest attraction was proving correct. At the height of the season, several thousand people an hour were queuing up to buy a ticket for twopence and briefly enter the weird and wonderful world of Colonel Barker.

And now, ladies and gentlemen, direct from Blackpool's Central Beach, a rare opportunity to step inside and get your tuppence worth.

But first, read those signs over the entrance:

I AM TAKING THIS STEP FOR THE WOMAN I LOVE
LOVE CALLING
COLONEL BARKER[33]

Now see what the posters on the side of the building say:

COLONEL BARKER IS HERE
COLONEL BARKER AND HIS OR HER BRIDE
HOW LONG CAN A LOVING COUPLE REMAIN UNDER
THESE CONDITIONS
BOARD THE GIRL PAT[34]

*(This last attraction, by the way, isn't as titillating as it sounds –
merely an invitation to take a trip on a Grimsby trawler.)*

What is Mr Luke Gannon trying to tell us with these cryptic
comments?

'During Whit I had a couple fasting here and those are the signs
I had made for them,' he says.[35]

So what if some of it isn't appropriate for his current show – he
isn't going to waste money by changing signposts. That isn't what
people are paying to see, is it?

They're paying to see this: it's a pit (actually a converted cellar),

A seaside attraction: Colonel Victor Barker, DSO

twelve feet deep, containing two single beds; Colonel Barker is in one, his 'bride' in the other. Next to each bed is a Belisha beacon. 'The Belisha beacons are a sign of futuristic love,' says Luke Gannon. 'People go so fast now in their courting and the beacon is a sign for them to pull up and go a bit slower.'[36] This probably made as much sense then as it does now.

Near each bed are some small tables; on these are scattered newspapers, books and Craven 'A' cigarettes; above the beds hangs a cardboard Cupid. Colonel Barker appears to have a bottle of something kept under his bed.

On the walls are more posters, declaring:

> HE'S THE SECRET HERO IN
> MANY WOMEN'S LIVES,

and

> A WOMAN MARRYING A WOMAN!
> INCREDIBLE! YET IT IS TRUE![37]

The Colonel wears red pyjamas with dark epaulettes; his bride has a Dalmatian puppy on her bed.

An attendant is on hand to bring curious onlookers up to date with the progress of Barker and bride: 'They don't cross to each other for 21 weeks. Oh yes, they are watched day and night. He's come here for a wager, to win, I believe, it's £250.'[38] Yes, the Colonel has put on a bit of weight since he's been stuck down there – about twenty pounds.

The guide decides that Barker's notoriety needs spicing up even more. 'The first person in the world to have the now-famous operation changing her sex from that of man to a woman,' he barks.

'The silly bugger,' says one boy.

'Pass no remarks, please,' the guide rebukes him.[39]

But remarks are passed.

'He never were a colonel.'

'He's getting some bloody easy money.'

'He looks very much like a he, doesn't he?'

'Eee, isn't it sensational?'

'What if they have nightmares and sleep-walk?'

'Anyone who mistook him for a man would be crackers.'[40]

The Colonel, trying to read a cheap novel, appears disturbed by the crowd's murmurings.

'He can't read his book – he's upset. Are you upset, love?'[41]

His bride takes no notice and carries on perusing her Daily Mirror.

And that's it, folks – that's all the sensation you get for tuppence. Show's over.

The cynosure of this tabloid tableau couldn't see the attraction. 'What sort of thrill people could get out of this set-up is beyond me,' he reflected. 'It was certainly the easiest ten pounds a week I ever earned.'[42]

Some of those overheard coming out of the show agreed with him. 'It's a waste of twopence, lad,' one woman told her boyfriend. But he felt satisfied with his tuppenceworth: 'She looked me in the eye, she looked up and smiled at me,' he said.[43]

As the season drew to a close, business at Luke Gannon's sideshow slackened considerably, and 'Mr and Mrs Barker' finally emerged from their pit of despondency on 25 October. They packed up and left their lodgings, a boarding house run by a Mr and Mrs Gallimore at 34 Larkhill Street. The Gallimores had rather enjoyed their little claim to fame; they couldn't wait to tell the next guest who came to stay with them that he would be put 'in Colonel Barker's bed – it's not everybody who can say they have slept in his bed'.[44]

However, the couple felt some resentment towards their most infamous visitor – and his wife. 'We had him for seven weeks. He left us last week and never paid us the last week's rent for himself and his woman,' said Mrs Gallimore. 'The woman he was living with was filthy. I think she's one of them women who like women – you know what I mean – but I don't know for certain.'[45]

Eva Norton was the woman's name. And John Hill, who had come to Blackpool to be Colonel Barker once more, had had another rummage in the name-bag, and signed in at the boarding house as 'Jeffrey Norton'; here, he shared a room with his wife, Eva, 'both of them in the same bed'.[46]

According to the Gallimores, 'That woman Colonel Barker is living with is the wife of another man; her husband comes from Manchester, but she ran away to Blackpool.'[47] They claimed that Eva's estranged husband had threatened to cite Norton as a co-respondent in the divorce but was told he would have to prove that Norton was a man. Other than that, they didn't know anything about her. Nor, it seemed, did anyone else.

The Gallimores had another grievance against Norton: an anonymous complaint was made to the Blackpool Health Office regarding rabbits allegedly kept at the Larkhill Street boarding house. Mr Norton was accused of being the complainant; he denied it vehemently and threatened to sue the Gallimores for defamation.

Despite this, Jeffrey Norton didn't seem to be averse to letting his hair down in front of the Gallimores and making an exhibition of himself. Mrs Gallimore claimed that one night she and her husband had got drunk with the Nortons and persuaded Jeffrey to give them a free peepshow – they wanted to see what he kept underneath his gentleman's attire. According to the Gallimores, he accepted the challenge and they, by all accounts, got their tuppenceworth of the 'artificial means' about which Elfrida Haward had so coyly told the police.

'He's a man and a woman,' declared Mrs Gallimore. 'You know he's got all that a woman has, big-busted, and he's gotten one of them there that a man can't go without. I call him a Gene. Jack [her husband] says he can be a man one minute and then be a woman. Christ knows how he does it. They should lock up that sort of person, they're no use to anybody.'[48]

However, that wasn't what Eva Norton was said to have told her landlady.

'She told me another time that Colonel Barker was good for it any time,' said Mrs Gallimore. 'What the hell can you make of him, he has breasts like any woman.'[49]

Leaving many questions unanswered, Mr and Mrs Jeffrey Norton took their leave of Blackpool, for an unknown destination.

A Mass-Observation volunteer, who had been amongst the spectators getting a tuppenny view of Barker and bride, came close to obscure profundity with his observation that 'The symbol of sexual repression is a true one, but the symbol, Colonel Barker, made only a pretence of remaining true.'[50]

9

⊰⊱⊷❦⊶⊰⊱

Heroes

It is known that a father is necessary, but not known how to identify him.

Germaine Greer, *The Female Eunuch*

On 31 August 1939, the mass evacuation of children from Britain's major cities began. War was looming, just four days away – on 3 September, Britain and France would officially declare that a state of war existed with Germany. But long before Neville Chamberlain made his grim announcement, the country had been preparing for what had seemed inevitable all the previous year.

As children were emptied from the cities and dispersed to areas considered safe from the bombing, rural communities had to adjust to an influx of urban strangers in their midst. But sometimes the strangers were already in their midst.

In Great Yarmouth, the schoolmates of sisters Marjory and Daisy Ferrows were concerned: they hadn't seen their friends for some months. The two girls had always been a worry to their teachers and fellow pupils – in their early teens, both sisters had 'developed characteristics that made them hold themselves aloof from other schoolchildren, and eventually forced them to sacrifice scholarships which they had won to Yarmouth Central School and Yarmouth High School for Girls'.[1] After this, Marjory, the elder sister, didn't leave the family home in Middlegate Street for over a year, and eventually, it became known that she and Daisy had left Yarmouth.

What their friends and family didn't know then was that they would never see the sisters again.

When Marjory and Daisy returned to Yarmouth in August 1939, they were brothers – 'no longer as girls but as young men'.[2]

During their absence, Marjory had had some unspecified treatment in hospital and both sisters had started to wear men's clothes. Now, with war just about to break out, they had returned: Marjory had become seventeen-year-old Mark Ferrow, 5ft 10in, who shaved and smoked a pipe, while Daisy was now brother David, a well-built fifteen-year-old. Not so much a 'man-woman' as a 'boy-girl'.

The French might have had a name for them. Some newspapers in France had been criticising female members of ENSA, the variety organisation that provided entertainment for British troops. And in the face of the atrocities being committed throughout Europe, what terrible war crime were these women guilty of?

Wearing trousers.

Garçonnes, the French press were calling them – 'tomboys'.

Everywhere, it seemed, women were daring to wear the trousers – even in Mayfair. Hertford Street, once the home of Ernest Wild (who had died in 1934), Victor Barker and other prominent gentlemen, was now attracting a different type of trouser-wearing character. Barbara Bell, then a young policewoman, stumbled upon a very high-class lesbian club in Hertford Street. Bell and her girlfriend were there off-duty the night it was raided by some of their colleagues from the Metropolitan Police. A few weeks later, the pair were summonsed to see their superintendent, who told them that, in future, if they wanted to go to 'that' sort of club, why, she could easily get them into hers. After all, they were already all part of the same 'club'.

Before the war was over, the 'club' lost its most famous 'member'.

On 7 October 1943, Radclyffe Hall died at her home in London's Dolphin Square. The *Daily Telegraph*'s 'Peterborough' diary chose to mark her passing not by celebrating any of Hall's literary achievements, or even her legal battles, but by recalling an incident said to have occurred in Rye's Flushing Inn some years earlier. On this occasion, the unnamed widow of a 'Victorian celebrity' was said to have told a waiter to 'Please ask that young man to remove his hat.'[3]

Looking at Hall on her deathbed, her partner Una Troubridge observed that 'No one in their senses could have suspected that anything but a young man had died.'[4] In the midst of grief, she conjured up an image of her dead lover as a young airman who had lost his life in the service of his country.

In September 1939, ration cards were issued to every man, woman and child in Britain, though they were not used until January 1940. To obtain the cards, a form had to be filled in by each person, giving their name and signature, and the national registration letters and number from their identity card; the form was then sent to the Local Food Office. It was, of course, an offence for anyone to put false information on this form, but some people did – just as they would to obtain those vital identity cards: they had no choice. These people had to keep their identity preserved, for their own sake and their families'. They were not traitors, or deserters, or 'Fifth Columnists' – they simply had a secret to keep. And sometimes a signature on a legally binding document was all it took.

During the war, the Government published leaflets bearing the stern reminder: 'Always Carry Your Identity Card – you must produce it on demand.' In June 1944, when new five-year ration books were issued, each citizen had to produce a signed ID card to obtain them.

Failing to report the loss of an identity card was an offence, but it was an even bigger crime to participate in forging one. Throughout the war, court cases involving forged credentials were common – a typical example occurred early in 1944, when a policeman in Paddington and an army deserter were sentenced to twelve months' imprisonment each for, respectively, forging and receiving an ID card.

The war left a number of civilian men facing an identity crisis. Cigarettes and tobacco were hard to come by throughout the war; beer was watered down. By March 1941, rationing was badly affecting some everyday requisites – razor blades and shaving cream, for example, were in short supply.

Despite this, some men were never seen sporting so much as a five o'clock shadow. But keeping a six-foot, eighteen-stone male frame suitably attired was a real challenge.

Clothes rationing came into effect in June 1941. Each man's allowance was: one pair of shoes every eight months; one shirt every twenty months; one jacket and one pair of trousers every two years; one pair of socks every four months; one vest and one pair of underpants every two years. From March 1942, extra measures were introduced to save on material: no double-breasted jackets were permitted, nor were zips or permanent turn-ups on trousers.

This was hard enough for an average man to cope with; faced with insurmountable sartorial difficulties, men who were outside the parameters of 'average' sometimes resorted to drastic action:

Girl Mistaken For a Boy

Wearing her hair short and dressed in male attire, Phyllis Elizabeth Stock (28), presser, Eccleston Square, SW1, pleaded guilty at Clerkenwell to stealing a coat, the property of John Maxwell, from a shop in Caledonian Road, N. She walked into the dock with a jaunty air and sat down.[5]

On 20 January 1944, around 1a.m., Stock had broken the shop window and taken the coat. The police were called and were in attendance at the shop premises when, at about 2.40 a.m., Stock, still carrying the coat she had taken earlier, returned to the scene of the crime and was arrested. One of the officers, Detective Sergeant Edwards, later said it appeared that the accused, 'who was thought at the time to be a boy', had 'returned to clear the window out'.[6]

Rationing, identity cards, food and clothing shortages: they all combined to make life somewhat complicated for a forty-four-year-old, almost menopausal gentleman known by the name of Jeffrey Norton – as if his life wasn't complicated enough already.

Still, at least Jeffrey still had his wife, Eva, the woman who had left her husband, run off to Blackpool and then thrown her lot in with him when he became a seaside attraction. A man with a loyal wife could get by, no matter the rather unique problems the war brought them.

Whatever happened, he mustn't resort to stealing clothes or food or anything else he needed to sustain himself – he couldn't risk another court appearance, even if it was under a different name. It wouldn't take long for the police or a canny solicitor or even a magistrate to make the connection between this Jeffrey Norton and John Hill, Victor Barker and Valerie Arkell Smith.

But while Jeffrey Norton had been able to wangle an identity for himself, he was less certain of what part he could play in the unfolding events. After all, what role could there be for a man like him in a justifiable war, which would require real heroes? His medals had gone, his uniforms had gone – but his son still believed in his father. Norton had made sure of that, if he had made sure of nothing else in his life. Despite the fact that his son had spent most of his life away at boarding schools, he still looked up to his 'Pops'. And whatever trouble Victor Barker or John Hill or Jeffrey Norton had got into, the boy had been kept in blissful ignorance of it all. In later years, his father, even when revealing details about his own life, took great care to conceal nearly everything about his son's.

According to Norton, he and Eva spent the early part of the war outside London, living in a rented cottage; he had a job working on the switchboard of the local hospital. He always took great care not to reveal to anyone exactly where this had been. It was easy to be untraceable, as no electoral registers were kept for the duration of the war – for reasons of national security.

Concerns about national security would provide Jeffrey

Norton with his first wartime role. Right from the onset of war, there had been fears of a German invasion by sea and air. As early as October 1939, Winston Churchill suggested that a British Home Guard be formed, consisting of half a million men aged forty and over.

By the end of 1939, the fear of invasion had abated slightly – but the surrender of the Netherlands and Belgium in the spring of 1940 raised the spectre again, and in particular, the possibility of German paratroopers invading from the skies.

On 14 May 1940, War Minister Anthony Eden made a radio broadcast:

> We want large numbers of men who are not at present engaged in military service between the ages of seventeen and sixty-five to come forward and offer their services to make assurance doubly sure . . . You will not be paid but you will receive uniform and will be armed. You will form part of the Armed Forces and your period of service will be for the duration of the war . . . This appeal is directed chiefly to those who live in small towns, villages, and less densely inhabited suburban areas.[7]

Within a week, 250,000 men had enrolled, J. B. Priestley and George Orwell among them; in Hertfordshire alone, 6,000 men enrolled in just three days. Nearly half of these early recruits were World War One veterans; one company formed in East Sussex had six former generals signing up to serve as privates.

What would become affectionately known as 'Dad's Army' nearly began life as 'The Lads' – the Local Auxiliary Defence Service was the first name mooted, before 'Local

Defence Volunteers' was agreed. The initials, LDV, gave rise to a number of derogatory nicknames, including 'Long Dentured Veterans', which was both unfair and inaccurate – in fact, the average age of the Home Guard was thirty-five. Jeffrey Norton himself was still only forty-four.

On enrolling, each man had to give his name, age and occupation; he was then asked if he was familiar with firearms, and whether he was prepared to serve away from home. Standing orders decreed that 'all enrolled members of the Corps will be subject to Military Law and must obey orders'.[8]

Those chosen to be company leaders were normally men already prominent in their local communities, and with some previous military experience. In rural districts, the 'feudal overlord' was usually appointed platoon commander, in overall charge of between thirty and a hundred men, and would then pick a number of junior commanders or section leaders. Section leaders had to visit patrols once a night, to 'see that they are alert, at their posts and in possession of their equipment'. This comprised a rifle and ten rounds of ammunition, a gas mask, notebook and pencil, a knife, torch, watch, cord and a handful of loose change.

When Winston Churchill had suggested the formation of a Home Guard, he said that a lack of materials or equipment shouldn't matter: 'If uniforms are lacking, a brassard [arm band] would suffice . . .'[9] And in the first few months of its existence, brassards had to suffice. For weapons, volunteers had to make do with shotguns (often unloaded), sticks and garden tools. But then the Government was always of the opinion that local defence forces were 'not designed for serious offensive fighting' – their function was to obstruct the enemy 'by any means in their power'.[10]

Captain Ingram of the West Kent Home Guard told his men, 'It is clear that our chief function will be that of armed watchers – in short, we can regard ourselves as part of a network of sentries for the military mobile units.' But while the Home Guard may have seemed like a harmless way of contributing to the war effort, it was not without its dangers: 1,206 members would die while on duty.

In the few first months of its existence, the primary functions of the Home Guard were to 'stand-to' at dusk, and, until dawn, watch for landings of parachute troops; and to man roadblocks, asking drivers for some ID and, where the situation warranted, searching vehicles. Despite being woefully short of rifles and ammunition during the summer of 1940, they still managed, in one month alone, to shoot four drivers whose only crime had been to object to the somewhat overzealous manner in which they and their vehicles were being scrutinised.

When not apprehending 'suspicious' drivers, the Home Guard members made themselves useful by placing large objects, such as old bedsteads and cars, on open spaces, to prevent possible landings by paratroopers who might try to drop in in gliders.

Despite the enthusiastic response to Eden's civilian call-to-arms, the initial uptake didn't satisfy the Government. On 29 June, William Mabane of the Ministry of Home Security called for more LDVs, emphasising that these units would be 'forging the shield against which the attacks of the enemy will fail to strike home'. Winston Churchill offered further encouragement: 'If the Nazi villains drop on us from the skies, you will have to make it clear to them that they have not alighted in the poultry run, or the rabbit farm, but in the lions' den.'[11] Edith Summerskill MP lobbied for women to be allowed to join the Home Guard, but it was not until April 1943 – long after any real threat of invasion had abated – that women were finally allowed to enrol.

Police and Home Guard representatives began to actively recruit new members, using their knowledge of local people to decide who would be suitable. Obviously, a man, such as Jeffrey Norton, with previous military experience would be invaluable; if he had served as an officer it was a bonus, as this would be particularly useful in training the non-military men.

In the fight against possible 'Fifth Columnists' who might, it was believed, seek to damage public morale and sabotage the war effort, the War Office prevented all known fascists and communists from joining the LDV. Local police were allowed to use their own discretion when it came to vetting.

When a policeman came knocking on Jeffrey Norton's door, he feared the worst. But this time there was no warrant, no arrest and no charges: he was simply being asked to join the local Home Guard. And why shouldn't he? After all, this Mr Norton hadn't been involved with fascists or communists, had he? And it was common knowledge that he had been on active duty in World War One. On the face of it, he was just the type of chap they were looking for to help instil a bit of military discipline and know-how into the motley crew of men who had signed up for the district Home Guard.

What else could Mr Norton do but agree to join?

And, after all, there would be some advantages: for a start, he would get a uniform, which would go some way to supplementing the paltry clothes allowance he was struggling to cope with. It was also no bad thing to be officially regarded as a respected and trusted figure in a minor position of authority when there were things about your life you would do anything to conceal. An acknowledged World War One veteran helping to train raw recruits was far less likely to come under scrutiny from suspicious neighbours or local police officers on the lookout for anyone behaving in an odd manner.

And in an odd twist of fate, it would provide a rare and ideal opportunity to be an 'authentic' military hero.

However, there was one slight risk: if this Mr Norton had been a serving officer, it was reasonable to expect him to know basic military drill and training procedures. Victor Barker had never been called upon to do anything except stand to attention and, occasionally, march on parade alongside other war veterans. If he was going to pull off this masquerade, Mr Norton would have to lay his hands on some military manuals and swot up before someone realised he wasn't quite the man for the job.

But for the present, all eyes were not on Mr Norton – they were trained up at the skies.

Pictures of what German paratroopers might look like to the unsuspecting eye portrayed an unlikely-looking figure, loaded down with a sub-machine-gun, a portable radio and a folding bicycle. It was also whispered that the German paratroopers were trained to be masters of disguise: a story came from Holland that some paratroopers had landed dressed as nuns, while Virginia Woolf noted in her diary that she had been warned about 'clergymen in parachutes'. The Home Office fuelled these rumours by issuing a warning that some paratroopers might disguise themselves as British police and ARP wardens. Even the most familiar faces in towns and villages were subject to suspicion.

The numbers of possible invaders from the sky were

exaggerated – by the spring of 1940, there were only 7,000 trained German paratrooopers from the four parachute schools, not the 100,000 that was rumoured. These crack parachute troops had to be of the highest calibre: 'Their behaviour on landing must be carefully taught: they must have special qualifications for their task, a knowledge of the language of the country . . . a specialised form of infantry training.'[12] One eighteen-year-old pilot who baled out over south-east England produced a photograph for his captors and said, 'This is my mother.' He had been told that, if he did this, the English would not shoot him.

British airmen baling out over their own home territory were in greater danger of being killed by so-called 'friendly fire', as trigger-happy Home Guard members, unable to differentiate between friend and foe, took pot-shots at them. Several suggestions were put forward to remedy this parlous state of affairs. Early in September 1940, Sir Jocelyn Lucas, MP asked the Secretary of State for Air

whether he will consider offering some small reward, say £5, to anyone capturing an enemy parachutist alive, thereby minimising the risk now taken by our own as well as enemy airmen shot down or escaping by parachute, since at present they are sometimes in danger of being shot in mid-air by over-zealous marksmen, despite orders to the contrary.[13]

Coincidentally, the commanding officer of a Home Guard unit in Hertfordshire had had a similar idea, offering his men five pounds for every German parachutist captured alive.

It was surely only a matter of time before Jeffrey Norton had a chance to land his very own prisoner.

> I had just got up one morning and was still in
> pyjamas when the siren sounded, followed by the
> crash of ack-ack fire. I went to the door and looked
> up to see a figure baling out from a burning plane
> which bore the Nazi emblem. I slipped a pair of
> trousers over my pyjamas, donned an overcoat and
> rushed across the fields.[14]

Had the moment finally arrived when he would have a
genuinely heroic tale to tell his proud son? Not if he was
telling the truth:

> It was not courage which lent speed to my slippered
> feet, but the prospect of getting the £5 reward
> offered to any member of the Home Guard who
> succeeded in taking prisoner a German pilot!
>   I was beaten to it by some troops of a Scottish
> regiment encamped near by. I was just in time to
> see them march their captive away.[15]

His chance for heroism – and a fiver – had passed him by.
    But there was a real hero in the family.
    In 1938, Norton's son had decided to try for a
commission in the Grenadier Guards. His father always
said what mixed feelings he had had after receiving a
letter from him explaining his reasons for wanting to join
up:

> Dear Pops,
>   You must remember how proud I have always
> been of your Army career, and it was this more than
> anything else which caused me to decide to join the
> Army.

If only I can do as well as you did, I shall be happy.[16]

After receiving his commission into the Guards, the young man had gone on to be chosen to train for service in the RAF. Then, 'The Few' really still were the few: between 1935 and 1939, only 7,000 men were recruited for initial flying training, involving basic navigation and how to carry out air attacks by day or night, in all weathers.

Now, with a son numbered amongst 'The Few', Jeffrey Norton was going to ensure that, however he might himself be remembered, his boy's reputation would not be besmirched by any folly or misdemeanour he had committed. He was determined the sins of the father would not be passed on, and to that end he would never reveal his son's surname, the name of his schools, the RAF depot where he was stationed, even the type of plane he flew. He would take those secrets to his grave.

Not long after his near-close encounter with a German pilot, Norton and his wife moved back to London; he was tired of life in the country, he said. Back in London, he went to work in a Hurricane factory. It might not have been as overtly heroic an occupation as that of the men, like his son, who flew the planes, but he could still play a vital part. By 1942, aircraft production was the biggest industry in the country, with 1.7 million workers producing 26,000 planes a year. One of the few advantages of being employed in such an essential industry was that the factory canteens received extra allowances of meat, cheese, butter and sugar.

However, while the factory food might have been an improvement on normal rations, Norton found the work was affecting his health. His legs were starting to worry him – they were often very painful – but he put it down to the long hours standing at the factory bench which his job entailed. He left and became the night porter at an expensive apartment building in Grosvenor Square.

Then came a bombshell bigger than any plane could have dropped – his son told him he was getting married. This development put Norton, as he had been so often in the past, on the 'horns of a dilemma': 'If I went to church for my son's wedding, he would expect me to go into the vestry after the ceremony to sign the marriage register as a witness.'[17]

It brought to mind another church wedding, nearly twenty years before, and another marriage certificate, to which a false signature had been added. This had led to further signatures – on summonses, arrest warrants and charge sheets. Now he was faced with another situation just as fraught with dangers.

> In the end I was driven to the conclusion that there was only one way in which all danger could be avoided. I must not be present at the actual ceremony. I must inadvertently be delayed in arriving at the church until the ceremony was over. What could be easier than to make a pretence of having got into the wrong train . . . a phone message to explain what had happened, and to say that I would be coming along at the earliest possible moment.[18]

There were other ways of avoiding danger, too: he would never reveal the name of his son's wife, where they were married, or even the date the wedding took place.

By the summer of 1944, Jeffrey Norton's son was a bomber pilot, flying missions as part of Bomber Command's 'Operation Crossbow'. The targets: flying-bomb (V2) launch sites situated at Siracourt, Domeleger, Marquise-Mimo, Watten, Bois Carré and Wizernes. A week after D-Day, on 13 June 1944, the Germans had launched their first Vergeltungswaffen (V1) at Britain from the northern coast of France. In only three days, seventy-three V1s fell on London. In response, Bomber Command pilots like Norton's son released 118,000 tonnes of bombs on V1 and V2 targets in just one month. However, the operation still failed to halt the bombardment of Britain: nearly 9,000 rockets and flying bombs were launched from France that summer.

Jeffrey Norton had seen at close range the results of that bombardment. He was working for the council in Paddington, one of the areas in London worst affected by the bombing. By the autumn of 1944, 4,654 properties had been damaged by flying bombs alone; prior to this, another 8,000 buildings had been damaged. The borough needed plenty of drivers for its 'incident lorries' – vehicles sent out during air raids to look for any signs of bomb damage and mark it out with red lamps – and Jeffrey Norton had decided to volunteer.

The job was dangerous: the drivers had to make their way through the borough's streets, with bombs falling around them. Norton described how he was driving near Regent's Park one night when the force of an explosion blew him out of his lorry. But all he could think about was his son, who 'night after night was flying over the Channel to bomb the enemy take-off sites. Not even his cheerful letters could stem the fear that gripped me.'[19]

Norton's son survived 'Operation Crossbow'. But as the Allied bombing of the Occupied Territory intensified in the wake of D-Day, danger was ever present. That September, much of the daylight bombing carried out by the RAF was devoted to reducing the German garrisons at Le Havre and Calais, and involved bombers having to fly dangerously low, sometimes below 2,000 feet.

During the last four months of 1944, Bomber Command carried out 27,030 sorties by day, and 38,235 by night; the respective losses totalled 221 and 554. These fatalities included airmen named Smith, Barker, Crouch, Pearce and Hill.

Some of them were called Tony, some Anthony and some Timothy.

One of them was the son born to Valerie Pearce Crouch, much loved by her – and the man she had become.

Many years later, veteran RAF pilots would struggle to speak about the horror of hearing the cries of their comrades over their radios, screaming as their stricken planes spiralled all the way to the ground. Jeffrey Norton never knew whether this had happened to his son. All he knew was that the most important person in his life had become a statistic – one in a total of 47,268 Bomber Command aircrew killed while on active duty during the war, his plane one of the 8,655 aircraft lost.

He received a telegram to tell him that his son had not returned from a sortie over France; this was followed by a letter of condolence on Buckingham Palace notepaper from the King:

> The Queen and I offer you our heartfelt sympathy in your great sorrow. We pray that your country's gratitude for a life so nobly given in its service may bring you some measure of consolation.[20]

The letter was signed, but it was a false signature: a facsimile of 'George RI'.

Norton was unequivocal: 'His death was the supreme tragedy of my life. No sorrow could have been more crushing. His letters to me up till the day of his death were always couched in the affectionate terms that a son would use to his "Pops".'[21]

What a bitter, cruel, ironic blow: Valerie Barker had joined the air force in World War I; the son she had given birth to had, unwittingly, followed her into the service. As Victor Barker, Jeffrey Norton had, without facing any real physical danger in a theatre of war, presented himself as a heroic figure to his son; now that son had outdone his father and become a hero by making the ultimate sacrifice.

In 1941, the German and British governments had made an agreement that fallen airmen's next-of-kin would be provided with photographs of their relative's grave through the International Red Cross. Jeffrey Norton benefited from this agreement: 'From the kindly French souls who live near where he lies, I received a photograph of his grave, flower-laden as any mother would love to see it. With the photograph came an invitation to visit the grave.'[22]

It was an invitation Norton never accepted: the villagers would have been expecting to receive a visit from the young airman's father, who would need a passport to make the journey. A passport that would, by necessity, contain false information about the holder and, again, bear a false signature. Jeffrey Norton simply couldn't bring himself to do it.

He could not, would not do anything that might bring shame upon his son, who had, in death, become the war hero he himself had only pretended to be most of his life. He had to make sure that this young man's reputation would not suffer by being connected with anything that Victor Barker or John Hill or Valerie Arkell Smith had

'What I have done has been solely for my boy':
the son who never knew his mother

done. To ensure this, he would never reveal the date of his son's death, or the type of plane he was flying, or whether he died alone, or even the name of the French village where he was buried.

Norton cared little about the rest of his own life, but as long as he lived, he was determined his son would rest in peace. He would bear a father's grief – and a mother's.

As for himself, he would try and find some peace – in obscurity.

10

A Menopausal Gentleman

That fear – it's a deep dark place. I think part of getting older and going through the menopause is that you want to be by yourself more. And it goes along with a lot of that world of passing women at that time, that it felt natural to become isolated and not have that many friends.

Peggy Shaw, November 2000

We are used to pieces of flotsam and jetsam like old driftwood turning up on the beach – but nothing like this.

The Guardian, 3 March 2000

Rawtenstall, Lancashire, 1948

For a small mill town, Rawtenstall has its fair share of eccentrics.
  There is sixty-eight-year-old widow Nancy Chadwick. She is known to locals as 'a bit of a miser . . . it was common knowledge that she carried plenty of money in her bag'. For the last ten years, Mrs Chadwick has worked as housekeeper to eighty-two-year-old John Whittaker; she also tells people's fortunes, using playing cards or tea leaves. Some time ago, she inherited four small houses

from a previous employer and is often seen in the local park, counting her rent money.

Then there's Maggie Allen. Or 'Bill', as she prefers to be called. Only five foot tall, she still cuts a striking figure in her usual attire of blue trousers, blue-striped collar and shirt, blue blazer and fawn mackintosh. She spends a lot of evenings at her local pub, drinking pints and playing darts and dominoes.

The twentieth of twenty-two children, she was put to work in the textile industry at the age of twelve; she also worked as a post-woman and a bus conductress. She was sacked from her job at the Middlesex Gun Company for stealing a notebook and some savings stamps and hasn't worked since January; she's had some sort of persistent bronchial illness, but she's seen the doctor for a number of things, including vertigo, dyspepsia, anaemia and general debility.

Allen also used to be plagued by dysmenorrhea – painful periods – and in 1935 she underwent surgical treatment for this condition. Since then, she's told people – the few who take any interest in her – that this 'surgery' in fact changed her sex. After this, she began to wear men's clothes and had her hair cropped short.

For many years, Margaret Allen and her mother lived at 137 Bacup Road, a rented house that was once a police station. Allen isn't interested in housework, and since her mother's death in 1943, her home has become increasingly neglected and filthy. Unable to work, she struggles to exist on eleven shillings a week National Assistance and twenty-two shillings National Health Benefit.

Her only real friend is Mrs Annie Cook, who is separated from her husband. Cook says that in the two years or more since they met, Allen has told her '. . . that she was father to a child of a woman evacuee that used to stay with her . . . she used to say to me, "Don't call me Maggie, call me Bill" . . . I have never known her to be dressed up in women's ways'.[1]

*The two women see each other almost every evening, meeting on
the corner of Bacup Road and Kay Street. Sometimes they go to a
pub, but mostly to Allen's house.*

*Mrs Cook will make a poignantly stark statement to the police
that tells the bare facts about their relationship:*

> *I have been going out with her regularly. I have slept at her
> house on 3 occasions. We slept together. The last time I slept
> with her she had pyjamas on, I had a nightgown. She said
> to me, 'We have been going out long enough now together.
> Can't we start having connections?' I told her, 'No. I am
> parted from my husband and I don't want to bother.' As
> far as I know, I don't know what she was going to have
> connections with from her point of view.*[2]

*The two women spent the Whitsun holiday week of 1948
together in Blackpool, where Margaret registered as 'Mr Allen'.
'She used the men's lavatories when she was there,' says Annie
Cook.*[3]

*But the frustrations of Margaret Allen's life are getting the
better of her – with her feelings towards Annie Cook unrecipro-
cated, and plagued by depression and lassitude, she makes a
melodramatic 'suicide' attempt in front of her friend: 'She got
angry and suggested I was trying to break our friendship,' says
Annie. 'She rushed to a gas jet, put a tube in her mouth and
turned the gas on. I took the tube from her.'*[4]

*Now it's the summer, and Allen's mental and physical health
don't look like improving: she often complains of crippling
headaches, dizziness and listlessness that no doctor appears to take
seriously. Despite Annie Cook's exhortations to 'pull yourself
together', Allen can't seem to bring herself to clean up her home,
and, still unable to work, she's fallen into debt: she owes £15 in
rent arrears and £8 electricity, and could be facing possible eviction.*

Life is closing in around her, and it's all getting too much.

On the morning of 28 August, something snaps.

Just as Margaret Allen is about to leave her house, Nancy Chadwick appears at the door. 'I told her to go and she could see me some time else,' Allen will say later. 'But she seemed to insist on coming in. At this time we were talking just inside the kitchen . . . I was in a nervy mood and she just seemed to get on my nerves . . . on the spur of the moment I hit her with the hammer.'[5]

Allen puts the body in her coal cellar; later that night, she will drag it out on to Bacup Road. The murder weapon, a hammer, will be found in the River Irwell; Allen later admits that she intended to put the body there too. Instead, the body of Nancy Chadwick is discovered by a bus driver in the early hours of Sunday morning.

Later that day, the police begin door-to-door enquiries and call on Margaret Allen, whose house is only yards from where the body was found. No, she tells them, she didn't hear or see anything unusual in the street that night. That afternoon, she stands with other onlookers as Mrs Chadwick's bag is pulled from the river – it contains no purse or money. Later, she meets Annie Cook for a drink at the Ram's Head Hotel: 'She kept laughing and sort of staring at me,' Annie will recall.[6] By a strange coincidence, Mrs Cook's estranged husband, Willie, has served divorce papers on her that very morning.

On Wednesday 1 September, Chief Inspector Stevens calls at 137 Bacup Road; there, he discovers bloodstained ashes, and further bloodstains on the wall and front door. Margaret Allen picks up her mackintosh and tells the detective, 'Come on, let's get out of here. I'll tell you all about it.'[7] Later that day, she is charged with the murder of Nancy Chadwick and, under caution, admits to the killing; she is remanded at Strangeways prison in Manchester.

The forensic evidence is overwhelming: some of the victim's

*hairs and fibres from her clothing are found on Allen's clothes;
ashes found in the house contain Mrs Chadwick's blood, and
ashes are also found on her body. At first, the police believe they
have an open-and-shut case, with robbery as an obvious motive
behind the killing.*

*But Margaret Allen's statements don't support this theory: 'I
didn't actually kill her for that,' she says. 'I had one of my funny
moods. I had no reason at all. It seemed to come over me.'*[8]

*After Allen is sent for trial at Manchester Assizes, there is
another twist in this tragic tale: within hours of being informed he
will be called as a prosecution witness, John Whittaker tells a
neighbour he 'couldn't face it' and drowns himself in a nearby
pond.*

*The five-hour hearing at Manchester Assizes takes place on
Friday 10 December. Allen pleads 'not guilty'. Her defence counsel,
William Gorman KC (later a High Court judge), admits to the
court that the killing was 'a senseless, unjustified and purposeless
crime'. He enters a plea of insanity on his client's behalf, and tells
the court that 'She was going through the change of life and in
that stage most extraordinary things can happen. It was extraordinary, a sudden break-out in a woman of that kind without any
sort of cause but a purely voluntary insane act.'*[9]

*Dr George Cormack, the Principal Medical Officer at
Strangeways, testifies that he has 'not detected any signs of insanity, although she was undergoing the change of life . . . [she]
complained of headaches and giddiness for two or three days before
her periods'. However, most fatally, he says, 'She showed no evidence of being likely to lose her control at that time.' In mitigation,
he makes the observation that 'She fully realises her position and
seems to regret the crime.'*[10]

*This evidence from a doctor seems to carry substantially more
weight in the courtroom than that given by Annie Cook,
who describes how her friend has been prone to depression and*

*irritability, and outlines the desperate suicide attempt – a clear
'cry for help' from an unhappy, scared woman if ever there was
one.*

*The jury of nine men and three women take only fifteen minutes
to reach their verdict: rejecting the defence's plea of insanity, they
find Margaret Allen guilty of murder, with no recommendation to
mercy.*

*The ever-loyal Annie Cook organises a petition, pleading for a
reprieve for her friend, which reads: 'We the undersigned knew
Margaret Allen . . . and are aware of her peculiarities, and respect-
fully request a reprieve be granted.'[11] Only 162 out of
Rawtenstall's 28,000 residents sign the petition.*

*Margaret Allen's fate now lies in the hands of Chuter Ede, the
Home Secretary, who reviews the case with all the evidence before
him. Unfortunately, this includes further reports from Dr
Cormack, who says that the prisoner 'was well-behaved . . . she is
described as being a leader among the women and they accepted
her as such. We had further evidence that she was a homosexual.'
In an earlier report to the Director of Public Prosecutions, the
doctor has said, 'She denies absolutely any homosexual or other
abnormal sexual tendencies.'[12]*

*Ede decides there are insufficient grounds to justify him over-
turning the death sentence. In vain, Allen's MP, Mr G. Walker,
makes a last-minute intervention to save her.*

*On Tuesday 11 January 1949, Annie Cook visits her doomed
friend for the last time: Margaret Allen tells her, 'You know the
time tomorrow morning? It is nine o'clock. Do me a favour and
stand at that time at the end of Kay Street.'[13]*

This is where they used to meet.

*And so, at 9 a.m. on Wednesday 12 January, that is where
Annie Cook stands, weeping and comforted by her sister, as
Margaret Allen becomes the first woman to be executed in Britain
for twelve years. According to the custom for prisoners who were*

hanged, she is buried in the prison grounds, in an unmarked grave known only to the Governor and the Home Secretary. The day after the execution, one newspaper reports that 'Opponents of capital punishment were arguing that . . . Parliament was under the impression that execution of the [death] sentence would be confined to the worst cases. They contend that in refusing to recommend a reprieve for Allen, Mr Chuter has not kept to this alleged understanding.'[14]

That same morning, Annie Cook receives a parcel containing her friend's few personal belongings that she bequeathed her – a gold wedding ring, a lighter, a crucifix and 4s. 5½d. in cash.

Only two other women will share Margaret Allen's fate: Mrs Christofi, in October 1954, for the murder of her daughter-in-law, Hella; and Ruth Ellis, in July 1955.

Eight days after Allen's death, Prime Minister Clement Attlee establishes a Royal Commission on capital punishment.

In 1964, Sidney Silverman's Murder (Abolishment of the Death Penalty) Bill begins its journey through Parliament; it becomes law in 1965, when capital punishment is finally abolished – ostensibly for a trial period. If Parliament dictates, it could be reintroduced at any time.

The killing of Nancy Chadwick was a tragically senseless one that ended up costing three lives. There is a strong argument that says this was a case where a manslaughter conviction could have been substituted for murder, and a custodial sentence for execution. Yet the police, the prosecutors, the jury, the judge and the Home Secretary seemed united in determination that this shouldn't happen. It was almost as though, when they looked at the defendant, they didn't like what they saw.

Whatever moral verdict might be passed on someone who kills an old woman in a fit of temper, it is unthinkable that a similar crime would now result in a murder charge, or a custodial sentence of more than ten years.

*Given the lack of a clear motive for the killing, and the medical
evidence that showed how much the menopause was affecting her
emotionally and physically, it is not inconceivable that Margaret
Allen could have been charged with manslaughter, not murder.
But her defence lawyers, funded by legal aid, did not pursue this
line. In a similar case, more than fifty years on, a team of reliable
'expert' witnesses would, as a matter of course, be able to plead mitigation on medical and psychological grounds.*

*In the end, her doctor's failure to take her 'funny moods' seri-
ously, the lack of proper medical treatment, and what her friends
called 'her peculiarities' almost certainly cost Margaret Allen any
chance of mercy.*

And so 'Bill' Allen had to take his punishment like a man.

Kessingland, Suffolk, 1948

This is a queer place to end up.

All manner of things are washed up here.

*Which probably explains why, at first, no one noticed him
amongst Kessingland's flotsam and jetsam, stranded like a
landed whale. There was no particular reason why anyone
would: it's not unknown for unusual creatures to be observed in
the vicinity, and not just on the beach. A few miles away is the
most easterly point in Britain. All in all, it's a perfect place for
those with something to hide – it might be themselves, or it might
be someone else.*

Up to the fourteenth century, Kessingland was a wealthy
port. This fishing village, four miles south of Lowestoft,
was once said to be the wealthiest village in England.

The prolific author Rupert Croft-Cooke fondly remembered Kessingland's parish church, St Edmund's, as
'one of those high-towered buildings which seem most

commonly to rise from flat country, like the belfries of Belgium'.[15]

Croft-Cooke spent a summer in Kessingland after leaving school in 1920; then, it was 'a lonely village of a few hundred people; cornfields spread almost to its church doors and on its beach were fishing boats drawn up with never a cabin for holiday-makers'. People got about on farm waggons, pony-and-trap and bicycles; cars were scarce. 'The telephone had six local subscribers. Farmers' wives churned their own butter . . . the names over the shops and the name of the village itself seemed to me to be of Saxon and Danish origin and there were many bright yellow heads and blue eyes among the children.'[16]

After the Second World War, Kessingland's fishing industry was receding while its attractions as a summer holiday resort for families were being exploited. By 1948, its population still numbered less than 2,000, and one local family, the Catchpoles, had quite a monopoly on the village's activities. There was Mrs E.M. Catchpole, the boat-owner; Edward Junior, the boot repairer; George, the proprietor of the Kessingland Holiday Camp, one of three such camps in the district; and Mrs Gertrude Catchpole, who ran the Hillcrest boarding house.

In 1948, the people of Kessingland's main concerns were the state of its sea defences and the price of herrings – the fishermen had had a bad season that year. Local shopkeepers, many of them ex-servicemen, were worried about the prospect of a Co-op opening in the village. There were other worries, too: the beach was still littered with bombs, and that July, a thirteen-year-old boy staying at the Holiday Fellowship Camp was killed by one of these lethal bits of flotsam and jetsam. Another bomb shell was found near Kessingland beach by the village bobby, PC

Harry Blythe – Blythe by name and blithe by nature, he calmly carried it home on his bicycle.

But mostly, life in Kessingland was undramatic: charity whist drives were held in the village hall, and sporting action was provided by Kessingland United Football Club, the bowls club and the darts club at the Queen's Head pub.

Frederick George Bligh and his wife Mildred ran the corner grocer's shop in the High Street. In such a small village, it was easy for shopkeepers to remember and recognise all their regular customers. The Blighs' daughter, Maureen, recalled one in particular, a man who used to come to the shop to buy cigarettes and tobacco. He was a tall figure, usually dressed in a hat and suit, who sometimes swore like a trooper. But Maureen didn't remember this man because of his language, but because of what someone once said about him as he left the shop one day when she was there: 'You'd never think she was a woman, would you?'

So, it seemed someone in the village knew the truth about fifty-three-year-old Geoffrey John Norton – formerly known as Victor Barker, Ivor Gauntlett, John Hill and Jeffrey Norton.

Geoffrey and Eva Norton lived at number 3 Wrights Cottages, 'in the last of a pair of quiet cottages standing back from the road, with grass before them, low wall and a gate each, furthest from the Lowestoft end'.[17] The couple kept themselves to themselves, although they were friendly with milkman Derrick Briggs and his wife Mabel, who had lived at 4 Wrights Cottages before moving to 4 Meadow View.

Geoffrey was also on cordial terms with PC Harry Blyth. 'He was a fattish man and had a deep man's voice,' recalled Blyth. 'He usually wore an ordinary navy blue suit and had his hair brushed back like a man. He told me he met his wife while they were both working in a London store.'[18]

The truth was, no one knew what the Nortons had been doing or where they had been living since the war ended. There was one story that said they had briefly lived at Laindon in Essex before moving to Suffolk in 1948, but they never told anyone and no one asked them. If they had been seeking a life of quiet obscurity, they certainly found it when they came to Kessingland.

But after eight years, the quiet obscurity was shattered again, through a combination of health and money problems.

Geoffrey's weight had burgeoned in recent years, and his legs, which had begun to play him up during the war when he was working in the Hurricane factory, definitely seemed to be getting worse. By March 1956, his mobility had become severely impaired, and his GP, village doctor Robert Peregrine, decided to have his patient admitted to Lowestoft Hospital. Initially, he was admitted to the men's ward, where his bed was surrounded by screens before he was moved to the women's ward.

There, Geoffrey Norton was transferred to what was then known as an 'amenity ward', where patients could pay for the privilege of having a room to themselves, although they did not receive treatment as a private patient. Norton's room, however, was paid for by the local authority.

The nursing staff who looked after Geoffrey Norton have never forgotten him – especially the nurse who, preferring to remain anonymous, spent the most time with this most memorable of patients.

In 1956, I was a staff nurse on the private and amenity wards and the operating theatre. This private room was not what you'd imagine from hospitals today. It was dark, it had a wooden floor, curtains at the window and a fireplace for a coal fire.

She lay there in the single bed like a landed whale. That's the only way I can describe her. Superficially, you'd think she was a man – cropped hair, reddy-blue jaw, I don't think she shaved but it was red and raw; and weighing approximately seventeen-plus stone. But really she had no physical resemblance to a man at all – she had big breasts that were basically flat. But then, in the twenties, when he started dressing like that, it was the age of 'the Flapper' and women used to bind themselves. Now, if she did the same, she would just look like a very large man, even under a singlet.

She was a nursing problem because she would not move and she would not help herself at all. In this day and age, there would be cranes and hoists – there were none then. She ruined my back from lifting!

She was there for about three to four weeks. The vast majority of nursing staff refused to go near her. But it was my job to be there. She did ring the bell constantly for a bedpan – we used to go in and give her a bedpan, and the matron used to go in and say, 'Good morning, Mr Norton, how are you?'[19]

While examining Norton and trying to make him comfortable, the nurse made a grim discovery.

The labia was excoriated – it was raw, sore and slightly inflamed. Now, whether that was due to wearing a male prosthesis of some sort, I don't know. We never saw that, obviously, but one of our first jobs was to sort her out and heal her up. She was so sore that she probably couldn't walk at all. Whether that was the start of her immobility, I don't know. Perhaps the Parkinson's was making itself manifest. There was nothing wrong with her arms. The consultant used to come and examine her but she didn't really have any specific treatment. I can't remember physiotherapists coming near her. As far as I know, there was never a definite diagnosis.[20]

Geoffrey Norton spent most of his days lying in his bed, alone with his thoughts. But whatever those might have been, he chose not to share them with his carers. His nurse recalls:

She was a strange character. You could not get near her – I did try, partly because I was so involved with her, I was that sort of nurse. There was a wall but behind that wall I felt she was terrified. She didn't talk about the son – not ever. I felt that a lot of her physical condition was just due to fear. Our dear auxiliary and I used to make her get up and lugged her out of bed and forced her to walk round and round the room, one on each side, until the doctors felt she was well enough to go home.[21]

During his stay at Lowestoft Hospital, Geoffrey Norton only had one real visitor, according to his nurse:

Her wife used to come and see her regularly from
Kessingland, which is indicative of caring – it was
quite a way to come in those days, you would need at
least two buses. She was a funny little wisp of a
woman: minute, drab, and she always used to come
in and say, 'Bums up.' That's about the only thing I
can remember about her. She used to sign in as 'Mrs
Norton'. She used to push him around in a wheel-
chair, which was no mean feat.[22]

Occasionally, there were other visitors for Geoffrey
Norton, but their interest in him was purely professional.
'She was also trying to sort out financial affairs, because
people used to come and see her,' remembers the nurse.
'She was obviously getting short of money and she was
attempting to make money; she was thinking about dying,
though she never talked to us about it, because she was
talking to solicitors.'[23]

It wasn't too long before the hospital staff discovered
exactly what Geoffrey Norton was planning as a short-term
solution to his financial worries. 'By a fluke, the theatre
porter went out one Sunday – it was snowing and he
bought every Sunday newspaper and of course one of
them was the *Empire News* – with her story! She had obviously done this to make money.'[24]

It may have seemed incredible but it was true: for the
third time in his life, Victor Barker was selling his story to
the press. The *Empire News and Sunday Chronicle* was a scandal sheet, a kindred spirit of the *News of the World* – the
paper which would eventually swallow up the title. As such,
it was the perfect home for a story like Barker's which so
readily lent itself to sensationalism:

I POSED AS A MAN FOR 30 YEARS!
MY AMAZING MASQUERADE
A WIFE CONFESSES
By Valerie Arkell Smith

This 'confession' ran in the paper from 19 February until 15 April 1956, and was lavishly illustrated with photographs of Valerie Arkell Smith and Victor Barker. There were pictures of Victor at an Old Contemptibles' reunion; laying the wreath at the Cenotaph; wearing his uniform and medals. There was even a picture of Elfrida Haward, though the face was blanked out, and a childhood one of Barker's son.

As the previous two 'life-stories' had contradicted each other, so did this third version contradict its predecessors. The chronology of certain events was presented in a different way from those of 1929 and 1937; scant details were given about Barker's time in Holloway prison and even fewer about his time as a seaside attraction in Blackpool. And the name 'Eva Norton' was conspicuous by its absence.

What did remain constant was Barker's insistence that nothing 'perverted' had caused him to choose the life he had, and that he had 'suffered no "tendency" to become a "man" . . . I have undergone no physical operation to turn me from woman into man, and physically I am, as I started out in life to be, 100 per cent woman. But so long have I lived as a man, that I have come to think as one, behave as one, and be accepted as one.' He was also at pains to reiterate – just as he had in his previous tellings – that whatever he had done, he had done for the sake of his boy, and for no other reason. 'I ask for no pity or sympathy,' he insisted. 'You may feel that I do not deserve it anyway and maybe you are right.'[25]

This serialised version of Barker's 'life story' was almost as intriguing for what it concealed as for what it revealed. It did not disclose the current whereabouts of Colonel Barker, or even that he had been living as Geoffrey Norton for some years. Although it revealed that he had been in the Home Guard, it didn't say where. And, once again, any details about his son, referred to as 'Tony', his RAF service and the exact circumstances of his death remained a secret.

Curiously, the local press in Suffolk didn't pick up on the story – perhaps they were too preoccupied with the state of herring fishing – but Norton's nurses, at least, found it a revelation. 'We knew more about her from reading that, because she had put up this real barrier.'[26]

The serialisation concluded with an account by writer Ursula Bloom of her face-to-face encounter with the 'woman who hoaxed the world'. Like the 'life story' that had preceded it, 'I Meet Colonel Barker' was short on fact and long on sentimentality and sensationalism.

'I wondered what kind of a woman was this who had always wanted to be a man,' Bloom pondered. 'And I wondered if she regretted her life of make-believe – a life of deliberate deception, because there was no physical change or glandular disorder in her case.'[27]

In Norton's bedroom, Bloom found

A grey-haired woman. A woman with the most dramatic eyes that I have ever seen. She wore ordinary striped flannel pyjamas, a man's grey cardigan about her shoulders; her thick grey hair was cropped, and she had a man's signet ring.

She is still Colonel Barker at heart. She is the social misfit, which is always a wretched condition

. . . Cultured and very virile, she is stimulatingly interesting. She says that if she had her life again, she would still do the same thing.

Had she been born forty years later, none of it would have mattered, for today dozens of women live like men. But in her case it went further. Deep down in that vital personality there is the delight of dramatic thrill. If the grandiose had not dazzled her, nothing more would probably have happened. Sensation intrigued her. She put too much icing on the cake and it went sour on her . . . She is the kind that could never have lived the dull, eventless life, and at heart she knows it.

She is a religious woman. She goes to church when she can. She prays. She believes in reincarnation . . . 'We live again,' she said. 'I believe in destiny, and in fate.' She has found it difficult to accept three of the fundamental bases of life, our birth, our sex, our death. She challenged the conditions of her own birth, she did everything that she could to change her sex, but I think she is more tolerant of death. Even if she realises that she flew in the face of fate, and none of it has availed her anything at all, her answer is that she is still living as a man, behaving as a man, and continuing as she began.

I said goodbye to her, wishing very much that something could have been done to help her, but there is little anyone can do. Probably the most tragic part of all was that today, further advanced in our civilisation, her sins would not have attracted so much comment, so much that must have hurt her badly. But she is not bitter about any of it, because the male mentality predominates in that. I cannot

think of her as a man, much as I am sure she would
want me to do so. I am uninterested in Sir Victor
Barker, and that unslakable thirst for adventure . . . I
have deep sympathy with the woman who is so much
alone and who prays. That is how I think all of us
should feel about her.[28]

However, it appeared that Bloom's piety and sympathy
towards Barker only went pen-deep: later, she would tell a
friend, 'I found her a bad egg alright but absolutely interesting. I saw his [the son's] letters to her beginning "Dear
Dad".'[29]

Bloom had visited Geoffrey Norton at 3 Wrights
Cottages: after a few weeks at Lowestoft Hospital everyone's patience had run out – including the patient's. The
nursing staff had had enough of this strange person who,
as far as they were concerned, appeared to be taking up a
bed for no good reason, and Norton's temper was becoming frayed – sometimes he would throw things at one of the
auxiliaries. The nurse who had most to do with Norton
noticed that 'She didn't like authority, even the small
authority I had. There was an unspoken battle of wills
between us. She must have hated being in hospital.'[30]

Eventually, to everyone's relief – including Norton's – he
was discharged from Lowestoft Hospital. 'She went back to
Kessingland to the care of this little woman,' said his nurse.
'But, funnily enough, one of my colleagues nursed the wife
on the women's ward later, when she was dying. I would
imagine she's buried in Kessingland as well.'[31] No one
seems to know what became of this shadowy Mrs Norton.

The exact nature of Geoffrey Norton's illness was not
diagnosed at this time, but within the next few years
it became obvious that he was suffering from the same

affliction that had blighted his mother's life: Parkinson's disease, with its familiar symptoms of shaking, stiffness and slow, restricted movement.

Back in Kessingland, Norton was to acquire a new ally: on 1 August 1956, the Reverend Thomas Drury became the Rector of Kessingland and was introduced to Geoffrey, which was what he always called his unconventional parishioner.

> She always wore men's clothes – I never saw her in anything else – but the village didn't see much of her as she was crippled and remained in a bath chair. She was a tall person of very good physique who easily passes as a man but I guessed that she was a woman. Obviously she thought I thought she was a man. She was a good churchman and although she could not attend church I used to call on her regularly. She was very well educated and well versed in affairs.[32]

The 'little woman' who was to die in Lowestoft Hospital within two years of her husband's stay there obviously found it hard to cope with caring for his increasing immobility. In 1957 he went into hospital again – this time, St Andrew's Hospital at Thorpe, near Norwich. He was admitted to the male ward but, again, was soon transferred to the female admission ward.

One nurse who worked at St Andrew's was intrigued by the new patient:

> My mother told me the story about her when I was a young girl so when she came into hospital, I was really interested about her, but she would never talk

about herself. I remember she was dressed in a shirt, neck-tie, a pinstripe suit . . . I think she is the most masculine woman I have ever seen in my life.

The sister asked another nurse and myself to bath her, and when I was drying her feet I asked her what size shoes did she wear; she said size seven but should be size ten. I remember she always had a photo of a nice-looking young man dressed in uniform of the RAF; she always said it was her son.[33]

Once back at home, Geoffrey Norton's 'little woman', who some locals nicknamed 'Brandy Lil', would wheel her husband to the pub in a bathchair where, weather permitting, he would have his drink outside.

After Eva's death, their old neighbour and friend, Mabel Briggs, would help to look after Geoffrey; he was also attended by a district nurse, and the Revd Drury visited occasionally. 'He was very ill towards the end,' said Mrs Briggs. 'He would rarely talk about the old days although he would occasionally mention his work on a farm or in the Home Guard.'[34]

Geoffrey Norton gradually sank into a coma, and Mrs Briggs was at his side when he died at home, on 18 February 1960, aged sixty-four. No death notices were placed in the local press.

Norton was laid to rest in the grounds of St Edmund's Church, Kessingland, on 23 February. By his own request, he was buried in an unmarked grave, in a coffin that bore no nameplate. At that time, no records for these unmarked plots had to be kept, so only the undertakers, the Rector and Mrs Briggs knew the location of the grave. They took this secret to theirs.

The Revd Drury conducted the short ceremony, with

only Mrs Briggs and the funeral directors in attendance. The Rector did notice a man he didn't recognise watching the proceedings from the edge of the churchyard, but when the priest approached him, he walked off. No one has ever admitted to being this mystery man.

On 1 March, Mrs Briggs registered the death of 'Geoffrey Norton otherwise Lillias Irma Valerie Arkell-Smith, shop assistant (retired)'. There appeared to be no will to be read; the Briggses acted as caretakers for the cottage. No one knows what became of the framed picture of the young airman, and the letters he wrote to his father, or the studio photographs taken of a tall, upright, handsome man in full officer's uniform, proudly sporting his medals.

Like Valerie Barker, Valerie Arkell Smith, Valerie Pearce Crouch, Victor Barker, Ivor Gauntlett, John Hill and Geoffrey Norton, they had been buried, once and for all.

On 6 May 1960, a headline appeared in the *Lowestoft Journal*: 'Woman Who Was Once Col. Barker Dies at Kessingland'. It appeared that, a few months before he died, Geoffrey Norton had told a local journalist who he was, and who he had been, but had managed to get them to agree not to reveal his death until a suitable period had elapsed.

Now, it seemed, the time had come.

The *Daily Express* also ran the story of the 'Woman Who Hoaxed the World' on 6 May, declaring: 'Col. Barker Was Man to the End'. The paper described him as a 'burly, 20-stone hard-drinker who took brandies and bitters in the village pub at lunchtime and took bottles of brandy home every day'.[35]

The revelation took some Kessingland residents totally by surprise. Harry Blyth, the bomb-carrying policeman, was shellshocked:

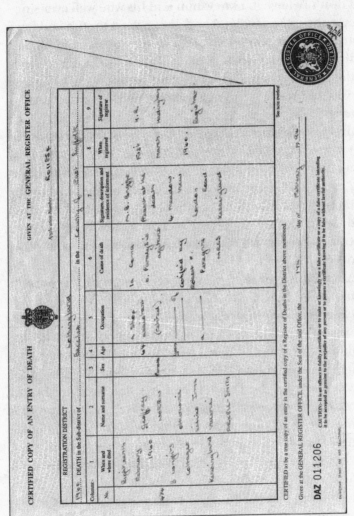

Death certificate for Geoffrey Norton, 1960

I don't believe it. I knew him and his wife well ever since they came to Kessingland and always used to stop and have a chat with him when I met him being wheeled in his chair in the village. Mrs Norton used to take a job in the summer at the holiday camps. Her husband couldn't work because he was an invalid. I will never believe he was a woman.[36]

Number 3 Wrights Cottages is gone now: the little row of tiny houses was demolished and became Scott's Close. Like other parts of Kessingland, new houses were erected in the 1960s and 70s, to meet the demands of the burgeoning holiday industry and the commuters working in Lowestoft and Great Yarmouth. The shop run by the Blighs, where Geoffrey Norton used to buy his tobacco, is now the car park of the Queen's Head pub.

A few miles up the coast, there's a sign in a Lowestoft public toilet that reads: *This attendant will carry out his/her duties in both male and female areas.*

Since 1947, Bailiffs Court farm has been the three-star Bailiffscourt Hotel. When Lord Moyne, Walter Guinness, bought the estate in 1927, he demolished the Georgian farmhouse that the Pearce Crouches had lived in. But in the hotel, there is still a black-and-white photograph in a frame, the only known picture that exists of the old farmhouse. It shows a man and a woman standing in front of the house. The woman is tall and well built – slightly taller, in fact, than her husband. He looks older than her. She is not looking at him, but seems more focused on the two dogs she is holding on leads in front of her. It is not a picture of a woman who is happy or content.

In Jersey, as elsewhere, Nazi collaborators sleep safely. In England, a group emerged in 2000 calling themselves the 'Friends of the Swastika' – motto, 'To hell with Hitler!'

Their aim was to reclaim this symbol that had originated from the Sanskrit word meaning well-being and good fortune. The group's leader was an artist, whose main body of work was the 200 tattoos adorning their own body.

This artist called themselves: 'ManWoman'.

Without the use of global electronic media and modern technology, Colonel Barker still managed to provide entertainment for the masses, and at a bargain price – in Blackpool, in 1937, he could be had for twopence; for little more than that, he was on sale in every major British newspaper in March and April 1929. He continued to fill columns right up to, even after, his death. There was no doubt: without meaning to be, he became a star attraction.

But long, long after Victor Barker was buried with Geoffrey Norton, there were other women who realised that if gentlemen preferred blondes, then many blondes preferred gentlemen.

When DJ Jo Purvis opened her legendary Rehearsal Club in Soho in the late 1960s, the club boasted weekly drag shows, featuring a mixture of old and new performers. In the early 1970s, club members were informed in their newsletter that a different kind of performer would soon be gracing the stage of the Rehearsal: Randy Knight.

The club had launched new acts before. But Randy Knight was a drag act with a difference – quite a big one. Because it was *Miss* Randy Knight. Or, if you prefer, Pearl. Or, as *she* preferred, Paul.

But more significant than what Randy chose to call herself was what Jo Purvis decided to call her. The Rehearsal Club faithful were informed that 'Unlike Hetty King and Vesta Tilley, and their imitators, whose acts are geared to

Victorian Music Hall, our "Drag King" has brought the whole thing up to date by adapting male impersonation to today's pop scene.'

Pearl had been dreaming of becoming Paul for years: she had been working on her male impersonations since she was fourteen: 'I'd rush home from school, wait till my family was out and then get into male clothes, put oil on my hair and practise in front of the mirror.'[37]

Throughout the 1970s, Randy Knight was still doing the cabaret circuit, though curiously, most of her performances were for all-female hen parties. In 1978, she revealed to *Gay News* that some of the women in her audiences seemed blissfully unaware what lay beneath her natty three-piece, as she mimed to numbers like 'I Want a Woman'. Others were a bit more in the know, sending her notes backstage asking, *Will I do?*

Other hazards came with the job: butch women offering her their girlfriends for the night, gay men who chatted her up for hours, and on one occasion, a straight man who yelled 'Lesbian!' at her throughout her set before turning up at the stage door with a knife.

In Japan, thousands of women still queue for five or six hours to catch a glimpse of their Takarazuka idols, or to festoon them with gifts. 'I wouldn't wait that long for a man,' they say. Many of them are married women, with children, who say they meet just to talk about their favourite male player: 'We come here secretly. Our husbands don't know we are here.'[38]

On stage, these women's idols are the tall figures with the wide padded shoulders, in natty suits or black tails and ties, with hair worn short and slicked-back or sporting Elvis quiffs. Their Western characters have names like 'Smithy' and 'Ralph'. Their devoted fans can still remember how they felt when they first saw these figures: 'I felt a surge of excitement. My mind exploded.'[39]

These idols are created at the Takarazuka music and drama school, where they spend two years being groomed to be ideal men. But it is usually only the taller girls or those with deep voices that get to be male players. The dance director tells them, 'I want the male players to look more powerful or you'll come across as girls. Try to be more sexy – that's what excites the audience. Be more aware of being male. Remember, it's your job.' Men from the local military are drafted in to teach them to walk 'the way soldiers do'. The female players complain, 'The male players can be more natural.'[40]

The women who make up nearly a hundred per cent of the Takarazuka audiences are under no illusions about what these 'men' give them:

> They give you a dream, so you can forget reality. The men on stage are endlessly kind to their women . . . show real sensitivity. If the actors were real men, the result would be coarse. But because women act the male roles, they can create the ideal man . . . that women really want. They *are* the ideal man.[41]

When Valerie Arkell Smith 'played' Victor Barker, the result was not coarse, either. And the reality, as Elfrida Haward saw it, was out of a dream: ' With me he was ideally kind, and a marvellous cavalier – the kind of companion that every girl dreams about.'[42]

In the 1990s, following in the footsteps of their 'father', Randy Knight, dozens of drag kings started to take to the floors and stages of lesbian clubs in America and Britain, delighting thousands of women with their versions of masculinity. American writer and performer Peggy Shaw presented her one-woman show, *Menopausal Gentlemen*; prior to this, Shaw spent several months living as a man in preparation for playing Billy Tipton, the jazz musician who was another 'woman who hoaxed the world'.

Any regular daytime TV viewer, either in the US or Britain, might agree that there doesn't seem to be much separating Colonel Victor Barker and his wife, who sold their stories to the tabloid press (three times, in his case), from the sad, attention-seeking creatures who expose themselves and their most intimate personal problems on those consensual humiliation exercises that we know as chat shows.

Elfrida Haward, as a 'wronged wife', would have made a splendid contributor to an edition of *Kilroy* which was entitled 'My husband's not the man I married'. It is also easy to imagine her appearing on the *Trisha* show, saying, as one woman did of her deceitful boyfriend, 'I thought he was my knight in shining armour. I thought, here's someone who really wants to marry me . . . he could have told me the truth.'[43]

Nineteen twenty-nine or 1999: the subjects are the same, only the medium has changed. In 1929, a thousand women thronged outside Holloway prison to gawk at the 'freak'; in 1937, they would pay tuppence to see the 'freak show'. In the new millennium, people don't have to leave their homes to be a spectator – they just switch on the television and watch Rikki and Trisha and Jerry and Montel and Robert wheel them on. Only camera crews and photographers would wait outside a prison now.

In all her incarnations, Valerie Barker chose not to make herself inconspicuous. She was an outstanding gentleman, the bon viveur in plush hotels, an actor; she marched with

Old Contemptibles and new fascists, had portraits taken to break into films, was the centrepiece of a Blackpool sideshow, where Victor Barker played himself and his wife played his wife. They would have made the perfect chat-show couple – the ideal sideshow to be gawped at and laughed at.

Ideal men turned into ideal whipping boys.

The posts might have been taken down, and the stocks dismantled, but there are still crimes, there is still punishment and there are still victims. They may not be called Mary Hamilton or Edward de Lacy Evans or Victor Barker, but while, as the writer Emma Donoghue observed, 'Lawmakers are still ready to believe that the non-cross-dressed "normal" woman is innocent of lesbian desire, and there is still infinite resentment against the woman who usurps what heterosexual men see as their clothes, their role, their access to women,' there will always be girls who were boys who as girls can be turned into whipping boys.[44]

Mariana Cetiner comes to mind: a Romanian woman imprisoned in 1998 for 'luring another woman into sexual intercourse'.[45]

And, of course, there was Brandon Teena, another 'ideal man': he received 'punishment' of the most brutal and extreme kind for his crime of usurping 'what heterosexual men see as their clothes, their role, their access to women'.

Brandon lived in Falls City, Nebraska, not as grand as its name implies. It was and is stereotypical smalltown America. In Falls City, he became friends with John Lotter and Tom Nissen, whom he met in a bar. To become one of the boys, Brandon tried to emulate his friends' redneck behaviour – but not in the way he treated women.

On New Year's Eve 1993, Brandon was shot twice and stabbed by Lotter and Nissen; the two men also killed

Brandon's friends Lisa Lambert and Phillip DeVine. Lotter was the ex-boyfriend of Brandon's girlfriend Lana Tisdel; a week earlier, on Christmas Eve, he and Nissen had discovered that Brandon had been born Teena, and beat him up and raped him.

Brandon went to the police and told them who his assailants had been. But the cops didn't arrest the two suspects – they wanted to check out Brandon's story first. Word got back to Lotter and Nissen that charges were being brought against them and they decided to silence Brandon for good.

John Lotter was sentenced to death for the triple murders; Nissen got life-without-parole, after doing a deal with the prosecution. Brandon Teena's mother, Jo Ann, sued the Nebraska County authorities on the grounds that they had failed to protect him by arresting the two suspects after he had reported the rape to the police. The judge in the civil case awarded Jo Ann $80,000 in damages, but said the county was only liable for $17,000 – the murderers were responsible for the rest.

At the age of fourteen, Brandon used to watch trashy TV chat shows; he first heard the word 'transsexual' on the Maury Povitch show. His murder prompted endless media speculation about who and what Brandon was. Kimberley Pierce, director of *Boys Don't Cry*, the film based on Brandon's story, said, 'I knew that he wanted to be with women and he wanted to dress as a boy. And where that might have led, I didn't want to speculate, because I couldn't be certain.'[46]

One thing was certain: as one of Brandon's ex-girlfriends told a reporter, 'He was a lot of girls' dream guy. He didn't push, he always gave.'[47]

Brandon struggled with the problems that Victor Barker

surely had – like periods. How did a man buy sanitary
towels without arousing suspicion? If it was hard enough
for Brandon to do in the 1990s, how much harder it must
have been for a memorable figure like Victor Barker to do
in the 1920s and 30s. Of course, his wife could always have
bought them for him – but then she believed he was a
man, didn't she? He could have taken some of his wife's
sanitary protection – but then she would have wondered
why items kept going missing, wouldn't she?

Acquiring the towels was hard, but disposing of them
was even harder. Where would he do it – in men's public
toilets?

Brandon Teena and Victor Barker had more than
period problems in common: in both cases, their identities
were unravelled by petty crimes – in Brandon's case, passing false cheques and violation of parole, in Barker's,
failure to pay a debt. They both ended up paying a heavy
price for their misdemeanours.

On 26 March, after Hilary Swank had received the
Academy Award for Best Actress for her portrayal of
Brandon Teena in *Boys Don't Cry*, she said, 'I pray for the
day when we not only accept our differences, but celebrate
our diversity.'[48]

> *She prays. She believes in reincarnation ... 'We live again,'*
> *she said. 'I believe in destiny, and in fate.'*

In 1995, Joyce Chester went to the weekly Sunday market
held in the car park of Brighton station. Browsing through
some sheet music, she discovered an old newspaper cutting, a full page folded in half, and noticed the word
'man-woman' in the headline.

The cutting was from the *News of the World*, the edition

dated 10 March 1929, and told the story of Colonel Victor Barker.

Chester bought the cutting for 10p and donated it to the Brighton Ourstory Project, who gave it pride of place in the BOP 1997 Brighton Festival exhibition, *Gay Girls and Bachelor Boys.*

Brighton's most famous bridegroom had returned, once more, to hold an audience spellbound. He lived again.

Thursday 2 March 2000

At about 7.15 a.m., a local woman is walking her dog along the beach beneath the cliffs at Kessingland. At the top of the cliffs is Rider Haggard Lane, named after the author whose holiday home was demolished in 1925, the house where his daughter, Lillias, saw a strange creature off the Kessingland coast.

All manner of things are washed up here.

Which probably explains why, at first, no one noticed him amongst Kessingland's flotsam and jetsam, stranded like a landed whale. There was no particular reason why anyone would: it's not unknown for unusual creatures to be observed in the vicinity, and not just on the beach. All in all, it's a perfect place for those with something to hide – it might be themselves, or it might be someone else.

But Kessingland, it seems, always gives up its secrets eventually.

In time-honoured fashion, just like the beginning of a crime novel, the unfortunate dog-walker stumbled upon the strange creature.

By the high-tide mark was a body. It was naked, and attached to it was a heavy chain, three 2.5kg, 6½ inch Spur Barbell gym weights and two padlocks. The police were alerted and the area was sealed off. The body was taken to the James Paget Hospital at Gorleston for a post-mortem. The police believed the body to be that of a woman, white, in her twenties to forties, of slim build and with brown collar-length hair; her left ear was pierced but there was no jewellery or, for that matter, any clothing found on the body. The police started to check their missing persons list.

By the end of the weekend, fingerprint tests had given them a name: Christine Chappel. Christine had been better known by her other name: Bryan Hooley.

The twenty-eight-year-old from Roxwell, Essex, paid £10,000 for a male-to-female sex change operation in 1994. In 1990 he had married Alison Halfacree, and the couple had a child. Three years later they separated, although Bryan continued, on and off, to live in the marital home after he became Christine.

In 1996, Christine Chappel lost a bitter court case with, of all people, the Revd Christopher Awdry, son of the late Revd Wilbert Awdry, author of the Thomas the Tank Engine books. Chappel claimed that she had had a two-year relationship with Christopher Awdry and had co-authored some of the books.

Sometimes he dressed and lived as Bryan Hooley, sometimes she dressed and lived as Christine Chappel.

When the body was discovered, no one could say for certain whether it had been Bryan or Christine who had been dumped in the sea: what was certain, according to the Home Office patholo-gist, was that the victim had been struck around the head with a flat object and was still alive when they went into the water – death was due to drowning.

Some of Bryan Hooley's clothes were known to be missing, including a navy suit and a pair of blue jeans. Detectives inves-tigating the murder said the victim 'could have been dressed as a man when he left home. It's a possibility someone may have found gents' clothing on the shoreline and not reported it.'[49]

The local press were quick to spot the analogies between fact and fiction: the Evening Star *said the grim discovery had all the hallmarks of a classic P.D. James mystery . . . the Suffolk-based author set many of her murder stories on remote beaches and other areas of East Anglia. In her classic detective story,* Devices and Desires, *police chief Adam Dalgliesh has to investigate the death of a young woman found naked on the local beach.'[50]*

They could also have pointed to a novel by another crime writer based on England's eastern coast: Ruth Rendell's A Sleeping Life. Based in Suffolk, the book's story involves the murder of a woman called Rhoda Comfrey; a man's wallet is found in her bag, one bought by a writer called Grenville West. It emerges that West and Comfrey are one and the same person – Comfrey lived as West for twenty years, during which time, a woman called Polly Flinders fell in love with him. It is she who turns out to be Comfrey's killer. The woman who loved Grenville West was the same woman who would ultimately destroy him.

One of the book's characters, pondering Comfrey's 'masquerade', observes that 'all her miseries came from being a woman . . . as a man, she had everything to gain . . . she had very little to lose'.[51]

As the Hooley/Chappel investigation progressed, a witness reported seeing a Volkswagen caravanette, driven by a white man with dark hair and a short dark anorak, parked at the end of Rider Haggard Lane at 4.45 p.m. on 28 February, near steps leading to the beach. The rented holiday cottages there were all empty. On 30 March, a man using a metal detector on the beach found another weight, identical to the three chained to Hooley's body.

Six months later, on 26 September 2000, Bryan Hooley's estranged wife, Alison, was charged with assisting an offender and perverting the course of justice. On 1 September, her brother, Charles Halfacree, had been charged with the murder of his brother-in-law.

One of Bryan Hooley's Essex neighbours told reporters: 'Life as a woman just didn't work out for him.'[52]

St Edmund's Churchyard, Kessingland, Suffolk, Thursday 22 June 2000

Dear Lillias/Valerie/Victor/Ivor/John/Jeffrey/Geoffrey, (I think that's all of you):

This was a queer place to end up.

Today, I walked along the desolate stretch of beach where they found the body that was never meant to be found. Covehithe Beach, it's called. Most of the journalists who came to report on the case had probably never heard of it, or of Kessingland.

But I'd heard of Covehithe Beach.

One day, I was sorting through some of my old papers and found some stuff from when I was involved in a youth theatre group, more than twenty years ago. A young woman had sent us a script and we were planning to stage it. I was going to direct it, I remembered, as I turned the pages over. It was a simple story, about a young girl's first sexual encounter on a deserted beach, during a holiday romance.

The couple joke about how easy it would be to murder someone in such an isolated place. 'If you washed me out to sea, I'd get washed up again,' the girl tells her boyfriend.

Then I looked again at where the young lovers are: 'Covehithe Beach, early morning'. The play is called Covehithe.

Finally, I am able to see this place. The place you came to to disappear.

Today, I stood by your grave. Or perhaps I should say, I stood on your grave. Because I probably did.

There are so many unmarked graves here, and there is no record of who lies in them. But you are here – you lie in one of them. One that was never meant to be found.

I looked at all of them, I stood by all of them – those eerie mounds of earth and grass that make it look as if a giant mole's been at work. I searched for some clue, some evidence – not the sort of evidence that would include men's clothing or a picture of a young airman.

But something.

You didn't weigh yourself down with chains or weights or place yourself in the sea. But you were determined you would never be found and you tried to make sure you left no evidence of your 'crimes'.

You spoke a great deal about your 'shame', but less about your pain.

And there was great pain for you.

You and I are very different people, from very different times, with very different beliefs. Though you have been with me all these years, there is much about you I still don't understand, still can't feel sympathy for.

But I have wept for you – when I stood on the site of your neglected grave; when I thought of another neglected grave somewhere in the French countryside; and whenever I reread the legal and moral judgment passed on you as you stood in the Old Bailey dock.

As a daughter, you were proud of your father.

As a father, you were proud of your son – and he knew it.

As a mother, you were proud of him – but he never knew it.

He was proud of his father. You knew this, but said you could feel no pride in it.

You were his hero, and he was yours. He died believing that, so maybe that was some comfort to you, as you lay, alone and frightened, in those hospital beds, with his picture at your side.

As successful as you were in concealing your own identities, you were more successful in concealing your son's identity.

You lie in a grave that you intended should never be seen.

He lies in a grave you never saw.

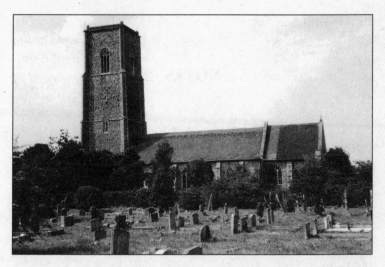

St Edmund's Church, Kessingland, Suffolk: no marker, no epitaph

You were never able to go and stand by his grave, and put flowers on it, and weep for him – and nor was anyone else.

If I had been the one to find him, I would have placed some flowers there for him, from you. From both of you. From the mother and father who loved you beyond reason.'

But you made sure no one could make even this one small gesture for you.

You have no marker and no epitaph. But if you had chosen one, what might it have been?

Perhaps, like someone else who landed at Kessingland, it could have been: 'Life as a woman just didn't work out for him.'

One thing is certain: it could not possibly be the one you and your family chose for your father: 'He was a simple gentleman.'

You were anything but a simple gentleman.

NOTES

PRO – Public Record Office

Dedication – quoted from Oscar acceptance speech, Hilary Swank, 26 March 2000

Prologue

1. 'Tommy Mary Walker', from *Broadsides*, anon., 1867, H. Disley, 57 St Giles High St, London.
2. Gladys Mitchell, *A Speedy Death*, p.24.
3. Browning, *Women Under Fascism and Communism*, p.1.
4. Paul Ferris, *Sex and the British*, p.45.
5. Faulkner and Hartman, *All the Best People*, p.11.

Chapter One

1. *Jersey Times*, 24 July 1897, p.2.
2. Norton, *Mother Clap's Molly House*, p.147.
3. *Empire News and Sunday Chronicle*, 19 February 1956, p.2.
4. *Jersey Express*, 7 March 1898, p.2.
5. *Jersey Express*, 8 March 1898, p.2.
6. Ibid.
7. Taylor, *Biographical Tracts 1750–1880, The History and Confession of the Man-Woman*.

8. Ibid.
9. Ibid.
10. Ibid.
11. Ibid.
12. Ibid.
13. *Jersey Express*, 11 June 1889, p.2.
14. *Jersey Express*, 27 June 1889, p.2.
15. *Jersey Times*, 8 September 1897, p.2.
16. Ibid.
17. Smith, *Edwardian Children*, p.145.
18. *Sunday Dispatch*, 10 March 1929, p.12.
19. *Empire News and Sunday Chronicle*, 19 February 1956, p.2.
20. *Sunday Dispatch*, 10 March 1929, p.12.
21. Ibid.
22. Dyhouse, *Girls Growing Up in Late Victorian and Edwardian England*, p.42.
23. *Daily Mail*, 3 March 1929, p.14.
24. *The Leader*, 11 September 1937, p.6.
25. Sally Mitchell, *The New Girl: Girls' Culture in England 1880–1915*.
26. *Girls' Home*, 19 November 1910, p.305.
27. *Girls' Home*, 3 December 1910, p.326.
28. *Girls' Home*, 19 November 1910, p.307.
29. Ibid.
30. *Girls' Home*, 3 December 1910, p.327.
31. *Girls' Home*, 10 December 1910, p.339.
32. *New York Times*, 19 January 1901, p.3.
33. Ibid.
34. Ibid.
35. *Daily Mail*, 3 March 1929, p.14.
36. *Empire News and Sunday Chronicle*, 19 February 1956, p.2.

37. *The Leader*, 11 September 1937, p.6.
38. Ibid.
39. *Daily Mail*, 3 March 1929, p.14.

Chapter Two

1. *Empire News and Sunday Chronicle*, 19 February 1956, p.2.
2. *Sunday Dispatch*, 10 March 1929, p.12.
3. Marwick, *Women at War 1914–18*, p.38.
4. Anon., *The WAAC*, p.32.
5. Bagnold, *A Diary Without Dates*, p.30.
6. Bishop, *Social History of the First World War*, p.82.
7. *Daily Sketch*, 27 January 1915, p.1.
8. *Empire News and Sunday Chronicle*, 19 February 1956, p.2.
9. Denny, *The Diggers*, p.147.
10. *Empire News and Sunday Chronicle*, 19 February 1956, p.2.
11. *Sunday Dispatch*, 10 March 1929, p.12.
12. *Empire News and Sunday Chronicle*, 19 February 1956, p.2.
13. Ibid.
14. *Sunday Dispatch*, 10 March 1929, p.12.
15. *The Times*, 4 July 1917, p.3.
16. *The Times*, 9 April 1917, p.3.
17. *The Times*, 21 January 1918, p.3.
18. Ibid.
19. Ibid.
20. PRO, AIR/1/681/21/13/2212.
21. *Sunday Dispatch*, 10 March 1929, p.12.
22. *Empire News and Sunday Chronicle*, 19 February 1956, p.2.

Chapter Three

1. From the inscription etched on the Brighton boundary pylon on the A23.
2. *Sunday Dispatch*, 10 March 1929, p.12.
3. Glendinning, *Vita*, p.106.
4. *Sunday Dispatch*, 10 March 1929, p.12.
5. Ibid.
6. *Daily Mail*, 3 March 1929, p.14.
7. Anon., *The History of the Times*, p.530.
8. *Sunday Dispatch*, 10 March 1929, p.12.
9. *The Times*, 16 August 1921, p.12.
10. *Hansard*, 4 August 1921, p.1801.
11. Ibid.
12. Ibid.
13. Davenport-Hines, *Sex, Death and Punishment*, p.153.
14. *The Times*, 16 August 1921, p.12.
15. *Empire News and Sunday Chronicle*, 26 February 1956, p.2.
16. Ibid.
17. *Sunday Dispatch*, 10 March 1929, p.2.
18. *Daily Mail*, 6 March 1929, p.3.
19. PRO, MEP 3 439.
20. *Sunday Dispatch*, 10 March 1929, p.2.
21. Ibid.
22. *Reynold's Illustrated Newspaper*, 12 March 1923, in Sieveking (ed.), *Man Bites Man*, p.13.
23. *Sunday Dispatch*, 10 March 1929, p.2.
24. *Empire News and Sunday Chronicle*, 4 March 1956, p.2.
25. *The Leader*, 11 September 1937, p.7.
26. *Empire News and Sunday Chronicle*, 4 March 1956, p.2.
27. *Sunday Dispatch*, 10 March 1929, p.2.
28. *Daily Telegraph*, 7 March 1929, p.14.

29. *Sunday Dispatch*, 10 March 1929, p.2.
30. Maitland, *Vesta Tilley*, p.93.
31. *The Leader*, 11 September 1937, p.7.
32. *Empire News and Sunday Chronicle*, 4 March 1956, p.2.
33. *The Leader*, 11 September 1937, p.8.
34. Mason, *The English Gentleman*, p.81.
35. *The Leader*, 11 September 1937, p.14.
36. Ibid.
37. Ibid.

Chapter Four

1. Flower, *The Old Ship*, p.149.
2. *The Leader*, 11 September 1937, p.14.
3. Ibid.
4. Ibid.
5. *Empire News and Sunday Chronicle*, 11 March 1956, p.2.
6. *Evening News*, 7 March 1929, p.1.
7. *Brighton Argus*, 6 March 1929, p.16.
8. *Empire News and Sunday Chronicle*, 11 March 1956, p.2.
9. Ibid.
10. *Sunday Express*, 10 March 1929, p.1.
11. Ibid., p.3.
12. Ibid.
13. *The Leader*, 18 September 1937, p.6.
14. *Empire News and Sunday Chronicle*, 11 March 1956, p.2.
15. Ibid.
16. *Sunday Express*, 10 March 1929, p.3.
17. West Sussex County Records Office, Episcopal Archives EP.II/3 1923.
18. Maitland, *Vesta Tilley*, p.111.
19. *The Leader*, 18 September 1937, p.6.
20. *Sunday Express*, 10 March 1929, p.3.

21. *The Leader,* 11 September 1937, p.6.
22. *The Leader,* 18 September 1937, p.6.
23. *Sunday Express,* 10 March 1929, p.3.
24. *Empire News and Sunday Chronicle,* 11 March 1956, p.11.
25. *Brighton & Hove Society & Hove Gazette,* 24 April 1924, p.6.
26. *Brighton & Hove Society & Hove Gazette,* 22 May 1924, p.6.
27. *Daily Mail,* 6 March 1929, p.3.
28. *Jersey Morning News,* 7 March 1929, p.1.
29. *Daily Herald,* 7 March 1929, p.1.
30. *Evening News,* 6 March 1929, p.1.
31. *Sunday Express,* 10 March 1929, p.3.
32. *Sunday Dispatch,* 10 March 1929, p.2.
33. *Daily Mail,* 6 March 1929, p.3.
34. *Sunday Dispatch,* 10 March 1929, p.2.
35. Peters, *Mrs Pat,* p.384.
36. Ibid., p.385.
37. *Empire News and Sunday Chronicle,* 18 March 1956, p.11.
38. Jacob Epstein, *An Autobiography,* p.90
39. Ibid.
40. Gardiner, *Epstein,* p.232.
41. *Empire News and Sunday Chronicle,* 18 March 1956, p.11.
42. *The Leader,* 18 September 1937, p.14.
43. *Southport Guardian,* 5 September 1925, p.8.
44. *Daily Mail,* 6 March 1929, p.3.
45. *Sunday Express,* 10 March 1929, p.3.
46. *Sunday Dispatch,* 10 March 1929, p.2.
47. *Sunday Express,* 10 March 1929, p.3.
48. Ibid.
49. *Daily Mail,* 6 March 1929, p.14.
50. Hirschfeld, *The Transvestites,* p.215.

Chapter Five

1. PRO, HO 144/21933.
2. *Oral History*, Spring 1996, p.57.
3. Skidelsky, *Oswald Mosley*, p.291.
4. Ibid.
5. *Daily Herald*, 31 July 1925.
6. *Brighton & Hove Herald*, 29 December 1923, p.6.
7. Cowling, *The Impact of Labour 1920–24*, p.36.
8. Rudlin, *The Growth of Fascism in Great Britain*, pp.117–18.
9. PRO, HO 144/19069.
10. Ibid.
11. Ibid.
12. Kushner and Lunn, *Traditions of Intolerance*, p.147.
13. *Empire News and Sunday Chronicle*, 25 March 1956, p.2.
14. *Sunday Dispatch*, 10 March 1929, p.2.
15. *Daily Mail*, 6 March 1929, p.14.
16. PRO, HO 144/19069.
17. *Empire News and Sunday Chronicle*, 25 March 1956, p.2.
18. Ibid.
19. PRO, HO 144/19069.
20. Ibid.
21. Ibid.
22. *Sunday Dispatch*, 10 March 1929, p.2.
23. PRO, HO 144/19069.
24. *Empire News and Sunday Chronicle*, 25 March 1956, p.2.
25. PRO, MEPO 3 439.
26. Ibid.
27. Ibid.
28. Ibid.
29. Ibid.
30. *Sunday Dispatch*, 10 March 1929, p.2.

31. *Daily Sketch*, 6 March 1929, p.3.
32. Ibid.
33. *Sunday Dispatch*, 10 March 1929, p.2.
34. *Evening News*, 7 March 1929, p.1.
35. Ibid.
36. Ibid.
37. *Evening News*, 6 March 1929, p.1.
38. Ibid.
39. *Daily Mail*, 3 March 1929, p.14.
40. *Evening News*, 7 March 1929, p.1.
41. Ibid.
42. Ibid.
43. Ibid.
44. *Sunday Dispatch*, 10 March 1929, p.2.
45. Ibid.
46. Ibid.
47. *Daily Sketch*, 6 March 1929, p.3.
48. Ibid.
49. *Evening News*, 7 March 1929, p.1.
50. *Sunday Dispatch*, 10 March 1929, p.2.
51. *Daily Mail*, 6 March 1929, p.3.
52. Ibid.
53. Ibid.
54. *Jersey Morning News*, 6 March 1929, p.1.
55. *Daily Sketch*, 6 March 1929, p.3.
56. *Sunday Dispatch*, 10 March 1929, p.2.
57. *Evening News*, 6 March 1929, p.1.
58. Ibid.
59. *Sunday Dispatch*, 10 March 1929, p.2.
60. *Daily Sketch*, 6 March 1929, p.3.
61. Ibid.
62. *Evening News*, 6 March 1929, p.1.

Chapter Six

1. PRO, MEPO 3 439.
2. *Sunday Dispatch*, 10 March 1929, p.12.
3. Size, *Prisons I Have Known*, p.99.
4. PRO, MEPO 3 439.
5. *Sunday Dispatch*, 10 March 1929, p.12.
6. Size, op. cit.
7. *Evening News*, 6 March 1929, p.1.
8. PRO, MEPO 3 439.
9. Ibid.
10. *Daily Herald*, 8 March 1929, p.1.
11. Size, op cit., p.100.
12. *The Leader*, 25 September 1937, p.7.
13. Size, op. cit., p.102.
14. *Jersey Morning News*, 6 March 1929, p.1.
15. Ibid.
16. *Brighton Argus*, 6 March 1929, p.12.
17. *Daily Mail*, 6 March 1929, p.3.
18. *Evening News*, 7 March 1929, p.12.
19. *News of the World*, 10 March 1929, p.9.
20. Ibid.
21. Letter to author, 1 June 1998.
22. *Sunday Express*, 10 March 1929, p.12.
23. *Sunday Dispatch*, 10 March 1929, p.12.
24. Baker, *Our Three Selves: A Life of Radclyffe Hall*, p.254.
25. *Evening News*, 7 March 1929, p.12.
26. *Brighton Argus*, 14 March 1929, p.5.
27. *Jersey Evening Post*, 12 March 1929, p.2.
28. PRO, MEP 3 439.
29. *News of the World*, 10 March 1929, p.9.
30. PRO, MEP 3 439.
31. *Sunday Dispatch*, 10 March 1929.

32. Ibid.
33. Ibid.
34. Ibid.
35. *Sunday Dispatch*, 24 March 1929, p.12.
36. *Sunday Dispatch*, 31 March 1929, p.12.
37. *Sunday Express*, 10 March 1929, p.2.
38. Ibid.
39. Ibid.
40. PRO, MEPO 3 439.
41. Ibid.
42. *The Times*, 25 April 1929, p.12.
43. PRO, MEP 3 439.
44. *The Times*, 25 April 1929, p.12.
45. Ibid.
46. *News of the World*, 31 March 1929, p.4.
47. Ibid.
48. Davenport-Hines, *Sex, Death and Punishment*, p.151.
49. Blackham, *Sir Ernest Wild*, p.152.
50. Ibid., p.176.
51. Davenport-Hines, op. cit., p.151.
52. *The Times*, 22 April 1929, p.5.
53. *Brighton Argus*, 25 April 1929, p.7.
54. *News of the World*, 28 April 1929, p.6.
55. Ibid.
56. *The Leader*, 25 September 1937, p.7.
57. *News of the World*, 28 April 1929, p.6.
58. Ibid.
59. Ibid.
60. Ibid.
61. *Brighton Argus*, 25 April 1929, p.7.
62. *News of the World*, 28 April 1929, p.6.
63. Ibid.
64. *The Times*, 25 April 1929, p.7.

65. Ibid.
66. PRO, MEPO 3 439.
67. *News of the World*, 28 April 1929, p.6.
68. *Brighton Argus*, 27 April 1929, p.7.
69. Fielding, *The Female Husband*, p.23.
70. Norton, *Mother Clap's Molly House*, p.237.
71. Mayne, *The Inter-Sexes*, p.12.
72. Hennegan (ed.), *The Lesbian Pillow Book*, p.152.
73. Ibid., p.157.
74. Ibid., p.159.
75. *The Sun*, 21 September 1991, p.3.
76. *The Sun*, 19 September 1991, p.4.
77. *The Sun*, 21 September 1991, p.3.
78. *News of the World*, 22 September 1991, p.13.
79. *Brighton Argus*, 28 April 1929, p.7.
80. Ibid.
81. Ibid.
82. Ibid.

Chapter Seven

1. PRO, MEPO 3 439.
2. *Birmingham Mail*, 10 May 1929, p.8.
3. Ibid.
4. Ibid.
5. PRO, MEPO 3 439.
6. *New York Times*, 5 May 1929, p.21.
7. *Birmingham Mail*, 15 May 1929, p.6.
8. *The Leader*, 2 October 1937, p.13.
9. Ibid.
10. Size, *Prisons I Have Known*, p.102.
11. *News of the World*, 12 May 1929, p.5.
12. Ibid.

13. Ibid.
14. *Birmingham Mail*, 5 June 1929, p.5.
15. *Empire News and Sunday Chronicle*, 1 April 1956, p.14.
16. Size, op cit., p.102.
17. Curtin, *We Can Always Call Them Bulgarians*, p.145.

Chapter Eight

1. *The Times*, 5 September 1934, p.14.
2. Ibid.
3. *The Leader*, 9 October 1937, p.13.
4. *Sussex Daily News*, 5 September 1934, p.4.
5. Ibid.
6. *The Leader*, 2 October 1937, p.15.
7. *The Times*, 28 September 1934, p.8.
8. Ibid.
9. Ibid.
10. Ibid.
11. Gardiner, *Epstein*, p.228.
12. *The Leader*, 9 October 1937, p.13.
13. Ibid.
14. Ibid.
15. Ibid.
16. *The Times*, 16 March 1937, p.13.
17. Ibid.
18. Sieveking (ed.), *Man Bites Man*, p.126.
19. Ibid.
20. Ibid.
21. Ibid.
22. Ibid.
23. *The Leader*, 9 October 1937, p.13.
24. *The Times*, 23 March 1937, p.13.
25. Ibid.

26. Mass-Observation, Worktown Collection Intersex I, Box W60/C.
27. Ibid.
28. Ibid.
29. Ibid.
30. *The Leader*, 11 September 1937, p.31.
31. Ibid., pp.6–7.
32. *Sunday Dispatch*, 31 March 1929, p.12.
33. Mass-Observation, Worktown Collection, Central Beach C31/8, Box 58.
34. Ibid.
35. Ibid.
36. Mass-Observation, Worktown Collection Intersex I, Box W60/C.
37. Ibid.
38. Ibid.
39. Ibid.
40. Ibid.
41. Ibid.
42. *Empire News and Sunday Chronicle*, 8 April 1956.
43. Mass-Observation, Worktown Collection Intersex I, Box W60/C.
44. Ibid.
45. Ibid.
46. Ibid.
47. Ibid.
48. Ibid.
49. Ibid.
50. Ibid.

Chapter Nine

1. Sieveking (ed.), *Man Bites Man*, p.41.

2. Ibid.
3. Faulkner and Hartman, *All the Best People*, p.263.
4. Baker, *Our Three Selves*, p.345.
5. *Paddington News*, 21 January 1944, p.2.
6. Ibid.
7. Mackenzie, op. cit., p.23.
8. East Sussex Record Office, 84/7/1, p.1.
9. Mackenzie, op. cit., p.19.
10. Ibid., p.42.
11. Lewis, *A People's War*, p.35.
12. Langdon Davies, *Parachutes Over Britain*, p.21.
13. Graves, *Home Guard of Britain*, p.96.
14. *Empire News and Sunday Chronicle*, 15 April 1956, p.4.
15. Ibid.
16. Ibid.
17. Ibid.
18. Ibid.
19. Ibid.
20. PRO, WO/32/4674.
21. *Empire News and Sunday Chronicle*, 15 April 1956, p.4.
22. Ibid.

Chapter Ten

1. *Bacup Times*, 11 December 1948, p.8.
2. PRO, MEPO 3/3024.
3. Ibid.
4. Ibid.
5. *Bacup Times*, 11 December 1948, p.8.
6. Ibid.
7. *News of the World*, 12 December 1948, p.3.
8. PRO, MEPO 3/3024.
9. *Bacup Times*, 11 December 1948, p.8.

10. PRO, MEPO 3/3024.

11. *Bacup Times*, 8 January 1949, p.4.

12. PRO, PCOM 9/1234.

13. *Bacup Times*, 8 January 1949, p.4.

14. Ibid.

15. Croft-Cooke, *The Drums of Morning*, p.168.

16. Ibid., p.169.

17. Letter, Ursula Bloom, date unknown.

18. *Lowestoft Journal and Mercury*, 6 May 1960, p.15.

19. Interview with author, 20 June 2000.

20. Ibid.

21. Ibid.

22. Ibid.

23. Ibid.

24. Ibid.

25. *Empire News and Sunday Chronicle*, 19 February 1956, p.2.

26. Interview with author, 20 June 2000.

27. Ibid.

28. *Empire News and Sunday Chronicle*, 22 April 1956, p.9.

29. Letter, Ursula Bloom, date unknown.

30. Interview with author, 20 June 2000.

31. Ibid.

32. *Lowestoft Journal and Mercury*, 6 May 1960, p.15.

33. Letter to author, August 1997.

34. *Daily Express*, 6 May 1960, p.11.

35. Ibid.

36. *Lowestoft Journal and Mercury*, 6 May 1960, p.15.

37. *Gay News*, no. 139, 23 March–5 April 1978, p.29.

38. *Dream Girls*, directed by Kim Longinotto and Jano Williams, 20th Century Vixen, 1995.

39. Ibid.

40. Ibid.

41. Ibid.
42. *Sunday Express*, 10 March 1929, p.3.
43. *Trisha*, ITV, 7 May 1999.
44. Donoghue, *Passions Between Women*, p.86.
45. *Pink Paper*, 27 March 1998, p.3.
46. *Curve*, February 2000, p.36.
47. *Diva*, April 2000, p.10.
48. Hilary Swank, Oscar acceptance speech, 26 March 2000.
49. *Evening Star*, 5 July 2000.
50. *Evening Star*, 2 March 2000.
51. Rendell, *A Sleeping Life*, p.536.
52. *East Anglian Daily Times*, 31 August 2000.

ACKNOWLEDGEMENTS

I would like to thank the following institutions and groups for their kind assistance: Brighton Local Studies Library; Brighton Ourstory Project; the British Library; the British Newspaper Library; Court Service; East Sussex County Record Office; Family Record Centre; Guildhall Library; Jersey General Register Office; Jersey Reference Library; Lowestoft Central Library; Public Record Office; Société Jersiase; Suffolk Record Office; the Theatre Museum; Westminster Archives Centre; West Sussex Record Office.

My thanks and gratitude also go to the following individuals for their kind assistance: John Alban, Norfolk Record Office; Mary Billot, Société Jersiase; Catherine Blake, Jersey Archive; Peter Burton; Peter Cherry; Joyce Chester; Nick Connell, Hertfordshire Archives & Local Studies; Mrs E. M. Doggett; Joy Eldridge, Mass-Observation Archive; Mrs Pat Evans, Godalming Joint Burial Committee; Stephen Freeth, Guildhall Library; Jonathan Gray, Theatre Museum; Wesley Hooper, NessPoint.com; Revd John S. Hunt; Francis King; Mrs Maureen Long; Andrew McEvoy, National Archives of Australia; Mrs Gillian Maddock; Richard Mangan, The Mander and Mitchenson Collection; Margaret Monod; Mrs Alice Myall; Julie Parker; Nick Patrick, Radio Suffolk; Mrs S. A. Penaluna, Registrar, Parish of St Clement; Mark Peters; Jo Purvis; Matt Radley, *Eastern Daily Press*; Anthony

Richards, Imperial War Museum; Gillian Rodgerson, for half the title; Tom Sargant; Peggy Shaw; Robert Smith, Bailiffscourt Hotel; Mrs H. E. Stevens, Witley & Milford Parish Council.

I am grateful to Dorothy Sheridan of the Mass-Observation Archive, the Trustees of the University of Sussex and the Curtis Brown Group for permission to quote from the Mass-Observation Archives.

Pictures 1, 3, 6–8, 10, 11, and 13–19 are copyright © The British Library and I am grateful for permission to reproduce them. The rest of the pictures are my own.

Thanks, as ever, to Cora Vesey and Ilan Shaffer at Fisher Phillips, and enormous gratitude also goes to Julia Lyndon and Gaby Kompalik, for their outstanding repair work on my tired and damaged body.

I am pleased to gratefully acknowledge the generous support of the Society of Authors; their Authors' Foundation grant funded the initial period of research on this book when it was little more than a faint idea. Without this support, it is unlikely it would have got any further than that.

I would also like to thank the Arts Council for their financial help – unfortunately, I cannot. In 1998 and 1999, I made consecutive unsuccessful applications for a Writers' Award; only fifteen are given by the Council each year. This is not merely a sour-grapes gripe, but a point made to highlight a worrying trend: in 1998, only two non-fiction writers were recipients of this funding; in 1999, only one. South-East Arts, my regional arts body, makes no financial provision whatsoever for non-fiction writers – this despite the fact that it is responsible for a geographical area with an exceptionally high concentration of biographical and historical writers.

The kind of long-term work needed to produce properly researched non-fiction books is woefully underfunded in the UK. It is the most expensive form of literature to produce: the costs of travel, photocopies, photographs, permissions, accommodation, professional and other fees do not decrease, and publishers' advances rarely cover more than a fraction of these costs.

In 2000, the Society of Authors published a survey, drawing on information provided by 1,700 authors. This survey showed what most established British authors knew: that almost half of us earn less than £5,000 a year – the national minimum wage – and that the lowest earners were in the specialist non-fiction field.

Until other funding bodies follow the fine example set by the Society of Authors, and recognise the enormous contribution made by non-fiction writers, those of us without private incomes, inheritances or jobs in academia will have to continue financing our work by running up huge credit card bills and selling our homes. While unorthodox histories and biographies are increasingly sought and valued by readers, they appear to be worthless to the majority of those with their hands on the coffers. It is a situation that is both ridiculous and scandalous, and one that needs to be addressed by government, funding bodies and publishers alike.

At Virago, my thanks go to Lennie Goodings and Sally Abbey, who guided this book through its formative stages, and especially to Antonia Hodgson, for her astute and sensitive editing. I am grateful for all their support, encouragement and belief, especially at those moments when they would ask, 'But exactly *how* are you going to do that?' – and answer came there none.

My strength and support has always come from those I

am fortunate enough to count as friends. The years during which I worked on this book were, as they know, particularly difficult and transitional ones for me – a period of upheaval, loss, uncertainty, change and development. Nothing would be possible without their love and support, for me and all the unlikely projects I undertake, so my special thanks, as always, go to: Jeff Baines, Thea Bennett, Paul Boyd, Sharon Boyd, Sue Brearley, Mark Bunyan, Peter Burton, Joyce Chester, Andrew Craig, Helen Dady, Mary Daly, Melita Dennett, Jill Gardner, Sandra Hounsham, Sheila Hutchinson, Chris Farrah-Mills, Rick Farrah-Mills, Chris Moller, Margaret Monod, Mark Peters, Gary Pulsifer, Tom Robinson, Gillian Rodgerson, Helen Sandler, Tom Sargant and Janice Smith.

Finally, there are two individuals who must be singled out for exceptional praise, above and beyond the call of duty.

Firstly, my extraordinary agent, Patrick Walsh – his patience, persistence and encouragement were instrumental in nurturing this book from the germ of an idea (mentioned by me in passing as I put my coat on to leave his office) into a project which threw up challenge after challenge, and taxed me to the nth degree. I owe him an enormous debt of gratitude for presenting me with those challenges, and ensuring I took them on when I would probably have preferred not to. I hope I have repaid his faith in me.

Secondly, my partner, Sally McMahon – whose tireless support and belief in me and my work are immeasurable. At one end of the scale, she accompanied me on a memorable research trip to Jersey, and was, I know, as relieved to leave there as I was. At the other, she has seen me through debt, wretchedness and despair – and cared enough to wait until there was light at the end of the tunnel. I can find no words adequate enough to express my gratitude to her.

Rose Collis,
Hove, February 2001

BIBLIOGRAPHY

Unless stated otherwise, all publishers are London.

Altman, Dennis (ed.), *Homosexuality, Which Homosexuality*, GMP, 1989

Anon., *The History of the Times*, 1952

Anon., *The Story of Bailiffscourt*, privately published, date unknown.

Anon., *The WAAC*, T. Werner Laurie, 1930

Anon., *We Also Served: The Story of the Home Guard in Cambridgeshire and Isle of Ely 1940–43*, privately printed, 1944

Aslet, Clive, *Country Houses*, Yale University Press, 1982

Bagnold, Enid, *A Diary Without Dates*, Virago, 1978

Baker, Michael, *Our Three Selves: A Life of Radclyffe Hall*, Hamish Hamilton, 1985

Barnes, James Thomas Strachey, *Fascism*, Thornton Butterworth, 1931

Barrow, Andrew, *Gossip 1920–1970*, Hamish Hamilton, 1978

Bell, Barbara, *Just Take Your Frock Off*, Ourstory Books, Brighton, 1999

Benewick, Robert, *The Fascist Movement in Britain*, Allen Lane/The Penguin Press, 1972

Benstock, Shari, *Women of the Left Bank*, Virago, 1987

Bishop, James, *Social History of the First World War*, Angus & Robertson, 1982

Blackham, Robert, *Sir Ernest Wild*, Rich and Cowan Ltd, 1935

Braybon, Gail, and Summerfield, Penny, *Out of the Cage*, Pandora, 1987

Brophy, John, *Britain's Home Guard*, G. G. Harrap & Co., 1945

Browning, Hilda, *Women Under Fascism and Communism*, Martin Lawrence Ltd, 1934

Burton, Sarah, *Impostors*, Penguin, 2000

Camp, John, *Holloway Prison*, David and Charles, 1974

Caprio, Frank S., *Female Homosexuality*, Peter Owen Ltd, 1957

Castle, Terry, *The Apparitional Lesbian*, Columbia University Press, New York, 1993

Chorley, W. R., *RAF Bomber Command Losses (5) 1944*, Midland Counties, Leicester, 1998

Cline, Sally, *Radclyffe Hall, A Woman Called John*, John Murray, 1997

Cowling, Maurice, *The Impact of Labour 1920–24*, Cambridge University Press, 1971

Croft-Cooke, Rupert, *The Drums of Morning*, Putnam, 1961

Cross, Robin, and Lynn, Vera, *We'll Meet Again*, Sidgwick and Jackson, 1989

Curtin, Kaier, *We Can Always Call Them Bulgarians*, Alyson Publications, Boston, 1987

Davenport-Hines, Richard, *Sex, Death and Punishment*, Collins, 1990

Dekker, Rudolf M., and van de Pol, Lotte C., *The Tradition of Female Transvestism in Early Modern Europe*, Macmillan, Basingstoke, 1989

Denny, W. J., *The Diggers*, Hodder & Stoughton, 1919

Dent, Alan H., *Mrs Patrick Campbell*, Museum Press Ltd, 1961

Donoghue, Emma, *Passions Between Women*, Scarlet Press, 1993

Dyhouse, Carol, *Girls Growing Up in Late Victorian and Edwardian England*, Routledge and Kegan Paul, 1981

Epstein, Jacob, *An Autobiography*, Vista Books, 1963

Epstein, Jacob, *Let There Be Sculpture*, Hulton Press, 1955

Epstein, Julia, and Straub, Kristina, *Body Guards*, Routledge, 1991

Escott, Sq. Leader Beryl E., *Women in Air Force Blue*, Patrick Stephens Ltd, Wellingborough, 1989

Faderman, Lilian, *Chloe Plus Olivia*, Penguin, 1994

Faderman, Lilian, *Surpassing the Love of Men*, Women's Press, 1985

Faulkner, Alex, and Hartman, Tom, *All the Best People*, George Allen & Unwin, 1981

Ferris, Lesley (ed.), *Crossing the Stage: Controversies on Cross-Dressing*, Routledge, 1993

Ferris, Paul, *Sex and the British*, Michael Joseph, 1993

Fielding, Henry, *The Female Husband*, M. Cooper, 1748

Fletcher, Lynne Yamaguchi, and Saks, Adrien, *Lavender Lists*, Alyson Publications, Boston, 1990

Flower, Raymond, *The Old Ship*, Croom Helm, 1986

Foster, Jeanette H., *Sex Variant Women in Literature*, Naiad Press, Talahassee, 1985

Garber, Marjorie, *Vested Interest*, Harper Perennial, 1992

Gardiner, Stephen, *Epstein*, Michael Joseph, 1992

Gilbert, Sandra M., and Gubar, Susan, *No Man's Land Vol.2: Sexchanges*, Yale University Press, 1989

Glendinning, Victoria, *Vita*, Penguin, 1983

Glover, Michael, *Invasion Scare 1940*, Leo Cooper, 1990

Graham, Alistair, *Fascism in Britain*, Badminton, 1966

Graves, Charles, *Home Guard of Britain*, Hutchinson, 1943

Hamilton, Alastair, *Fascism in Britain*, Blond, 1966

Harrison, Tom, *Living Through the Blitz*, Collins, 1976

Hennegan, Alison (ed.), *The Lesbian Pillow Book*, Fourth Estate, 2000

Hirschfeld, Magnus, *Sexual Anomalies and Perversions*, Encyclopaedia Press Ltd, 1959

Hirschfeld, Magnus, *The Transvestites*, Prometheus Books, Buffalo, NY, 1991

Hotchkiss, Valerie, *Clothes Make the Man*, Garland, 1996

Jalland, Pat, *Women, Marriage and Politics 1860–1914*, OUP, 1986

Jay, Karla, *The Amazon and the Page*, Indiana University Press, Bloomington, 1988

Katz, Jonathan, *Gay American History*, Avon Books, New York, 1978

Krafft-Ebing, Richard von, *Psychopathia Sexualis*, Staples Press Ltd, 1959

Kushner, Tony, and Lunn, Ken, *Traditions of Intolerance*, Manchester University Press, 1989

Langdon Davies, John, *Parachutes Over Britain*, Pilot Press Ltd, 1940

Lee, Stephen J., *Aspects of British Political History 1914–45*, Routledge, 1996

Lewis, Peter, *A People's War*, Methuen, 1986

Lowerson, John, *Victorian Sussex*, BBC, 1972

Mackenzie, S. P., *The Home Guard*, OUP, 1996

Maitland, Sara, *Vesta Tilley*, Virago, 1986

Marlow, Joyce (ed.), *The Virago Book of Women and the Great War*, Virago, 1998

Martin, Christopher, *English Life in the First World War*, Wayland Publishers, 1974

Marwick, Arthur, *The Deluge*, Macmillan, 1965

Marwick, Arthur, *Women at War 1914–18*, Fontana, 1977

Mason, Philip, *The English Gentleman*, Pimlico, 1993

Mayne, Xavier, *The Inter-Sexes*, privately printed, 1908

Middlebrook, M., and Everitt, Chris, *Bomber Command War Diaries*, Viking, 1985

Mitchell, David, *Women on the Warpath*, Jonathan Cape, 1966

Mitchell, Gladys, *A Speedy Death*, Victor Gollancz, 1929

Mitchell, Sally, *The New Girl: Girls' Culture in England 1880–1915*, Columbia University Press, 1995

Mosley, Nicholas, *Rules of the Game*, Secker and Warburg, 1994

Munt, Sally R., *Butch/Femme Inside Lesbian Gender*, Cassell, 1998

Musgrave, Clifford, *Life in Brighton*, Faber and Faber, 1970

Norton, Rictor, *Mother Clap's Molly House: The Gay Subculture in England 1700–1830*, GMP, 1992

Payne, Stanley G., *A History of Fascism 1914–45*, UCL Press, 1995

Pearce, Robert, *Facism and Nazism*, Hodder and Stoughton, 1997

Peters, Margot, *Mrs Pat*, Bodley Head, 1984

Ramsey, Winston G. (ed.), *The Blitz: Then and Now*, Battle of Britain Prints International, 1988

Raverat, Gwen, *Period Piece: A Cambridge Childhood*, Faber and Faber, 1952

Rendell, Ruth, *A Sleeping Life*, Hutchinson, 1978

Richards, Dell, *Lesbian Lists*, Alyson Publications, Boston, 1990

Rowbotham, Sheila, *Century of Women*, Penguin, 1999

Rudlin, W. A., *The Growth of Fascism in Great Britain*, Unwin Bros Ltd, 1935

Sampson, Mark, *Brighton*, Alan Sutton Publishing Ltd, Stroud, 1994

Sieveking, Paul (ed.), *Man Bites Man*, Jay Landesman Publishing, 1980

Silber, Evelyn, *Rebel Angel*, Birmingham Museums and Art Gallery, 1980

Size, Mary, *Prisons I Have Known*, G. Allen and Unwin, 1957

Skidelsky, Robert, *Oswald Mosley*, Papermac, 1990

Smith, Joanna, *Edwardian Children*, Hutchinson, 1983

Spencer, Colin, *Homosexuality A History*, Fourth Estate, 1995

Street, Arthur, *From Dusk Till Dawn*, Harrap & Co., 1942

Taylor, T. H., *Biographical Tracts 1750–1880, The History and Confession of the Man-Woman*, J. G. Edwards, Sandhurst, Victoria, Australia, 1880

Tey, Josephine, *To Love and Be Wise*, Pan Books, 1965

Tosh, John, *A Man's Place*, Yale, 1999

Wheelwright, Julie, *Amazons and Military Maids*, Pandora, 1989

Woodhouse, Annie, *Fantastic Women: Sex, Gender and Transvestism*, Macmillan, 1989

Newspapers and Magazines

Bacup Times
Beccles and Bungay Journal
Birmingham Gazette
Birmingham Mail
Blackpool Gazette and Herald
Blackpool Times
Brighton Argus
Brighton Examiner
Brighton & Hove Herald
Brighton & Hove Society & Hove Gazette
Curve
Daily Express

Daily Herald
Daily Mail
Daily Mirror
Daily Sketch
Daily Telegraph
Diva
East Anglian Daily Times
Eastern Daily Press
Empire News and Sunday Chronicle
The Era
Evening News
Evening Standard
Evening Star
Fascist Bulletin
Gay News
Girls' Home
Glasgow Herald
Halifax Courier and Guardian
Herts and Essex Observer
Isle of Wight Guardian
Jersey Evening Post
Jersey Express
Jersey Morning News
Jersey Times
The Leader
Lowestoft Journal and Mercury
News of the World
New York Times
Oral History
Oxford Times
Paddington News
Pink Paper
Southampton Observer and Hampshire News

Southampton Times
Southern Echo
Southport Guardian
The Stage
The Stock-Keeper
The Sun
Sunday Dispatch
Sunday Express
Sussex County Magazine
Sussex Daily News
Theatre World
The Times
Weekly Dispatch

INDEX

Numbers in italics refer to photographs.